Classical Subjects Crea

Spanish for Children

Learn more than how to order a taco™

Primer B

Julia Kraut with Grant Durrell

Spanish for Children Primer B

Version 1.0

ISBN: 978-1-60051-052-6

Classical Academic Press
515 S. 32nd St.
Camp Hill, PA 17011

www.ClassicalAcademicPress.com

Illustrations by:
Jason Rayner

Book design by:
Lenora Riley

PGP.08.18

TABLE OF CONTENTS

INTRODUCTION TO STUDENTS

¡Hola!

Welcome, **estudiante**, to your second year of Spanish. We think you are going to enjoy this year even more than the first! *Spanish for Children Primer B* is filled with new exercises, readings, translations, and fun things to do and learn. You should find this book quite familiar. Its setup is very similar to that of *Primer A*, but it is a thicker book because there are more pages per chapter.

If you have completed *Primer A*, you already know some important tips for learning Spanish well. The following are some additional tips that will help you become an even better student of the Spanish language.

- Do your exercises faithfully and well. Your assignments should not be too long, but you will have at least two every week.
- Speak Spanish as often as you can, even while you are still gaining confidence.
- Ask questions whenever you are not sure of something.
- Memorize your Spanish words. You will only have to learn about ten new words a week. Here are some tips that will help you memorize your Spanish words:
    - Chant or sing your words, just as you will learn them in this course. It is much easier to remember what you sing or chant.
    - If you purchased the video that accompanies this book, sing and chant along with the students.
    - Review your Spanish words every day (or night) for five to fifteen minutes. A little bit of review every day is very, very helpful. Keep reviewing words from earlier chapters to make sure you have really mastered them.
    - Make Spanish vocabulary cards and put them on a ring. You can put the Spanish word on one side and the English word on the other. Take these cards with you wherever you go so you can review almost any time.
    - Make up silly or fun ways to remember Spanish words. For instance, the Spanish word **casa** means "house." You could make up a sentence such as this: "My **casa** is a castle!" This will help you remember that **casa** means "house."
    - Quiz your classmates or anyone else you know who is also taking Spanish. Quiz your teacher or parent, and have that person quiz you. Have contests to see who can get the most right or who can give the answers fastest. Make your own written test, and see how many you can get right.

- Visit www.HeadventureLand.com for fun and creative ways to practice your Spanish. Review your vocabulary by playing Spanish FlashDash—the game that tests your vocabulary chapter by chapter.

We hope that you will find your study of Spanish this year rewarding and enjoyable. Please contact us with questions about Spanish via the "Ask the Magister" form on our website at www.ClassicalAcademicPress.com.

¡Adios!

Christopher A. Perrin, PhD
Publisher

Canto:
Review of Verb Endings

	Present-Tense -ar Verb Endings	Present-Tense -er Verb Endings	Present-Tense -ir Verb Endings
1st-person singular (**yo**)	**-o**	**-o**	**-o**
2nd-person singular (**tú**)	**-as**	**-es**	**-es**
3rd-person singular (**él/ella/usted**)	**-a**	**-e**	**-e**
1st-person plural (**nosotros**)	**-amos**	**-emos**	**-imos**
2nd-person plural (**vosotros**)[1]	**-áis**	**-éis**	**-ís**
3rd-person plural (**ellos/ustedes**)	**-an**	**-en**	**-en**
	Preterit-Tense -ar Verb Endings	**Preterit-Tense -er/-ir Verb Endings**	**Future-Tense Verb Endings**
1st-person singular (**yo**)	**-é**	**-í**	**-é**
2nd-person singular (**tú**)	**-aste**	**-iste**	**-ás**
3rd-person singular (**él/ella/usted**)	**-ó**	**-ió**	**-á**
1st-person plural (**nosotros**)	**-amos**	**-imos**	**-emos**
2nd-person plural (**vosotros**)	**-asteis**	**-isteis**	**-éis**
3rd-person plural (**ellos/ustedes**)	**-aron**	**-ieron**	**-án**

1. As you may remember from *Spanish for Children Primer A* (*SFCA*), the second-person plural familiar form is only used in Spain. In Latin America, when people want to say "you all," they use the third-person plural form. From this point on, the second-person plural familiar form will appear in gray text to remind you that you will only use it if you travel to Spain.

Vocabulario:

Vocabulario nuevo

Spanish	English
desayunar: desayuno, desayuné, desayunaré	to eat breakfast: I eat breakfast, I ate breakfast, I will eat breakfast
cortar: corto, corté, cortaré	to cut: I cut, I cut, I will cut
el lápiz	pencil
el bolígrafo	pen
el papel	paper
el cuaderno	notebook
las tijeras	scissors
la mochila	backpack
la palabra	word
la página	page

Vocabulario de repaso

Spanish	English
hablar: hablo, hablé, hablaré	to speak: I speak, I spoke, I will speak
cantar: canto, canté, cantaré	to sing: I sing, I sang, I will sing
bailar: bailo, bailé, bailaré	to dance: I dance, I danced, I will dance
correr: corro, corrí, correré	to run: I run, I ran, I will run
abrir: abro, abrí, abriré	to open: I open, I opened, I will open
vivir: vivo, viví, viviré	to live: I live, I lived, I will live

Welcome back! Let's start this course by reviewing some of the main things you learned in *Spanish for Children Primer A*. In this chapter, we're going to talk about verbs.

What Are Verbs?

A verb is a **part of speech**, the grammatical way of saying "a category of words." Verbs are words that name actions, such as "run," "swim," "read," or "think." Verbs can also name a state of being. This means they are words that tell you *what* something is. In sentences such as "I *am* happy," "We *are* silly," or "He *is* upside-down," the terms "am," "are," and "is" are forms of the verb "to be."

Quick Quiz 1: Write three verbs in *English* that you like:

__________________ __________________ __________________

Quick Quiz 2: Write three verbs in *Spanish* that you like:

__________________ __________________ __________________

Different Verb Forms

In English, our verbs don't always change a lot: We say things such as "I *go*," "you *go*," "I will *go*," and "I did *go*." We add other words such as "I," "you," "will," and "did" to tell us more about who is doing the action in the sentence and when that action happens. In Spanish, instead of adding extra words, you show **who** is doing the action and **when** the action happens by changing the last few letters (the ending) of a verb. Changing the ending of a verb to show who is doing the action and when the action happens is called **conjugating**.

Before we conjugate a verb, we start with something called the **infinitive**. In English, we sometimes use the word "to" to show that a word is in its infinitive form: "to talk," "to eat," "to live." Infinitives in Spanish end in **-ar**, **-er**, or **-ir**, such as this: **habl*ar*** (to talk), **com*er*** (to eat), **viv*ir*** (to live). When we want to conjugate a verb in Spanish, we take off the last two letters to find the stem of the verb. Then we add the ending that will show who is doing the action and when the action happens!

Quick Quiz 3: Look at the three Spanish verbs you wrote down a second ago. Rewrite them here, and circle the last two letters of each verb. Did you choose "**-ar**," "**-er**," "**-ir**" verbs or a combination of them?

__________________ __________________ __________________

Quick Quiz 4: Write down the stems of your three verbs:

__________________ __________________ __________________

(Did you choose a verb that's "irregular," such as **ser**, **ir**, or **ver**? If you did, try a different verb. We'll look at irregulars in the next chapter.)

How Do You Choose the Right Verb Ending?

There are three different characteristics of a verb that you have to think about when you're conjugating it. Do you remember what they are? That's right: person, number, and tense. Let's start with tense.

Tense

"Tense is time." Do you remember saying that? In the previous book, you learned quite a few tenses. The **present tense** is for verbs happening right now. The **preterit (past) tense** is for actions that happened in the past. And what about the **future tense**? Well, those actions happen in the future, of course! For each tense, there is a different set of endings. Do you remember what they are? See if you can fill in this chart. Watch out for the future tense—remember, we add future-tense endings to the infinitive without chopping off any letters first!

	Present-Tense -ar Verb Endings	Present-Tense -er Verb Endings	Present-Tense -ir Verb Endings
yo (I)	**habl__**	**corr__**	**viv__**
tú (you)	**habl__**	**corr__**	**viv__**
él/ella/usted (he/she/you, formal)	**habl__**	**corr__**	**viv__**
nosotros (we)	**habl_____**	**corr_____**	**viv_____**
vosotros (you all)	**habl*áis***	**corr*éis***	**viv*ís***
ellos/ustedes (they/you all)	**habl__**	**corr__**	**viv__**
	Preterit-Tense -ar Verb Endings	**Preterit-Tense -er/-ir Verb Endings**	**Future-Tense Verb Endings**
yo (I)	**bail__**	**abr__**	**cantar__**
tú (you)	**bail____**	**abr____**	**cantar___**
él/ella/usted (he/she/you, formal)	**bail__**	**abr__**	**cantar__**
nosotros (we)	**bail_____**	**abr_____**	**cantar_____**
vosotros (you all)	**bail*asteis***	**abr*isteis***	**cantar*éis***
ellos/ustedes (they/you all)	**bail____**	**abr_____**	**cantar___**

Now, once you know *when* an action happens, you know which set of tense endings to choose. Then, it's time to figure out which specific verb ending in that set will tell exactly who is doing the action. That's where **number** and **person** come in.

Number

Number is pretty easy. It is the grammatical way of saying "how many" of something. In "real life," it makes a big difference whether you have two cookies or eight cookies. **In grammar, all we care about is whether there is just one of something or more than one.** If there's just one of something, we say that it's **singular**. Once you have more than one, that's **plural**. When you're choosing a verb ending, you have to ask yourself, "How many people are doing this action?" If it's just one person, you choose a singular ending. If it's more than one person, you choose a plural ending.

Quick Quiz 5: Circle the words that are **plural** (that mean "more than one person"), and underline the words that are **singular**.

yo (I) **ustedes** (you all) **nosotros** (we) **ellos** (they) **ella** (she)

Quick Quiz 6: Here are a bunch of different conjugated verbs. Circle the ones that are **plural** (more than one person is doing the action), and underline the ones that are **singular** (just one person is doing the action).

hablaré	**como**	**vivimos**	**salió**	**cantaron**
bailé	**corriste**	**necesitan**	**compraremos**	**leerás**

Person

"Person" is a fancy grammar word we use to explain the relationship between the one doing the action (the subject) and the one saying the sentence (the speaker). If a verb is in the **first person**, that means the speaker and the subject are the same guy (or girl). If a verb is in the **second person**, the speaker is talking right to the subject of the sentence. The speaker will use words such as "you" to talk directly to a second-person subject. That means the "second person" is the listener or reader. When I write a sentence in this book to you, there are two of us, right? Me and you. That makes you the second person, the one listening to or reading the words of the speaker.

What about **third person**? Third person is when the subject of the sentence is neither the speaker nor the reader/listener. It's some other person. A sentence with a third-person subject isn't said or written *to* the third person; it's said or written *about* the third person. Here's the diagram we used in the previous book to help you understand person in verbs:

Quick Quiz 7: Draw moustaches on all the people in the pictures.

Recap

So, let's do a quick recap: Verbs have a basic form, called an infinitive. When you conjugate a verb, you take off the last two letters of the infinitive form in order to add endings. The endings you add will show you the verb's person and number (who's doing the action and how many people are doing it), as well as the verb's tense (when the action is taking place). In *SFCA*, you learned the endings for three tenses: present tense, preterit tense, and future tense. Future tense is a little different because you add the endings right to the infinitive instead of taking off the **-ar**, **-er**, or **-ir** to find the stem first.

Three Extra Tenses

In *SFCA*, you learned about three tenses that use a verb conjugated in the present tense with an extra verb added on to indicate the action you wish to describe. Do you remember them?

1. Near-Future Tense

This tense is for actions that are going to happen soon. It's like saying "I'm going to eat ice cream" instead of "I will eat ice cream." You make this tense with the verb **ir** (to go) conjugated in the present tense, plus the word **a**, plus the verb the subject is going to do.

ir + a + infinitive

Voy a cantar. (I'm going to sing.)
Vas a caer. (You're going to fall.)
Vamos a llorar. (We're going to cry.)
Van a desayunar. (They're going to eat breakfast.)

Quick Quiz 8: Finish the sentence to say what you are going to do after you finish this grammar chapter. Use a verb in the infinitive form.

Voy a ____.

2. Near-Past Tense

This tense is for actions that just happened. It's like saying "I just ate ice cream" instead of "I ate ice cream." The cool thing about this tense is that even though it shows a past action, you just use a present-tense form of the verb **acabar** (to finish). You conjugate **acabar** in the present tense to match your subject, then you add the word **de** and the infinitive of your verb.

acabar + de + infinitive

Acabo de cantar. (I just sang.)
Acabas de caer. (You just fell.)
Acabamos de llorar. (We just cried.)
Acaban de desayunar. (They just ate breakfast.)

Quick Quiz 9: Finish the sentence to tell something you just did. Use a verb in the infinitive form.

Acabo de ______________________________.

3. Present-Progressive Tense

Similar to the present tense, the present-progressive tense is for things that are happening right now. But with the present-progressive tense, you emphasize that an action is right in the middle of happening as you speak. How do you make this tense? You use the verb **estar** (to be) conjugated in the present tense. Then you add something called a **present participle**, which is your verb with the last two letters chopped off and **-ando** (for **-ar** verbs) or **-iendo** (for **-er**/**-ir** verbs) added onto the end.

estar + verb stem **+ -ando/-iendo**

Estoy comiendo. (I'm eating.)
Estás trabajando. (You're working.)
Él está bailando. (He's dancing.)
Estamos escribiendo. (We're writing.)
Están esperando. (They're waiting.)

Quick Quiz 10: Turn an infinitive verb into a present participle!

1. Write your infinitive: ______________________________
2. Chop off the last two letters to find the stem: ______________________________
3. Add **-ando** if it's an **-ar** verb or **-iendo** if it's an **-er** or **-ir** verb:

____

Quick Quiz 11: Put your present participle into a sentence to say what you're doing right now (even if it's not true):

Estoy ______________________________.

Quick Quiz 12: Draw a picture of a person to illustrate the sentence you just wrote. Make a speech bubble coming out of the person's mouth in the drawing, and write your present-progressive tense sentence in the speech bubble.

A. Translation:

1. **desayunaré**	______________	9. **word**	______________
2. **to cut**	______________	10. **la página**	______________
3. **pencil**	______________	11. **hablé**	______________
4. **pen**	______________	12. **canto**	______________
5. **el papel**	______________	13. **bailar**	______________
6. **el cuaderno**	______________	14. **I will run**	______________
7. **scissors**	______________	15. **I opened**	______________
8. **la mochila**	______________	16. **I lived**	______________

B. **Canto**: List the present-, preterit-, and future-tense endings.

	Present-Tense -ar Verb Endings	Present-Tense -er Verb Endings	Present-Tense -ir Verb Endings
yo (I)	**habl__**	**corr__**	**viv__**
tú (you)	**habl__**	**corr__**	**viv__**
él/ella/usted (he/she/you, formal)	**habl__**	**corr__**	**viv__**
nosotros (we)	**habl_____**	**corr_____**	**viv_____**
vosotros (you all)	**habl*áis***	**corr*éis***	**viv*ís***
ellos/ustedes (they/you all)	**habl__**	**corr__**	**viv__**

	Preterit-Tense -ar Verb Endings	Preterit-Tense -er Verb Endings	Future-Tense Verb Endings
yo (I)	**bail__**	**abr__**	**cantar__**
tú (you)	**bail____**	**abr____**	**cantar___**
él/ella/usted (he/she/you, formal)	**bail__**	**abr__**	**cantar__**
nosotros (we)	**bail_____**	**abr_____**	**cantar_____**
vosotros (you all)	**bail*asteis***	**abr*isteis***	**cantar*éis***
ellos/ustedes (they/you all)	**bail____**	**abr_____**	**cantar___**

C. Grammar:

1. What is tense? Circle one:
   a. The feeling you get when you didn't memorize your **canto**, and the teacher asks you to sing it
   b. The number of people doing an action
   c. A part of speech, such as a noun or a verb
   d. The grammatical way of saying "the time in which an action happens"
   e. Both a and d
2. What do all verbs have? Circle one:
   a. Person and number
   b. Person, gender, and tense
   c. Person, number, and tense
   d. Mommies who love them
3. In this list of jumbled words, write a "1" over first-person words, a "2" over second-person words, and a "3" over third-person words. Some words are in Spanish, and some are in English. Spanish words are **bold**, and English words are *italicized.*

canto	*I*	**bailamos**	*you all*	**tú**	*they*	*we*	**correrán**	*she*	**viviste**

Extra Tenses:

1. Write the formulas for the three extra tenses you reviewed in this chapter.

   a. The **near-past** tense: ____________ + ______ + infinitive

   b. The **near-future** tense: __________ + ______ + _________________

   c. The **present-progressive** tense: **estar +** ____________ _________________
2. The following are sets of three sentences. Write a "1" over the sentence that already happened. Write a "2" over the sentence that is happening right now. Write a "3" over the sentence that will happen.

   a. **Voy a cantar. Acabo de bailar. Estoy corriendo.**

   b. **Acabas de vivir en Nueva York. Estás viviendo en California. Vas a vivir en las montañas.**

   c. **Estoy pensando. Acabo de abrir el cuaderno. Voy a escribir.**[2]

2. Do you remember these words? You learned them in *SFCA*, but most of them are in the glossary in case you've forgotten. Guess what: You can do this exercise anyway, without knowing what these words mean!

A. New and Review Vocabulary:

Spanish	English
______________	to speak: I speak, I spoke, I will speak
cantar: canto, canté, cantaré	______________
______________	to dance: I dance, I danced, I will dance
correr: corro, corrí, correré	______________
abrir: abro, abrí, abriré	______________
______________	to live: I live, I lived, I will live
______________	to eat breakfast: I eat breakfast, I ate breakfast, I will eat breakfast
cortar: corto, corté, cortaré	______________
______________	pencil
______________	pen
el papel	______________
el cuaderno	______________
______________	scissors
______________	backpack
la palabra	______________
______________	page

B. Canto:

List the present-, preterit-, and future-tense endings.

	Present-Tense -ar Verb Endings	Present-Tense -er Verb Endings	Present-Tense -ir Verb Endings
yo (I)	**habl__**	**corr__**	**viv__**
tú (you)	**habl__**	**corr__**	**viv__**
él/ella/usted (he/she/you, formal)	**habl__**	**corr__**	**viv__**
nosotros (we)	**habl_____**	**corr_____**	**viv_____**
vosotros (you all)	habl*áis*	corr*éis*	viv*ís*
ellos/ustedes (they/you all)	**habl___**	**corr___**	**viv___**
	Preterit-Tense -ar Verb Endings	**Preterit-Tense -er/-ir Verb Endings**	**Future-Tense Verb Endings**
yo (I)	**bail__**	**abr__**	**cantar__**
tú (you)	**bail____**	**abr____**	**cantar___**
él/ella/usted (he/she/you, formal)	**bail__**	**abr__**	**cantar__**
nosotros (we)	**bail_____**	**abr_____**	**cantar_____**
vosotros (you all)	bail*asteis*	abr*isteis*	cantar*éis*
ellos/ustedes (they/you all)	**bail_____**	**abr_____**	**cantar___**

C. Grammar:

1. What are the three characteristics of a verb we talked about in this chapter?

____

2. What is "number" when we're talking about grammar?

____

____

3. What does a verb's tense tell you?

____

4. If a sentence is written in third person, the one doing the action is (circle one):
   a. The speaker
   b. The listener
   c. Somebody else
   d. Batman

5. Fill in the blanks to complete all of the tenses of the verb **cantar**. The present and present-progressive tenses have been provided for you.

   Preterit tense: **Yo ______________.**

   Near-past tense: **Acabo ___ cantar.**

   Present tense: **Yo canto.**

   Present-progressive tense: **Estoy cantando.**

   Near-future tense: **Voy ___ ______________.**

   Future tense: **Yo ______________.**

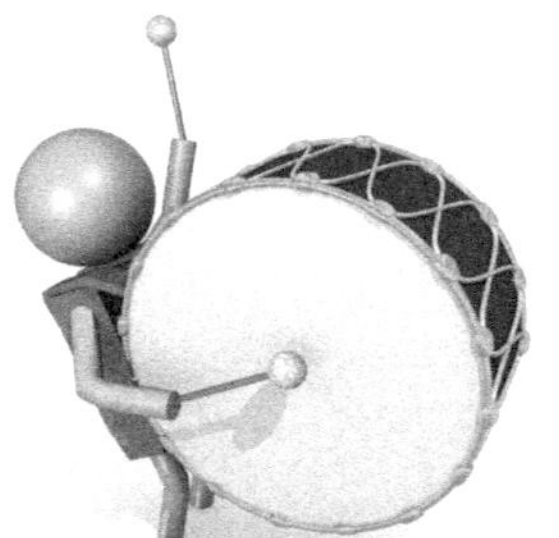

Canto:

Review of **Ser** (to be), **Estar** (to be), and **Ir** (to go) Present-Tense Forms

	Singular	Plural
Ser (to be: characteristics and "permanent" qualities)		
1st person	**soy** (I am)	**somos** (we are)
2nd person	**eres** (you are)	**sois** (you all are)
3rd person	**es** (he/she/it/**usted** is)	**son** (they/you all are)
Estar (to be: location, condition, and "temporary" qualities)		
1st person	**estoy** (I am)	**estamos** (we are)
2nd person	**estás** (you are)	**estáis** (you all are)
3rd person	**está** (he/she/it/**usted** is)	**están** (they/you all are)
Ir (to go)		
1st person	**voy** (I go)	**vamos** (we go)
2nd person	**vas** (you go)	**vais** (you all go)
3rd person	**va** (he/she/it/**usted** goes)	**van** (they/you all go)

Vocabulario:

Vocabulario nuevo

Spanish	English
mostrar: muestro, mostré, mostraré	to show: I show, I showed, I will show
bajar: bajo, bajé, bajaré	to go down: I go down, I went down, I will go down
venir: vengo, vine, vendré	to come: I come, I came, I will come

Spanish	English	Spanish	English
el almuerzo	lunch	**la fruta**	fruit
el desayuno	breakfast	**las verduras**	vegetables
la fiesta	party	**el postre**	dessert
la bebida	drink		

Vocabulario de repaso

Spanish	English
querer: quiero, quise, querré	to want/love: I want/love, I wanted/loved, I will want/love
tener: tengo, tuve, tendré	to have: I have, I had, I will have
poder: puedo, pude, podré	to be able to: I can, I could, I will be able to
poner: pongo, puse, pondré	to put/place: I put/place, I put/placed, I will put/place
hacer: hago, hice, haré	to make/do: I make/do, I made/did, I will make/do
ver: veo, vi, veré	to see: I see, I saw, I will see

Irregular Verbs

OK, so you've gotten the hang of conjugating verbs, and you're probably pretty good at it by now. But what about those big bad dudes, the irregulars? **Irregulars** are verbs that don't follow the regular rules of conjugation. Some of them have their own rules instead, and some don't follow any rules at all. To be a real pro at conjugating verbs, you have to know what to do when an irregular crosses your path. Do you? Let's find out. In this chapter, you can test your brain against the irregulars in the present and future tenses. In the next chapter, you'll go head-to-head with the irregulars in the preterit tense.

Irregulars That Break All the Rules

There are some irregular verbs that are "way out there"—they don't seem to follow any rules at all. Do you remember them? They are verbs such as **ser**, **estar**, **ir**, and **dar** in the present tense. What can you do about these guys? Memorize them! Many of the really common irregulars were **cantos** in the previous book. Do you remember them? Let's see! Fill in the following charts. To help you, the first chart has been completed for **dar**.

Dar (to give)
Present-Tense Forms

	Singular	Plural
1st person	**doy**	**damos**
2nd person	**das**	**dais**
3rd person	**da**	**dan**

Ser
Present-Tense Forms

	Singular	Plural
1st person	____________	____________
2nd person	____________	**sois**
3rd person	____________	____________

Estar
Present-Tense Forms

	Singular	Plural
1st person	____________	____________
2nd person	____________	**estáis**
3rd person	____________	____________

Ir
Present-Tense Forms

	Singular	Plural
1st person	____________	____________
2nd person	____________	**vais**
3rd person	____________	____________

Yo-Form Irregulars

In *SFCA*, you studied a lot of verbs that are only a little bit irregular. For instance, some verbs are only strange in the **yo** form, the first-person singular form. These **yo**-form irregulars are either **-go** verbs or **c » zc** verbs. **Tener**, **salir**, **caer**, and **poner** are all **-go** verbs. What are the **yo** forms of these verbs? **Tengo**, **salgo**, **caigo**, and **pongo**! As you can see, these verbs end in **-go** instead of just **-o** in their **yo** forms.

Obedecer, **traducir**, and **conducir** are **c » zc** verbs. The **yo** forms of these verbs get an extra little *z* added before the last *c*. They look like this: **obedezco**, **traduzco**, and **conduzco**.

Quick Quiz 1: Some of the forms in these conjugation charts are wrong! Cross out the incorrect verb forms. Write the correct verb forms in their places. Here's a hint: There are two mistakes in each chart.

Salir Present-Tense Forms

	Singular	Plural
1st person	**salgo**	**salimos**
2nd person	**salges**	**salís**
3rd person	**salge**	**salen**

Poner Present-Tense Forms

Singular	Plural
pono	**ponemos**
pones	**ponéis**
pone	**pongen**

Conocer Present-Tense Forms

	Singular	Plural
1st person	**conoco**	**conocemos**
2nd person	**conoces**	**conocéis**
3rd person	**conozce**	**conocen**

Stem-Change Verbs

Do you remember these guys? **Stem-change verbs** are those tricksters that change their stems when you try to conjugate them in the present tense (and sometimes other tenses). We also call these "boot verbs" because if you look at the following chart of a conjugated stem-change verb and fill in all the boxes where the verb changes its stem, you see the shape of a boot:

Querer

	Singular	Plural
1st person	**quiero**	**queremos**
2nd person	**quieres**	**queréis**
3rd person	**quiere**	**quieren**

Do you remember the four categories of stem-change verbs? In the following tables, a few verbs are listed with their present-tense conjugations. You are going to fill in the verb categories! The first one is done for you.

Verb	Conjugations		Category of Stem-Change Verbs
sentir (to feel)	**siento** **sientes** **siente**	**sentimos** sentís **sienten**	e » ie

Verb	Conjugations		Category of Stem-Change Verbs
pedir (to ask for)	**pido** **pides** **pide**	**pedimos** pedís **piden**	________________

Verb	Conjugations		Category of Stem-Change Verbs
poder (I can)	**puedo** **puedes** **puede**	**podemos** podéis **pueden**	________________

Verb	Conjugations		Category of Stem-Change Verbs
jugar (to play)	**juego** **juegas** **juega**	**jugamos** jugáis **juegan**	________________

Did you figure out the other three stem-change verb categories? They were **e » i**, **o » ue**, and **u » ue**.

Stem-Change Verbs "Plus"

Sometimes a verb isn't just a stem-change verb or a **yo**-form irregular. Sometimes it's both! Verbs such as **tener** and **venir** are stem-change verbs *and* **-go** verbs.

Quick Quiz 2: Tener and **venir** are stem-change verbs *and* **-go** verbs.

Circle one: True False

Quick Quiz 3: "Go verbs" is a special cheer you have to yell when you are conjugating verbs.

Circle one: True False

Future Irregulars

Guess what: Not only is the future tense really easy to conjugate, it also has a very easy set of irregulars! Remember, you make the future tense by adding the ending to the infinitive instead of to the stem. This means that there's no hassling with stem-change verbs in the future tense. The only irregular business in the future tense is a handful of verbs that do something "fancy." Instead of getting their future endings stuck on to their infinitives, these verbs have fancy new stems that they use just for the future tense. These fancy "future stems" are the same no matter the person and number of the verb. They're the same in the **yo** form as they are in every other form. That means you already have them memorized! Here they are, all in one convenient place. The **yo** forms have been completed for you. Fill in the **tú** forms (the first one is filled in to get you started).

Infinitive	Fancy Future Stem	Future-Tense yo Form	Future-Tense tú Form
decir	**dir-**	**diré**	**dirás**
haber[1]	**habr-**	**habré**	______________
hacer	**har-**	**haré**	______________
poder	**podr-**	**podré**	______________
poner	**pondr-**	**pondré**	______________
querer	**querr-**	**querré**	______________
saber	**sabr-**	**sabré**	______________
salir	**saldr-**	**saldré**	______________
tener	**tendr-**	**tendré**	______________
venir	**vendr-**	**vendré**	______________

Quick Quiz 4: How do you say "you will know" in Spanish? ______________

1. You haven't learned this verb yet, but don't worry—you will soon. It means "to have," as in "I *have* eaten anchovies." It doesn't mean "to have," as in "to have anchovies in your stomach." We'd use **tener** for that. You will learn more about this in chapter 16.

A. Translation:

1. **I will want/love**	__________	9. **I come**	__________
2. **tendré**	__________	10. **lunch**	__________
3. **I can**	__________	11. **breakfast**	__________
4. **puse**	__________	12. **party**	__________
5. **hacer**	__________	13. **la bebida**	__________
6. **veo**	__________	14. **fruit**	__________
7. **I show**	__________	15. **vegetables**	__________
8. **bajar**	__________	16. **el postre**	__________

B. Canto:

Ser (to be: characteristics and "permanent" qualities)

	Singular	Plural
1st person	__________	__________
2nd person	__________	**sois** (you all are)
3rd person	__________	__________

Estar (to be: location, condition, and "temporary" qualities)

	Singular	Plural
1st person	__________	__________
2nd person	__________	**estáis** (you all are)
3rd person	__________	__________

Ir (to go)

	Singular	Plural
1st person	__________	__________
2nd person	__________	**vais** (you all go)
3rd person	__________	__________

C. Grammar:

1. What are the different kinds of stem-change verbs?

____

2. Give an example of each kind of stem-change verb.

____

3. Which verbs are irregular in the future tense?

____

4. When a verb has a funky new stem in the future tense, is it the same in all the verb's future-tense forms (**yo**, **tú**, **él**, **nosotros**, etc.)?

____

D. Time Traveling!

In the following chart there are four verbs provided, and each one is in one of the three tenses we practiced in this chapter. Provide the missing forms for the other two tenses (stick with first-person singular forms). Use this as an opportunity to figure out which verbs you *don't* remember.

Infinitive	tener	poder	cortar	correr
Preterit	**yo tuve**	**yo pude**	**yo** __________	**yo** __________
Present	**yo** __________	**yo** __________	**yo corto**	**yo** __________
Future	**yo** __________	**yo** __________	**yo** __________	**yo correré**

A. New and Review Vocabulary:

Spanish	English
mostrar: muestro, mostré, mostraré	______________________
bajar: bajo, bajé, bajaré	______________________
venir: vengo, vine, vendré	______________________
el almuerzo	______________________
el desayuno	______________________
la fiesta	______________________
la bebida	______________________
la fruta	______________________
las verduras	______________________
el postre	______________________
querer: quiero, quise, querré	______________________
tener: tengo, tuve, tendré	______________________
poder: puedo, pude, podré	______________________
poner: pongo, puse, pondré	______________________
hacer: hago, hice, haré	______________________
ver: veo, vi, veré	______________________

B. Canto:

You know the drill—fill in the boxes!

Ser Present-Tense Forms

	Singular	Plural
1st person	______________	______________
2nd person	______________	**sois** (you all are)
3rd person	______________	______________

Estar Present-Tense Forms

	Singular	Plural
1st person	________________	________________
2nd person	________________	**estáis** (you all are)
3rd person	________________	________________

Ir Present-Tense Forms

	Singular	Plural
1st person	________________	________________
2nd person	________________	**vais** (you all go)
3rd person	________________	________________

C. Grammar:

See if you can fill in the blank spaces of this chart.

Infinitive	Fancy Future Stem	Future-Tense yo Form	Future-Tense tú Form
decir	**dir-**	**diré**	____________
hacer	**har-**	____________	**harás**
____________	**podr-**	**podré**	**podrás**
poner	____________	**pondré**	**pondrás**
querer	**querr-**	**querré**	____________
saber	**sabr-**	____________	**sabrás**
salir	**saldr-**	**saldré**	____________
____________	**tendr-**	**tendré**	**tendrás**
venir	**vendr-**	**vendré**	____________

Canto nuevo:

Ser Preterit-Tense Forms

	Singular	Plural
1st person	**fui** (I was)	**fuimos** (we were)
2nd person	**fuiste** (you were)	**fuisteis** (you all were)
3rd person	**fue** (he/she/it/usted was)	**fueron** (they/you all were)

Ir Preterit-Tense Forms

	Singular	Plural
1st person	**fui** (I went)	**fuimos** (we went)
2nd person	**fuiste** (you went)	**fuisteis** (you all went)
3rd person	**fue** (he/she/it/**usted** went)	**fueron** (they/you all went)

Vocabulario:

Vocabulario nuevo

Spanish	English
empezar: empiezo, empecé, empezaré	to begin: I begin, I began, I will begin
almorzar: almuerzo, almorcé, almorzaré	to eat lunch: I eat lunch, I ate lunch, I will eat lunch
conducir: conduzco, conduje, conduciré	to drive: I drive, I drove, I will drive
reducir: reduzco, reduje, reduciré	to reduce: I reduce, I reduced, I will reduce
creer: creo, creí, creeré	to believe: I believe, I believed, I will believe
el aeropuerto	airport
el avión	airplane
el autobús	bus
el barco	boat
la maleta	suitcase

Vocabulario de repaso

Spanish	English
decir: digo, dije, diré	to say/tell: I say/tell, I said/told, I will say/tell
saber: sé, supe, sabré	to know: I know, I knew, I will know
estar: estoy, estuve, estaré	to be: I am, I was, I will be
dormir: duermo, dormí, dormiré	to sleep: I sleep, I slept, I will sleep
pedir: pido, pedí, pediré	to ask for: I ask for, I asked for, I will ask for

The Preterit Puzzle: Preterit Irregulars

In the middle of all this reviewing, we're going to stop and do something new. We will take a look at the preterit tense again, and this time we're going to look at some irregulars.

You might be asking, "What is the preterit tense?" You probably finished *SFCA* thinking that the preterit tense is *the* past tense. But guess what—it's not! It's *a* past tense. In Spanish, there's more than one way to talk about actions that happened in the past, so we have more than one past tense. We'll get to that a bit later in the book. For now, you need to know why we're going to stop calling this tense "the past tense" and only call it "the preterit tense."

Preterit-tense conjugations have *tons* of irregulars—so many that we're not going to try to cover all of them in one chapter. Instead, you will be sent on a treasure hunt.

You've been doing so well learning Spanish that your **familia** decides to take you on **un viaje** to Mexico so you can get some extra practice. You're excited because you've always wanted to see the Mayan ruins. The ancient Mayans built **pirámides**, just as the Egyptians did. After spending a few **días** at the capital, Mexico City, your family rents a **carro** and drives deep into the jungle to **un pueblo** where Mayan people—the descendents of the ancient empire—still live. After going on jaguar-spotting hikes, riding a zip line through the jungle canopy, and having lots of chances to practice your Spanish with your tour guide, it's finally the day you've been waiting for: the day you visit **las ruinas**!

Paula, your tour guide, says that this is a special place to visit because **los turistas** are still allowed to climb on **las ruinas** and even go inside them. And there's another reason these **ruinas** are special: There's a mystery here.

Your visit to **las ruinas** starts in a little clearing. Just beyond the clearing there's a soaring **pirámide** with a tiny temple on top. Paula lets you climb up and see out over the jungle canopy. But the view from **el pirámide** isn't the best part. Paula presses a hidden switch, and a door in the back of the temple slowly slides open, revealing a steep stairway into the heart of **el pirámide**. After making sure everyone has a working flashlight, Paula tells everyone to follow her down the narrow stone stairway.

As you descend, Paula tells you that **el pirámide** was made for a great Mayan ruler, who instructed that the inside be constructed like a giant maze of crisscrossing corridors. According to ancient writings, this ruler hated his father, the previous ruler, and wished to destroy a valuable statue made of him, which featured diamonds for its eyes. The people had loved his father, however, so he dared not harm the statue but instead hid it in a secret chamber in **el pirámide**. To this day, no one has been able to find it.

At the bottom of the steps you see a maze of hallways stretching out in three directions. Paula points to a carving on the wall beside you and explains that it features a map of **el pirámide**. The ruler never revealed the location of the hidden treasure, but he did leave behind a set of puzzles that lead to it. Every time there is a fork in the path in the maze, each choice is marked by **una piedra** with a symbol on it. Each puzzle reveals the symbol of **la piedra** for the correct way to go. If someone were able to choose the correct **piedras** to follow, in order, he could follow the correct path and find the lost statue.

Paula mentions that many have tried, but so far no one has found the treasure. She looks your way and gives you a wink, asking, "Wanna give it a shot?"

Las piedras, young adventurer, are hidden in this book—and it is up to you to find them!

How are you going to find them? It's simple: Learn the preterit irregulars. Scattered throughout this book are eight "puzzle piece" sections. In each of these sections, you will be given a group of irregular verbs. Memorize their conjugations. Then, use what you know to choose a **piedra** by solving the provided exercises. Once you've discovered what all of the **piedras** are, you'll be able to find your way through the maze. Where does the treasure lie? The only way to find out is by solving the preterit puzzle.

La primera piedra:
First Preterit Puzzle Piece—Your First Clue

In this chapter, we're going to give you three **piedras** to get you started. Here's **la primera**.

How Do You Usually Form the Preterit Tense?

To earn this **piedra**, show that you know how to conjugate regular verbs in the preterit tense. You know the drill: Find the verb stems (for each verb, start with the infinitive, then chop off the last two letters) and add the preterit endings. What are your preterit endings? Let's list them again:

-ar Preterit Endings

	Singular	Plural
1st person	-___	-___ ◯ ___ ___
2nd person	-◯ ___ ___ ___	**-asteis**
3rd person	-___	-___ ___ ___ ◯

-er/-ir Preterit Endings

	Singular	Plural
1st person	-__	-__ __ __ __
2nd person	-__ __ __ __	**-isteis**
3rd person	-__ (◯)	-__ __ __ __ __

Now show that you know how to use regular preterit verbs. Finish each sentence with the verb given—make sure you conjugate for person and number.

Los estudiantes __ __ __ __ __ __ __ __ __ __ (◯) (*contestar*) **a las preguntas.**

Ayer mis hermanos y yo __ __ (◯) __ __ __ __ __ (*ayudar*) **a nuestra vecina** (neighbor).

En mi cumpleaños, __ (◯) __ __ (*abrir*) **regalos.**

Yo __ __ __ (◯) __ __ __ (*aprender*) **a decir mi nombre en chino** (Chinese) **.**

Tú __ __ __ __ (◯) __ __ (*comer*) **la carne.**

Now copy the letters from the circles on the previous page and above. Keep them in order (starting with the first-person plural in the **-ar** preterit endings chart), and you'll find a description of the hieroglyphs on your first **piedra**.

The **piedra** has a picture of a __ __ __ __ and __ __ __ __ __.

La segunda piedra:

Second Preterit Puzzle Piece

Preterit Verbs and –IR Stem Changes

To earn your second **piedra**, you have to learn about stem changes in the preterit tense. You don't have to worry about **-ar** and **-er** verbs, because even if they have stem changes in the present tense, they never do in the preterit tense. Did you get that? Remember, ***-ar* and *-er* verbs don't have stem changes in the preterit tense**. However, **-ir** verbs are a different story. They're a bit strange. Watch the stem change in the following table:

Pedir Preterit-Tense Forms

	Singular	Plural
1st person	**pedí**	**pedimos**
2nd person	**pediste**	**pedisteis**
3rd person	**pidió**	**pidieron**

Did you see that? That was a stem change—but only in the third-person singular and plural forms. The only verbs that change their stems in the preterit tense are ***-ir* verbs**, and they **only change their stems in the *él*, *ella*, *ellos*, *usted*, and *ustedes* forms**. Got that? Let's see it again with another stem-change verb.

Dormir Preterit-Tense Forms

	Singular	Plural
1st person	**dormí**	**dormimos**
2nd person	**dormiste**	**dormisteis**
3rd person	**d_u_rmió**	**d_u_rmieron**

Wait a minute . . . that wasn't even a real stem change! Usually when **dormir** has a stem change, the *o* changes to a *ue*. Here, the *o* just changed to a *u*. In the preterit, stem-change verbs that end in **-ir** only have a little bit of a stem change. **They only get the first vowel of their "new stem" vowels.** So, for example, an **o » ue** verb just gets a *u* in the preterit, and an **e » ie** just gets an *i*.

Are you ready to earn your next **piedra**? Then, fill in the blanks with the following:

The present-tense **yo** form of **servir**: ___ ___ ___ ___ ___

The present-tense **nosotros** form of **servir**: ___ ___ ___ ___ ___ ___ ___ (_)

The preterit-tense **nosotros** form of **servir**: ___ ___ ___ ___ ___ ___ ___ ___

The preterit-tense **yo** form of **servir**: ___ (_) ___ ___ ___

The preterit-tense **ella** form of **servir**: ___ ___ (_) ___ ___ ___

The present-tense **yo** form of **preferir**: (_) ___ ___ ___ ___ ___ ___ ___

The preterit-tense **yo** form of **preferir** (remember, there is no stem change in the preterit-tense **yo** form): ___ ___ ___ ___ ___ ___ (_)

The preterit-tense **ustedes** form of **preferir** (remember, just use the first vowel of the stem change): ___ ___ (_) ___ ___ ___ ___ ___ ___ ___ (_)

The present-tense **él** form of **morir**: ___ ___ ___ ___ ___

The preterit-tense **él** form of **morir**: ___ ___ ___ ___ ___

The preterit-tense **tú** form of **morir**: ___ ___ ___ ___ ___ (_) (_)

Once you've filled in all the blanks, write out the circled letters in order.

The design on the next **piedra** is a ___ ___ ___ ___ ___ ___ ___ ___ ___.

La tercera piedra:

Third Preterit Puzzle Piece

The Irregular Preterit-Tense Verbs

We're going to give you one last chance in this chapter to earn a **piedra**, and this will be the hardest one yet. These verbs are so irregular that you'll just need to memorize them. You're ahead of the game because you've already learned the **yo** form of each of them. From the **yo** form, you can basically guess what the other forms will be. And there's another added bonus: The verbs **ser** and **ir** have exactly the same forms in the preterit tense! And there's one more thing: **These really irregular guys don't have any accents in the preterit form.**

Preterit-Tense Forms

	Ser and **Ir**		**Dar**		**Ver**	
	Singular	Plural	Singular	Plural	Singular	Plural
1st person	**fui**	**fuimos**	**di**	**dimos**	**vi**	**vimos**
2nd person	**fuiste**	**fuisteis**	**diste**	**disteis**	**viste**	**visteis**
3rd person	**fue**	**fueron**	**dio**	**dieron**	**vio**	**vieron**

Are you ready to earn your puzzle piece? Translate the following phrases into Spanish.

1. I gave: ___ ___

   I saw: ___ ___

   I went: ___ ___ ___

   I was: ___ ___ ___

2. you gave: ◯ ___ ___ ___ ___

   you saw: ___ ___ ___ ___ ___

   you went: ___ ◯ ___ ___ ___ ___

   you were: ___ ___ ___ ___ ___ ___

3. he gave: ___ ___ ___

   she saw: ___ ___ ___

   you **usted** went: ___ ___ ◯

   it was: ___ ___ ___

4. we gave: ___ ___ ___ ___ ___

   we saw: ___ ___ ___ ___ ___

   we went: ___ ___ ___ ___ ___ ___ ___

   we were: ___ ___ ___ ___ ___ ___

5. they gave: ___ ___ ___ ___ ___ ___

   they saw: ___ ___ ___ ◯ ___ ___

   you all **ustedes** went: ___ ___ ___ ___ ◯ ___

   you all **ustedes** were: ___ ___ ___ ___ ___ ___

Write out the letters from the blank spaces in circles: ___ ___ ___ ___ ___

But that word doesn't make any sense! Use this decoder to find out what symbols are on your next **piedra**. The top row of letters on the decoder corresponds to the letters from the circles you've written out. The bottom row of letters is what the corresponding letters from the top line should be. For example, if one of the letters written from the circles was *a*, then you would need to change the *a* to an *x* because *x* is underneath the *a* on the decoder.

a	b	c	d	e	f	g	h	i	j	k	l	m	n	o	p	q	r	s	t	u	v	w	x	y	z
x	y	z	a	b	c	d	e	f	g	h	i	j	k	l	m	n	o	p	q	r	s	t	u	v	w

So, the next **piedra** has a picture of an ___ ___ ___ ___ ___. (Hint: It needs an accent!)

A. Translation:

1. **I began**	__________	9. **boat**	__________
2. **to eat lunch**	__________	10. **la maleta**	__________
3. **conduzco**	__________	11. **decir**	__________
4. **reduje**	__________	12. **sé**	__________
5. **creo**	__________	13. **estuve**	__________
6. **airport**	__________	14. **I slept**	__________
7. **el avión**	__________	15. **to ask for**	__________
8. **bus**	__________		__________

B. **Canto**:

Ser Preterit-Tense Forms

	Singular	Plural
1st person	__________	__________
2nd person	__________	**fuisteis**
3rd person	__________	__________

Ir Preterit-Tense Forms

	Singular	Plural
1st person	__________	__________
2nd person	__________	**fuisteis**
3rd person	__________	__________

C. Grammar:

1. What kinds of verbs do *not* do a stem change in the preterit tense? Circle one:
   a. **-ar** verbs only
   b. **-ir** verbs
   c. Lazy verbs
   d. **-ar** and **-er** verbs

2. When a stem-change **-ir** verb is conjugated in the preterit, which forms have a stem change? Circle one:
   a. The **yo** form and the **nosotros** forms (first-person singular and plural forms)
   b. The **tú** and **usted** forms (first- and third-person singular forms)
   c. The **él/ella/usted** forms and the **ellos/ustedes** forms (third-person singular and plural forms)
   d. All of them
   e. None of them

Quick Quiz: When an **-ir** verb *does* change its stem in the preterit tense, what ends up missing? Circle one:
   a. The verb ending
   b. The second vowel of the new stem
   c. The first letter of the verb
   d. All the fun

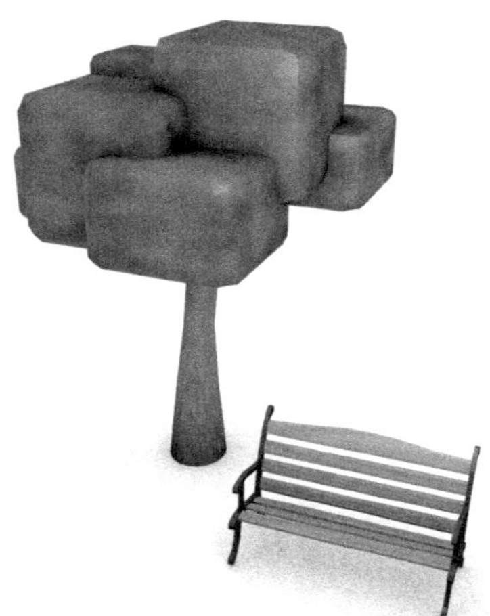

A. New and Review Vocabulary:

Spanish	English
______________	**to begin: I begin, I began, I will begin**
______________	**to eat lunch: I eat lunch, I ate lunch, I will eat lunch**
______________	**to drive: I drive, I drove, I will drive**
______________	**to reduce: I reduce, I reduced, I will reduce**
______________	**to believe: I believe, I believed, I will believe**
______________	**airport**
______________	**airplane**
______________	**bus**
______________	**boat**
______________	**suitcase**
______________	**to say/tell: I say/tell, I said/told, I will say/tell**
______________	**to know: I know, I knew, I will know**
______________	**to be: I am, I was, I will be**
______________	**to sleep: I sleep, I slept, I will sleep**
______________	**to ask for: I ask for, I asked for, I will ask for**

B. Canto:

Ser Preterit-Tense Forms

	Singular	Plural
1st person	______________	______________
2nd person	______________	fuisteis
3rd person	______________	______________

Ir Preterit-Tense Forms

	Singular	Plural
1st person	______________	______________
2nd person	______________	**fuisteis**
3rd person	______________	______________

C. Bad Conjugations!

A student wrote a bunch of sentences using irregular preterit verbs. He was really sleepy and made an error in every verb. His teacher corrected his work on another sheet of paper . . . but then her pet turtle chewed it up! Help her put the paper back together by *circling* the correct sentences and *crossing out* the incorrect ones.

1. a. **Encontraste a un amigo.** b. **Encuentraste a un amigo.**
2. a. **Susana dormió mal.** b. **Susana durmió mal.**
3. a. **Nosotros imos a nuestra casa.** b. **Nosotros fuimos a nuestra casa.**
4. a. **Yo vi un avión en el aeropuerto.** b. **Yo ví un avión en el aeropuerto.**
5. a. **Tú diste un regalo a tu abuelo.** b. **Tú daste un regalo a tu abuelo.**

Canto:

Review of Articles and Adjective Endings

	Definite Articles		Indefinite Articles		Adjective Endings	
	Singular	Plural	Singular	Plural	Singular	Plural
Masculine	**el**	**los**	**un**	**unos**	**-o**	**-os**
Feminine	**la**	**las**	**una**	**unas**	**-a**	**-as**

Vocabulario:

Vocabulario nuevo		Vocabulario de repaso	
Spanish	English	Spanish	English
limpio/a/os/as[1]	clean	**grande/es**	big
sucio/a/os/as	dirty	**pequeño/a/os/as**	little
feliz/felices	happy	**bueno/a/os/as**	good
triste/es	sad	**malo/a/os/as**	bad
divertido/a/os/as	fun		
aburrido/a/os/as	boring		
difícil/difíciles	difficult		
fácil/fáciles	easy		
diferente/es	different		
mismo/a/os/as	same		
yo mismo/yo misma	myself		

1. In *SFCA*, adjectives were presented in their full form for each person and number, for example, **gordo/gorda/gordos/gordas**. In this book, adjectives will be presented in a slightly different manner—the previous example would be formatted as **gordo/a/os/as**. Only the full form of the singular masculine will be given, but immediately following it will be the feminine ending, provided that the term is an adjective that changes forms in the feminine (remember, only adjectives ending in **-o** or **-dor** will change forms). For an adjective ending in **-o**, in order to change it to its feminine form, you simply drop the **-o** ending and replace it with an **-a** (e.g., **gordo** » **gorda**). The lexical form for this type of adjective would be **gordo-a**. For an adjective ending in **-dor**, you simply add an **-a** (e.g., **hablador** » **habladora**). The lexical form would then appear as **hablador-a**. No plural forms will be given. In order to make any adjective plural, you simply add an **-s** ending if it ends in a vowel (e.g., **gordo** » **gordos**) or an **-es** ending if it ends in a consonant (e.g., **leal** » **leales**).

Word Jobs: Nouns, Articles, and Adjectives

What's That Word's Job?

We just spent a lot of time (three whole chapters!) talking about verbs. Now it's time to talk about some other kinds of words, other *parts of speech*. First, let's create a sentence we can use to see all the different parts of speech. How about, "Inés sings a song"? That will work. Let's put it in Spanish: **Inés canta una canción.**

First let's look at our verb. What is it? It's **canta**, right? Singing is the action that Inés is doing.

Let's turn that last point around: Who is doing the action? Inés is. That makes her the subject of the sentence. **The *subject* of the sentence is the noun that does the action.**

What part of speech is "Inés"? Well, you might be thinking, *Inés is about four feet tall, she has dark hair and bangs, and she's wearing a purple sweater.* Those things might be true, but that doesn't matter when we study grammar. All that matters right now is that **Inés is a "person, place, or thing," which makes her a *noun*.**

More About Nouns: Number

Once we know Inés is a noun, there's a lot more we have to think about. In Spanish and English, **nouns have number**. You know what number is—the difference between *singular* (just one) and *plural* (more than one). In both languages, a plural noun usually ends in *-s*. In Spanish, when a singular noun ends in a consonant, we usually give it an **-es** ending to make it plural, as in the following examples:

cuaderno + -s = cuadernos **avión + -es = aviones**

Inés is a funny example, because her name ends in the letter *s*—but is she singular or plural? What do you think?

Quick Quiz 1: Write an *S* over all the nouns that are singular. Write a *P* over all the nouns that are plural.

canción	**lápices**	**bebida**	**papeles**	**frutas**	**maleta**	**aviones**

Quick Quiz 2: Make these singular nouns plural.

1. **canción** ______________
2. **papel** ______________
3. **autobús** ______________
4. **aeropuerto** ______________
5. **barco** ______________

More About Nouns: Gender

In Spanish (but not English), nouns also have **gender**. That means they are either **masculine** ("boy" words) or **feminine** ("girl" words). We know that some nouns are things that really do have gender, such as people and animals. We call that **natural gender**. Words such as **chico** and **chica** (boy and girl) have natural gender because the things those words are talking about have gender, too. In these cases, the grammatical gender just matches the natural gender of the noun. For example, my **abuelo** (grandfather) is a man, and in Spanish the word for grandfather is a masculine word. It has an **-o** ending because **-o** is the **masculine noun ending**. My **abuela** (grandmother) is a woman, and the word **abuela** is feminine. It has an **-a** ending, the **feminine noun ending** in Spanish.

What about a noun that doesn't have a natural gender? What about, say, a mountain? Or a car? Or a sled? When a noun doesn't have a natural gender in Spanish, it has an **assigned gender**. As the Spanish language was developing, people "assigned" words as having either one gender or the other. That's because in Spanish nouns always have to be either masculine or feminine; there are no nouns in Spanish that are **neuter** (neither masculine nor feminine). Gender has nothing to do with what the thing itself is. A pink, frilly **vestido** (dress) is still a masculine noun, and it has that masculine **-o** ending.

But let's get back to Inés. We know her gender: She's a girl, so words that match her will have to be feminine. Let's use another noun. How about **amiga** (friend)? It's going to have that **-a** on the end, since she is a friend who is a girl.

Mi amiga Inés canta una canción. (My friend Inés sings a song.)

Amiga is a noun, and it's a feminine noun. Now we're going to get fancy and describe that noun.

Words That Describe Nouns: Adjectives

When we want to describe a noun, we use an adjective. **Adjectives** are words that describe nouns. In Spanish, **adjectives usually go *after* nouns** (not before, as in English), **and they must have the same number and gender as the nouns they describe**. So, what do you do to make your adjective agree? Why, add the proper adjective ending, of course! Most adjectives come with an **-o** on the end, because we tend to use the masculine singular ending as a default. So, you'll have to take off that **-o** before you put another ending on. Let's see it in action.

The gender of **amiga** is feminine, and it doesn't have an **-s** on the end, so we know it's singular. That means we need a **feminine singular adjective**. How about the adjective **cómico** (funny)? We'll need to change the **-o** on the end to an **-a** before we use it with **amiga**.

Mi amiga cómica, Inés, canta una canción. (My funny friend, Inés, sings a song.)

Neuter Adjectives

Some adjectives never end in **-a** or **-o**. Instead, as with the words **grande** (big) or **triste** (sad), they end in an **-e** or another letter. When an adjective doesn't end in **-a** or **-o**, it doesn't have gender. It's called neuter (without gender), and it can match any kind of noun—as long as it has an **-s** on the end if the noun is plural.

mi amiga triste **mis amigas tristes**

mi amigo triste **mis amigos tristes**

When an adjective ends in a consonant, to make it plural you have to add **-es** instead of just **-s**.

la tarea difícil **las tareas difíciles**

Got it? Now let's talk about another little part of speech that has to match a noun in gender and number: articles.

Articles: Matching Nouns in Gender and Number

What are **articles**? The articles in English are "the," "a," "an," and "some" ("some" is the English equivalent of the Spanish indefinite articles **unos** and **unas**). Their main job is to go in front of a noun and tell you whether it's talking about something specific or something general. Watch:

Inés sings *the* song. Inés sings *a* song.

In the first sentence, we used a **definite article**. A definite article has to indicate a specific noun—the noun must be a specific thing. With the definite article "the" in that first example sentence there, Inés is definitely singing *the* song, not just any old song, not a song she chose at the last minute, but a very specific song: *the* song!

In the second example sentence, Inés is just singing *a* song—any old song. It doesn't matter which song; in fact, maybe we don't even know it. That's why we use the indefinite article "a." Remember, **indefinite articles** indicate a *general* (not specific) category of nouns.

Do you remember the definite and indefinite articles in Spanish? Put them in *the* chart (not any old chart, *the* one right here). Then do *a* dance. It doesn't have to be the "Dance of the Sugarplum Fairy." Any old dance will do!

	Definite Articles		Indefinite Articles	
	Singular	Plural	Singular	Plural
Masculine	________	________	________	________
Feminine	________	________	________	________

Now, we return to our sentence about Inés.

Mi amiga Inés canta una canción. (My friend Inés sings a song.)

Let's look at the noun **canción**. It doesn't have the usual **-a** or **-o** ending. But can you tell the gender of the noun by the gender of its article? They have to match. So, what is the gender of **canción**? Is it masculine or feminine? And is **una** a definite or indefinite article?

You got it—**canción** is feminine, and **una** is an indefinite article. Good job!

A. Translation:

1. **same**	______	9. **happy**	______
2. **myself**	______	10. **sad**	______
3. **good**	______	11. **fun**	______
4. **bad**	______	12. **boring**	______
5. **big**	______	13. **difficult**	______
6. **little**	______	14. **easy**	______
7. **clean**	______	15. **different**	______
8. **dirty**	______		

B. Canto:

You know how to do it! Fill in the boxes with this week's **cantos**.

	Definite Articles		Indefinite Articles	
	Singular	Plural	Singular	Plural
Masculine	______	______	______	______
Feminine	______	______	______	______

Adjective Endings

	Singular	Plural
Masculine	______	______
Feminine	______	______

C. Grammar:

1. What is the subject of a sentence?

____

2. What are the two characteristics of nouns?

____

3. What are the two kinds of articles? Circle one:
   a. Masculine and plural
   b. Definite and feminine
   c. Definite and indefinite
   d. Singular and indefinite
   e. Past-tense and present-tense
4. What does it mean that articles and nouns have to "agree"?
   a. They have to have the same gender and tense.
   b. They have to have the same tense.
   c. They have to have the same gender and number.
   d. They have to play nice.
5. Circle the word that has assigned gender: **chico** **mamá** **canción**
6. Circle the words that could agree with the word **casa**.

   Articles: **el** **la** **los** **las** **un** **una** **unos** **unas**

   Adjectives: **pequeña** **bueno** **grande** **sucias** **limpios**

D. Practice Out Loud!

Here are a few nouns. Read through the following list and say each noun with all of the new vocabulary words (from the beginning of this chapter) that are adjectives. To make it easy, the gender and number are provided for you. Remember, the noun will come first. Make sure you say the right form of the adjective—it has to have the same gender and number as your noun.

1. **casa** (house) – feminine, singular
   (Hint: To begin, you should say, "**Casa *limpia*, casa *sucia*, casa *feliz*** . . .")
2. **casas** (houses) – feminine, plural
3. **perro** (dog) – masculine, singular
4. **perros** (dogs) – masculine, plural
5. **chico** (boy) – masculine, singular
6. **chica** (girl) – feminine, singular

A. New and Review Vocabulary:

Spanish	English
limpio/a/os/as	________________
sucio/a/os/as	________________
feliz/felices	________________
triste/es	________________
divertido/a/os/as	________________
aburrido/a/os/as	________________
difícil/difíciles	________________
fácil/fáciles	________________
diferente/es	________________
mismo/a/os/as	________________
yo mismo/yo misma	________________
grande/es	________________
pequeño/a/os/as	________________
bueno/a/os/as	________________
malo/a/os/as	________________

B. Canto:

	Definite Articles		Indefinite Articles	
	Singular	Plural	Singular	Plural
Masculine	________	________	________	________
Feminine	________	________	________	________

Adjective Endings

	Singular	Plural
Masculine	______	______
Feminine	______	______

C. Grammar:

1. What does an adjective do? Circle one:
   a. It describes a verb.
   b. It describes a noun.
   c. It takes the place of a noun.
   d. It does the action of the sentence.

2. What does the subject of a sentence do? Circle one:
   a. It does the action of the sentence.
   b. It describes a verb.
   c. It takes the place of a verb.
   d. It does anything it wants to.

3. What two qualities do nouns have? Circle one:
   a. Number and tense
   b. Number and order
   c. Number and gender
   d. Gender and tense

4. What is gender? Circle one:
   a. Whether or not a word is a "bad word"
   b. A part of speech
   c. Whether a word is masculine or feminine
   d. Whether a toy is owned by a girl or a boy

5. What does it mean when words "agree" with each other?

____

Canto: Review of Prepositions

Preposiciones sobre la ardilla
(Prepositions About the Squirrel)

La ardilla va:	*(The squirrel goes:)*
de mi casa	*(from my house)*
sin descanso	*(without a rest)*
por el parque	*(through the park)*
para su hogar	*(to its home)*
en el árbol	*(in the tree)*
al lado del lago.	*(beside the lake.)*
Llega a su nido	*(It arrives at its nest)*
con una nuez	*(with a nut)*
después de correr	*(after running and)*
antes de comer.	*(before eating.)*

Vocabulario:

Vocabulario nuevo	
Spanish	English
siempre	always
nunca	never
todavía	still
también	also
tarde	late
temprano	early
tampoco	neither
sólo	only
solo/a/os/as	alone
demasiado	too (plus an adjective)
demasiado/a/os/as	too much, too many

Vocabulario de repaso	
Spanish	English
por	for, by, through
para	for, toward
a	at, to
de	from, of
con	with
sin	without

Adverbs and Prepositions:

Do you remember talking about Inés in the last chapter in such sentences as **Inés canta una canción** (Inés sings a song)? Since we had so much fun hanging out with Inés, let's discuss her again in this chapter using some other example sentences. Now we're going to talk about **adverbs** and **prepositions**. Do you remember them?

Adverbs: Describing Verbs

Adverbs are words that describe verbs. Some examples of these are **bien** (well), **mal** (poorly), **rápidamente** (quickly), and **lentamente** (slowly). Adverbs answer the question, "*How* was the action done?" In Spanish, adverbs go after the verbs they modify. Let's plug one in to our sentence. In fact, you can do it yourself. Fill in the blank:

Mi amiga Inés canta __________. (My friend Inés sings ____________.)

Why was that so easy? Because **adverbs don't have gender, number, tense, or anything like that**. That means you don't have to worry about making them agree with any other words.

More Adverbs

That was so much fun! Let's look at some more adverbs. You might not think of these guys as adverbs, but they are. Adverbs can answer the questions "how?" "where?" or "when?"

también (too):	**La hermana de Inés canta también.**	(Ines' sister sings, too.)
muy (very):	**Inés canta muy bien.**	(Ines sings very well.)
siempre (always):	**Ella siempre ensaya por las tardes.**	(She always practices in the afternoon.)
todavía (still):	**¡Y ella juega todavía al fútbol!**	(And she still plays soccer!)

Adverb Building Blocks

You can even make your own adverbs. Do you remember learning how to make adverbs from adjectives? Here's the rule:

1. For adjectives ending in **-o**, change the **-o** to an **-a** and add **-mente**.
   perfecto (perfect) » **perfect- + -a + -mente** » **perfectamente** (perfectly)
2. For adjectives ending in **-a**, **-e**, or a consonant, just add **-mente**.
   fácil (easy) » **fácil + -mente** » **fácilmente** (easily)
   fuerte (strong) » **fuerte + -mente** » **fuertemente** (strongly)

Prepositions: Like Adverbs and Adjectives, Only Cooler

Do you remember **prepositions**? They are little words that get a bunch of their friends (other words) together to act like adverbs and adjectives. When a preposition is with a bunch of his word-buddies, the whole group of them is something called a **prepositional phrase**. A prepositional phrase works as a giant adverb or adjective. The preposition is the team captain of all his buds, so he's the first word of the prepositional phrase.

Why do we say prepositions are like adverbs and adjectives? Here's why: Prepositional phrases can describe nouns (like an adjective) *or* verbs (like an adverb). Let's put one of each kind into our sentence about Inés. Here's our original sentence:

Mi amiga Inés canta una canción. (My friend Inés sings a song.)

Let's start by adding a phrase that acts like an adverb. It will tell us *how* she sings because it will be describing the verb. Let's see . . . how does Inés sing? Or better yet, *where* does she sing? How about this:

Mi amiga Inés canta una canción <u>en la ducha</u>. (Inés sings a song <u>in the shower</u>.)

Did you see that? That little preposition **en** got the other words, **la** and **ducha**, to work together. All three of them do the job of telling us where Inés sings: She sings in the shower.

Now let's add a preposition that acts like an adjective. Let's describe Inés. We'll have the prepositional phrase modify the word **amiga**.

Mi amiga <u>de mi clase</u>, Inés, canta una canción. (My friend <u>from my class</u>, Inés, sings a song.)

A. Translation:

1. **for, by**	____________	10. **still**	____________
2. **para**	____________	11. **also**	____________
3. **to**	____________	12. **tarde**	____________
4. **from, of**	____________	13. **temprano**	____________
5. **with**	____________	14. **tampoco**	____________
6. **without**	____________	15. **only**	____________
7. **always**	____________	16. **alone**	____________
8. **nunca**	____________	17. **too (plus an adjective)**	____________
9. **too much, too many**	____________		

B. **Canto**: Prepositions

Write the Spanish word or phrase that means the same thing as the English words on the left.

English	Spanish	English	Spanish	English	Spanish
about, over	____________	to, for, toward	____________	with	____________
from	____________	in, on	____________	after	____________
without	____________	beside	____________	before	____________
through, for	____________	at, to	____________		____________

C. Grammar:

1. What questions can an adverb answer?

____

2. What kind(s) of words do adverbs modify (describe)?

____

3. Do adverbs have to agree in number and gender with other words?

____

4. What do prepositions do?

____

5. What is your favorite Spanish preposition? Use it in a sentence.

____

A. New and Review Vocabulary:

Spanish	English
siempre	_______________
nunca	_______________
todavía	_______________
también	_______________
tarde	_______________
temprano	_______________
tampoco	_______________
sólo	_______________
solo/a/os/as	_______________
demasiado	_______________
demasiado/a/os/as	_______________
por	_______________
para	_______________
a	_______________
de	_______________
con	_______________
sin	_______________

B. **Canto**: Prepositions

Fill in the prepositions. On the lines to the right, write the English translation of each preposition.

Spanish	English
Preposiciones __________ la ardilla	____________________
La ardilla va:	
____________________ **mi casa**	____________________
____________________ **descanso**	____________________
____________________ **el parque**	____________________
____________________ **su hogar**	____________________
____________________ **el árbol**	____________________
_______ _____________ _______ **lago.**	____________________
Llega ________ **su nido**	____________________
____________________ **una nuez**	____________________
______________ ________ **correr**	____________________
______________ ________ **comer.**	____________________

C. Grammar:

1. What does an adverb do? Circle one:
   a. It describes a verb.
   b. It takes the place of a noun.
   c. It describes a noun.
   d. It does anything it wants to.

2. A preposition gets a bunch of other words to work together and act like a(n)______________ or a(n) ______________.

Canto: Review of Pronouns

	Subject Pronouns	Direct-Object Pronouns	Indirect-Object Pronouns
1st-person singular	**yo** (I)	**me** (me)	**me** (me)
2nd-person singular	**tú** (you)	**te** (you)	**te** (you)
2nd-person formal	**usted** (you formal)	**lo/la** (you formal)	**le** (you formal)
3rd-person singular	**él/ella** (he/she)	**lo/la** (him/her/it)	**le** (him/her/it)
1st-person plural	**nosotros/nosotras** (we)	**nos** (us)	**nos** (us)
2nd-person plural	**vosotros/vosotras** (you all)	**os** (you all)	**os** (you all)
2nd-person plural formal (Latin American "you all")	**ustedes** (you all)	**los/las** (you all)	**les** (you all)
3rd-person plural	**ellos/ellas** (they)	**los/las** (them)	**les** (them)

Vocabulario:

Vocabulario nuevo

Spanish	English
temer: temo, temí, temeré	to fear: I fear, I feared, I will fear
escoger: escojo, escogí, escogeré	to choose: I choose, I chose, I will choose
enviar: envío, envié, enviaré	to send: I send, I sent, I will send

Spanish	English	Spanish	English
las noticias	news	**el problema**	problem
la flor, las flores	flower, flowers	**el idioma**	language
el parque	the park	**el programa**	program
la carta	letter	**el poema**[1]	poem

1. **Problema**, **programa**, **idioma**, and **poema**—what do you notice about these terms? These nouns all end in **-a**, but they're all masculine! Nouns that end in **-ma** are usually masculine because they come from Greek rather than Latin.

Vocabulario de repaso

Spanish	English
gustar: me gusta, me gustó, me gustará	to be pleasing: it is pleasing to me, it was pleasing to me, it will be pleasing to me
tirar: tiro, tiré, tiraré	to throw: I throw, I threw, I will throw
usar: uso, usé, usaré	to use: I use, I used, I will use
beber: bebo, bebí, beberé	to drink: I drink, I drank, I will drink
recibir: recibo, recibí, recibiré	to receive: I receive, I received, I will receive

Pronoun Review

There's one really important part of speech we haven't reviewed yet: **pronouns**. Pronouns are words that take the place of nouns. We use pronouns because sometimes we don't want to say the same noun over and over and over again. That's why you don't say, "Jorge eats guacamole with Jorge's brother in Jorge's house while Jorge watches Jorge's favorite TV show." That would be boring! Pronouns save us from utter boredom in sentences.

When you want to get rid of a noun and put a pronoun in its place, you need to know what job in the sentence the noun is doing. That way, you can use the right kind of pronoun. In this chapter, we'll review the different jobs nouns do in a sentence and the different kinds of pronouns that can take their places.

Subject Pronouns

Subject pronouns are words such as "I," "you," "we," "he," "she," "it," and "you all." They take the place of a noun that is the subject of a sentence. That means these subject pronouns are what you use for the one (or ones) doing the action of the sentence. The subject pronouns in Spanish are **yo**, **tú**, **usted**, **él**, **ella**, **nosotros/nosotras**, **vosotros/vosotras**, **ustedes**, and **ellos/ellas**. In Spanish, the verbs are conjugated in a way that tells you who is doing the action, so you only need to use a separate word for the subject if the subject is not clearly determined by the information provided in the rest of your sentence.

Subject pronouns have to agree in person and number with the noun they replace. Some subject pronouns have to agree in gender, too. Look at **nosotros**, **vosotros**, and **ellos**. They each refer to a group of people, right? We know that because each term is plural, and that's what plural means. If the group of people is all guys, or some guys and some girls, or even mostly girls and just one guy, these pronouns stay just the way they are. But if there isn't a single guy in the whole group, guess what: It's "girly time"! And what does your pronoun do when it's just girls? Put on makeup? Dress up? Wear high heels? Nope, it just switches that last **-o** for an **-a**. This way, you'll have a feminine pronoun to match a group of feminine nouns.

Fill in the missing **-o** and **-a** insertions in this chart to practice turning regular pronouns into girly-time pronouns.

	Masculine Plural Pronoun	Feminine Plural Pronoun—It's Girly Time!
1st person	**nosotros**	**nosotr___s**
2nd person	**vosotr___s**	**vosotras**
3rd person	**ell___s**	**ell___s**

The only other two subject pronouns that make you pay attention to gender are **él** and **ella**, which mean "he" and "she," respectively.

Being Polite

In Spanish, there are two sets of second-person pronouns. There's one set of "you" words for people who are *familiar* to you: your buddies, your cat, your mom and dad, and little kids. There's another set of "you" words for people you treat more *formally*, such as your teachers, adults, and strangers. Do you remember which pronouns are familiar and which pronouns are formal? **Tú** and **vosotros** are the familiar pronouns, and **usted** and **ustedes** are the formal ones. In Spain, people use **vosotros** to refer to a group of their buddies and **ustedes** to refer to a group of respected people. In the rest of the Spanish-speaking world (including the United States), people don't use **vosotros** at all. Regardless of who they talk to, they just use **ustedes** as the plural form of "you."

The tricky thing about **usted** and **ustedes** is that even though they are second-person pronouns, they get matched with third-person verbs. Do you remember the chart we use to show the person and number of verbs or pronouns? It usually has three rows of verbs or pronouns, but it can be done with four rows. Let's use the verb **hablar** as an example:

	Singular	Plural
1st person	**yo hablo**	**nosotros hablamos**
2nd-person familiar	**tú hablas**	**vosotros habláis**
2nd-person formal	**usted habla**	**ustedes hablan**
3rd person	**él/ella habla**	**ellos hablan**

If we did our chart in this manner, we would put the second-person formal form between the second-person familiar and the third-person forms, because even though it's a second-person pronoun, it acts like the third-person pronoun and goes with third-person verbs. In *SFCA*, we did our charts the "traditional way," with **usted** lumped together with **él** and **ella**, and **ustedes** lumped with **ellos**. In this book, we can do it either way, depending on which kind of chart will be the best for what we're studying. Got it? OK, on to more pronouns!

Direct-Object Pronouns

The direct- and indirect-object pronouns are a bit tricky because the rules for using them are slightly different in Spanish compared to how they are in English. Let's start with answering the question, "What is a direct object?" Do you remember? **A *direct object* is the noun or pronoun to which the verb does its action**, or the noun or pronoun that gets "acted upon." You can really get an idea for what a direct object is when it's missing from a sentence. Here are some sentences that *should* have direct objects, but the direct objects aren't there! Fill in some direct objects yourself. Just put a noun on each line.

Yo tiro ____________________**.** (I throw ____________________.)

Yo uso ____________________**.** (I use ____________________.)

Yo temo ____________________**.** (I fear ____________________.)

Have you chosen your direct-object nouns? Do you see how, in every case, the action of the verb is being done to the noun you filled in? That's what happens to a noun that is a direct object.

Now, what do you do if you want to put pronouns in place of the nouns? First, you decide your noun's person, number, and gender. Then, you find a pronoun that has the same person, number, and gender. Remember, **if your noun is a direct object, the only pronoun that can take its place is a *direct-object pronoun*.** Here are the direct-object pronouns:

	Singular	Plural
1st person	**me**	**nos**
2nd person	**te**	**vos**
3rd person	**lo/la**	**los/las**

Here's an example sentence using a noun:

Yo bebo una limonada. (I drink a lemonade.)

We want to just say, "I drink it." So, let's put a pronoun in for the lemonade. **Limonada** is a feminine singular noun, so I'll use the feminine singular direct-object pronoun **la**.

Yo la bebo.

Where does the direct-object pronoun belong? If the verb is conjugated (such as **bebo**), the direct-object pronoun goes *before* the verb. If the verb is in the infinitive form (such as **beber**), the pronoun goes *on the end of* the verb.

Let's take your first example sentence and give it some pronouns. First, figure out the gender and number of your noun. Then, choose the pronoun that goes in its place. Now plug your pronoun into the sentence. Remember, it goes before the conjugated verb:

Yo ____________________ tiro.

Now, add it to the end of an infinitive-form verb:

Yo quiero tirar_____.

Indirect-Object Pronouns

An *indirect object* is the noun or pronoun in the sentence that receives the direct object. For example, when we say, "You give your dog a biscuit," what is the thing you're giving? It's the biscuit, right? That makes the biscuit the direct object. Who gets that yummy direct object? Your dog does. That makes your dog the indirect object. If you look at a sentence and ask yourself, "for whom?" or "to whom?" then the indirect object will be the noun that answers your question. "*To whom* do you give a dog biscuit?" Why, to your *dog*, of course!

An indirect object is represented by an *indirect-object pronoun*. You probably were able to guess that! Remember, almost all of the indirect-object pronouns are the same as the direct-object pronouns—except for the third-person pronouns. Here they are in a chart. The third-person row has been completed for you, now you do the rest:

	Singular	Plural
1st person	__________	__________
2nd person	__________	**os**
3rd person	**le**	**les**

In Spanish, when you have an indirect object, you *also* have an indirect-object pronoun. Just like direct-object pronouns, indirect-object pronouns go before conjugated verbs. If a verb is in the infinitive form, the indirect-object pronoun attaches onto the end of the verb. So, let's see these pronouns in action. Here's an example sentence:

Le envío una carta a mi mamá. (I send a letter to my mom.)

In this sentence, "mom" is the indirect object, since she's the one getting the direct object (the letter). Because she's the indirect object, she needs a pronoun. Gender doesn't matter with indirect-object pronouns, so we can just use **le**, the third-person singular pronoun. There it is, in front of **envío**.

What if I want to get rid of the phrase **a mi mamá**? That's easy to do! Because the indirect-object pronoun is already in place, we can just drop the indirect-object noun, no problem. Here's what that looks like:

Le envío una carta. (I send her a letter.)

Where Do We Place Object Pronouns?

This question is really important, so we're going to answer it one more time. You know that when you have a direct- or an indirect-object pronoun, it goes in front of your verb, right? That is, unless your verb is in the infinitive form.

When we take out our nouns and put in pronouns, this is how it looks:

	Our verb is just in one part, and it's conjugated. So, we put the object pronoun *before* the verb.	Our verb is in two parts, and one part is in the infinitive form. So, we put our object pronoun *on the end* of the infinitive verb.
Let's put a direct-object pronoun in for una carta.	**La envío a mi mamá.**	**Quiero enviarla a mi mamá.**
Let's put an indirect-object pronoun in for mi madre.	**Le envío una carta.**	**Quiero enviarle una carta.**

But what if we want to take out *both* nouns? If we have an indirect-object pronoun (IO) *and* a direct-object pronoun (DO), they sit right next to each other, and **the indirect-object pronoun goes first.**

Se[3]	**la**	**envío.**
IO	DO	Verb

3. Did you forget this form? Keep reading, and you'll see that it's really a **le** in disguise!

But wait! What happened to our indirect-object pronoun? Remember, we never have **le la** or **le lo** together because those word combinations are too twisty for your tongue—too many *l* sounds! Whenever a third-person indirect-object pronoun (**le** or **les**) is next to a **la** or a **lo**, **le** turns into **se**. And what if we had a verb that was in the infinitive? Well, then our sentence would look like this:

(Verb) (2nd Verb)(IO)(DO)

Quiero enviársela.

The other indirect-object pronouns, such as **me**, **te**, and **nos**, won't change. They don't have to because they don't start with *l*.

Pronouns After Prepositions

We've barely spent any time on pronouns after prepositions because they're really easy! They are the same as the subject pronouns, except for the **yo** and **tú** forms. Here are some example sentences with pronouns after prepositions. See if you can tell what the "special after-preposition pronouns" are in the first- and second-person singular forms.

	Singular	Plural
1st person	**Juan corrió hacia *mí*.** (Juan ran toward *me*.)	**Tú llegaste antes de *nosotros*.** (You got here before *us*.)
2nd-person familiar	**Este regalo es de *ti*.** (This present is from *you*.)	**Viajo a Madrid con *vosotros*.** (I travel to Madrid with *you all*.)
2nd-person formal	**Quiero hablar con *usted*.** (I want to talk to *you*.)	**Quiero pasar un rato sin *ustedes*.** (I want to spend a little while without *you all*.)
3rd person	**Recibí unas noticias de *él*.** (I got some news from *him*.)	**Las galletas son para *ellos*.** (The cookies are for *them*.)

Did you figure it out? The **yo** and **tú** forms are **mí** and **ti**.

A mí me gustan los verbos.

Do you remember how to say, "I like" in Spanish? It looks like this:

Me gusta el parque. (I like the park.)

Me gusta caminar. (I like to walk.)

Me gustan las flores. (I like the flowers.)

When we say "I like ________" in Spanish, we are really saying, "________ is pleasing to me." Instead of being the subject of the sentence, you're the object. That's why we use an indirect-object pronoun (**me**) instead of a subject pronoun (**yo**) with the forms of **gustar**. If you look *really* closely, you'll see that the verb **gustar** is conjugated to agree in number with the thing you like: It's singular when you like "the park," and it's plural when you like "the flowers."

A. Translation:

1. **to fear**	______	9. **el idioma**	______
2. **I choose**	______	10. **program**	______
3. **I send**	______	11. **poem**	______
4. **news**	______	12. **it is pleasing to me**	______
5. **flower**	______	13. **tiraré**	______
6. **the park**	______	14. **I use**	______
7. **la carta**	______	15. **I will drink**	______
8. **problem**	______	16. **to receive**	______

B. Canto:

	Subject Pronouns	Direct-Object Pronouns	Indirect-Object Pronouns
1st-person singular	______	______	______
2nd-person singular	______	______	______
2nd-person formal	______	______	______
3rd-person singular	______	______	______
1st-person plural	______	______	______
2nd-person plural	**vosotros/vosotras** (you all)	**os** (you all)	**os** (you all)
2nd-person plural formal (Latin American "you all")	______	______	______
3rd-person plural	______	______	______

C. Grammar:

1. Pronouns take the place of (circle one):
   a. Verbs
   b. Adjectives
   c. Any kind of word
   d. Nouns
2. Subject pronouns take the place of the ______________________ of a sentence.
3. Which subject pronouns have to agree in gender with the noun they replace?

   ____

4. What is the subject pronoun you use to talk to an adult? ____________________
5. What is the subject pronoun you use to talk to a group of people if you are anywhere but

   Spain? ________________________________
6. What is the subject pronoun you use to talk to **un amigo**?____________________
7. The action of the verb is done to (circle one):
   a. The subject of the sentence
   b. The direct object
   c. The indirect object
   d. The verb ending
8. The indirect object is the one that answers the question (circle one):
   a. "Why?"
   b. "Who is doing the action?"
   c. "To whom?" or "For whom?"
   d. "Can I be done now?"
9. You can have a sentence with an indirect-object noun and have no indirect-object

   pronoun anywhere else in the sentence. Circle one: True False
10. When you put direct- and indirect-object pronouns together, what goes first?

    ____
11. Which sentence is correct? Circle one:
    a. **Te doy un regalo.** (I give you a present.)
    b. **Doyte un regalo.** (I give you a present.)
12. Which sentence is correct? Circle one:
    a. **Voy te a dar un regalo.** (I'm going to give you a present.)
    b. **Voy a darte un regalo.** (I'm going to give you a present.)

A. New and Review Vocabulary:

Spanish	English
___	to fear: I fear, I feared, I will fear
___	to choose: I choose, I chose, I will choose
___	to send: I send, I sent, I will send
___	news
___	flower, flowers
___	the park
___	letter
___	problem
___	language
___	program
___	poem
___	to be pleasing: it is pleasing to me, it was pleasing to me, it will be pleasing to me
___	to throw: I throw, I threw, I will throw
___	to use: I use, I used, I will use
___	to drink: I drink, I drank, I will drink
___	to receive: I receive, I received, I will receive

B. Canto:

	Subject Pronouns	Direct-Object Pronouns	Indirect-Object Pronouns
1st-person singular	__________	__________	__________
2nd-person singular	__________	__________	__________
2nd-person formal	__________	__________	__________
3rd-person singular	__________	__________	__________
1st-person plural	__________	__________	__________
2nd-person plural	**vosotros/vosotras** (you all)	**os** (you all)	**os** (you all)
2nd-person plural formal (Latin American "you all")	__________	__________	__________
3rd-person plural	__________	__________	__________

C. Grammar:

Here are some sentences with lots of nouns and pronouns. For each sentence, write *S* over the subject, *DO* over each direct object, and *IO* over each indirect object. Be careful! Not all of the sentences have direct and indirect objects. You'll have to think hard about this one.

1. **Yo le envié una carta a mi madre.** (I sent a letter to my mom.)

2. **Marcos recibe un regalo de su amigo. Marcos le dice "gracias."**
   (Marcos receives a present from his friend. Marcos tells him, "Thanks.")
   Note: Be careful—**de su amigo** is a prepositional phrase.

3. **Lupe te dijo las noticias.** (Lupe told you the news.)

4. **¿Quires tú una bebida? Ella te la dará.** (Do you want a drink? She will give it to you.)

5. **Abuelo necesita una flor. Yo voy a dársela.** (Grandpa needs a flower. I am going to give it to him.)

6. **¿Te gustan los poemas?** (Do you like poems?)

Repaso de vocabulario

Now that you've learned more than ninety new vocabulary words, as well as reviewed many words you learned in *SFCA*, here's a chance to see how much you remember! Check the boxes of each word you don't know. Then review those words as much as you need to in order to master them.

Chapter 1

☐	1. **to eat breakfast**	☐	5. **paper**	☐	9. **word**	☐	13. **to dance**
☐	2. **to cut**	☐	6. **notebook**	☐	10. **page**	☐	14. **to run**
☐	3. **pencil**	☐	7. **scissors**	☐	11. **to speak**	☐	15. **to open**
☐	4. **pen**	☐	8. **backpack**	☐	12. **to sing**	☐	16. **to live**

Chapter 2

☐	17. **to show**	☐	21. **breakfast**	☐	25. **vegetables**	☐	29. **to be able to**
☐	18. **to go down**	☐	22. **party**	☐	26. **dessert**	☐	30. **to put/place**
☐	19. **to come**	☐	23. **drink**	☐	27. **to want/love**	☐	31. **to make/do**
☐	20. **lunch**	☐	24. **fruit**	☐	28. **to have**	☐	32. **to see**

Chapter 3

☐	33. **to begin**	☐	37. **to believe**	☐	41. **boat**	☐	45. **to be**[1]
☐	34. **to eat lunch**	☐	38. **airport**	☐	42. **suitcase**	☐	46. **to sleep**
☐	35. **to drive**	☐	39. **airplane**	☐	43. **to say/tell**	☐	47. **to ask for**
☐	36. **to reduce**	☐	40. **bus**	☐	44. **to know**		

1. Hint: You know two words for "to be"!

Chapter 4

☐	48. **clean**	☐	52. **fun**	☐	56. **different**	☐	60. **little**
☐	49. **dirty**	☐	53. **boring**	☐	57. **same**	☐	61. **good**
☐	50. **happy**	☐	54. **difficult**	☐	58. **myself**	☐	62. **bad**
☐	51. **sad**	☐	55. **easy**	☐	59. **big**		

Chapter 5

63. **always**	68. **early**	72. **too (plus an adjective)**	76. **at, to**
64. **never**	69. **neither**	73. **too much, too many**	77. **from, of**
65. **still**	70. **only**	74. **for, by, through**	78. **with**
66. **also**	71. **alone**	75. **for, toward**	79. **without**
67. **late**			

Chapter 6

80. **to fear**	84. **flower, flowers**	88. **language**	92. **to throw**
81. **to choose**	85. **the park**	89. **program**	93. **to use**
82. **to send**	86. **letter**	90. **poem**	94. **to drink**
83. **news**	87. **problem**	91. **to be pleasing**	95. **to receive**

Story Jumble (Chapters 4 and 5)

Here's a story for you to read, but it looks as though you shook your book too hard and all the adverbs and adjectives fell out! They're in a big pile, and you need to decide where in the story each of them should go. Pick terms from the adverb and adjective pile to fill in the blanks in the story. In the following paragraph, little arrows will indicate which word each blank space is describing. Adverbs should describe ______________, and adjectives should describe ______________.

Remember, if you use an adjective, it needs to match its noun in gender and number.

Adverb and Adjective Pile:

feliz **diferente** **limpio** **aburrido** **sucio** **siempre** **fácil** **triste** **divertido** **difícil** **nunca** **también** **tarde** **temprano** **demasiado** **lentamente** **rápidamente** **fácilmente** **cómicamente**

Mi amigo ←______________________ llegó ←______________________ a mi casa. Su cara estaba ←______________________, y él entró ←______________________. Yo le

pregunté: "¿Tú estás ←_________________________?" Pero él me dijo, "No, ¡yo estoy ←_________________________!"

Conjugating in the Future Tense (Chapters 1 and 2)

Here's another story, and this time all the *verb endings* fell off! Figure out who is doing each action and then add the correct verb endings. The verbs are in parentheses beside each blank. Insert the complete verb form, with its ending, in each blank.

Mañana, ¡mi familia (*ir-*) ____________________ a Barcelona! Nosotros (*hablar-*) ____________________ español y yo (*ver-*) ____________________ a mis amigos. ¡Ellos (*dir-*) ____________________ que yo hablo muy bien el español! Nosotros (*jugar*) ____________________ en el parque. Mis padres (*visitar-*) ____________________ el Museo Picasso. Mi mamá (*comprar-*) ____________________ una pintura. ¡Tú (*querr-*) ____________________ ir conmigo!

Preterit Irregulars (Chapter 3)

Uh-oh, someone didn't learn their conjugations properly! This student left two possible answers in each sentence, because he wasn't sure how to properly conjugate these terms—they are italicized in parentheses. Finish this student's work by circling the correct conjugation in each sentence.

¡Marcos (*haco, hizo*) un gol!

Mis amigos y yo (*imos, fuimos*) al parque para un picnic.

Los estudiantes (*leieron, leyeron*) *Don Quijote*.

Yo (*dormí, durmí*) en una hamaca.

La maestra (*dijo, deció*) adiós.

Yo (*queré, quise*) ir con ustedes.

Mi padre (*sabió, supo*) la verdad (the truth).

¿(*Estiste, Estuviste*) en el parque?

¿(*Tenieron, Tuvieron*) ellas las flores?

Prepositions (Chapter 5)

1. When a preposition is followed by a number of other words—a prepositional phrase—it can function as a(n) ______________________________.
2. Prepositions in the Blender:
   You were trying to make a **batido** (a smoothie) while you did your Spanish homework, and you accidentally put the bananas in your backpack and your homework in the blender. See if you can draw lines to put the pieces back together and make complete sentences.

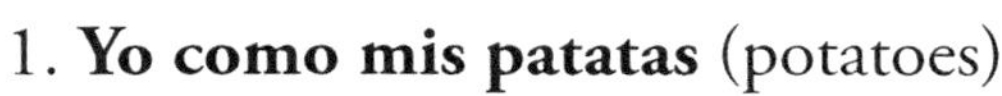

1. **Yo como mis patatas** (potatoes)	**en el restaurante.**
2. **Gracias**	**para su mamá.**
3. **Cenamos**	**con ketchup.**
4. **Yo le doy unas flores**	**por el ketchup.**
5. **Las flores son**	**a mi amiga.**

Algo más
(Something More)

Contractions

Do you know what contractions are? **A contraction is two words squished together to form one word** (such as “don’t” and “can’t”). There aren’t nearly as many contractions in Spanish as there are in English. All you need to worry about now are these four:

a (to) + **el** (the) = **al** (to the)	**con** (with) + **mí** (me) = **conmigo** (with me)
de (of) + **el** (the) = **del** (of the)	**con** (with) + **ti** (you) = **contigo** (with you)

Now, you try it! For each of the following sentences, circle the option that will form a *contraction*. Then, write out the sentence two ways, using both of the provided options. This way you’ll practice making sentences with contractions and without them.

1. **Voy a** ________
   a. **la escuela.**
   b. **el banco.**

Finished Sentences:
____
____

2. **Ella es la amiga de** ________
   a. **el presidente.**
   b. **la actriz.**

Finished Sentences:
____
____

3. **Mi hermano viene con** ________
   a. **nosotros.**
   b. **mi.**

Finished Sentences:
____
____

4. **Quiero jugar con** ________
   a. **Juan.**
   b. **ti.**

Finished Sentences:
____
____

Mucho and Poco

Usually when you memorize a word on your vocabulary list, you know which part of speech it is. We list verbs with several of their conjugations (such as **cantar: canto, canté, cantaré**), and nouns always come with articles in front of them (such as **el lápiz**, **la mochila**). You also know when a term is an adjective because we list it with the adjective endings, like this: **alto/a/os/as**.

But there are some words that can be many different parts of speech. Let's look at two of them: **mucho** and **poco**.

They can be *adjectives*:

Tengo *muchos* amigos. (**mucho** = many, a lot of)
Tengo *pocos* lápices. (**poco** = few, not many)

They can be *adverbs*:

Te quiero *mucho*. (**mucho** = a lot, very much)
Yo estudio *poco*. (**poco** = little, not much)

They can even be *pronouns*:

¿Tienes amigos? Sí, tengo *muchos*. (**mucho** = many, a lot)
¿Hablas español? Sí, hablo *un poco*. (**un poco** = a little bit)

You'll notice that these kinds of words tend to follow the rules for whatever part of speech they are at the time. When they're adjectives, they agree with their nouns in gender and number. When they're adverbs, they don't have to agree

with any other words. Keep your eyes open, and see how many part-of-speech changing words you can spot. You'll be surprised how many you'll come across!

Putting on a Play (Chapter 6)

A great way to get some extra practice in Spanish is to put on little plays. Even if you're all by yourself, you could always make some puppets and put on a Spanish puppet show. The more you practice speaking Spanish out loud, the better you will be! Here's a starter for you—the short script of a play with two characters: **el chico** and **el policía** (the police officer). There's just one problem: The person who wrote this play didn't know that in Spanish, people use the **tú** form when they are speaking to a child, a friend, or someone they know very well. Nor did the writer know that people use the **usted** form when they are speaking to an adult, a stranger, or someone they respect. So, which character do you think will use **tú** when he is talking to the other person? Which character will use **usted**? The following are their lines. Circle the correct pronouns, and conjugate the verbs. Remember, when you use the **usted** form, you will use third-person singular verbs and special pronouns. When you've finished the grammar, you can put on the play!

Policía: Buenos días.

Chico: Buenos días, señor.

Policía: ¿Qué (*hacer*, present tense**)** ____________ **(*tú*, *usted*) aquí?**

Chico: Yo busco a mi perro. ¿Lo (*ver*, preterit tense**)** ____________ **(*usted*, *tú*)?**

Policía: ¿Es grande (*su*, *tu*) perro?

Chico: Sí.

Policía: ¿Tiene un collar verde?

Chico: Sí.

Policía: ¿Es blanco y negro?

Chico: ¡Sí! Señor, ¡(*Usted*, *Tú*) (*ver*, preterit tense**)** ____________ **a mi perro!**

Policía: No, no lo vi.

Chico: ¿Qué?

Policía: No, no estoy en plan de broma. (I'm just kidding.) **(*Tu*, *Su*) perro está en la comisaría** (police station)**. Él (*le*, *te*) echa de menos.** (He misses you.)

Chico: Muchas gracias, señor. Y yo sé que mi perro le dirá gracias a (*ti*, *usted*) también.

What Do You Like? (Chapter 6)

Do you remember how to use the verb **gustar**? Practice talking about what you like!

1. Make a list of eight things you like. If you want to say that you like an activity, you can leave the verb in the infinitive form (for example, "I like *to run*," "**Me gusta *correr***").

   a. ______________________________

   b. ______________________________

   c. ______________________________

   d. ______________________________

   e. ______________________________

   f. ______________________________

   g. ______________________________

   h. ______________________________

2. Turn the first four into written sentences. Remember to write **me gusta** if the thing you like is singular, and **me gustan** if the thing you like is plural.

   a. ______________________________

   b. ______________________________

   c. ______________________________

   d. ______________________________

3. Use the last four things on your list to make four more sentences; but this time, don't write anything. Just say them out loud. Use the same grammar rules!

Cantos

You know the drill! Fill in your **cantos**. If you have any trouble, make sure you practice, practice, practice. You're going to need to know these as we move on!

Canto: Review of Verb Endings (Chapter 1)

	Present-Tense			Preterit-Tense		Future-
	-ar Verb Endings	-er Verb Endings	-ir Verb Endings	-ar Verb Endings	-er/-ir Verb Endings	Tense Verb Endings
1st-person singular (**yo**)	______	______	______	______	______	______
2nd-person singular (**tú**)	______	______	______	______	______	______
3rd-person singular (**él/ella/usted**)	______	______	______	______	______	______
1st-person plural (**nosotros**)	______	______	______	______	______	______
2nd-person plural (**vosotros**)	-áis	-éis	-ís	-asteis	-isteis	-éis
3rd-person plural (**ellos/ustedes**)	______	______	______	______	______	______

Canto: Review of **Ser** (to be), **Estar** (to be), and **Ir** (to go) Present-Tense Forms (Chapter 2)

	Ser (to be: characteristics and "permanent" qualities)		**Estar** (to be: location, condition, and "temporary" qualities)	
	Singular	Plural	Singular	Plural
1st person	______	______	______	______
2nd person	______	**sois** (you all are)	______	**estáis** (you all are)
3rd person	______	______	______	______

Ir (to go)

	Singular	Plural
1st person	______________	______________
2nd person	______________	**vais** (you all go)
3rd person	______________	______________

Canto: Review of Ser and Ir Preterit-Tense Forms

Ser Preterit-Tense Forms (Chapter 3)

	Singular	Plural
1st person	______________	______________
2nd person	______________	**fuisteis** (you all were)
3rd person	______________	______________

Ir Preterit-Tense Forms

	Singular	Plural
1st person	______________	______________
2nd person	______________	**fuisteis** (you all went)
3rd person	______________	______________

Canto: Review of Articles and Adjective Endings (Chapter 4)

	Definite Articles		Indefinite Articles		Adjective Endings	
	Singular	Plural	Singular	Plural	Singular	Plural
Masculine	________	________	________	________	________	________
Feminine	________	________	________	________	________	________

Canto: Review of Prepositions (Chapter 5)

Fill in the prepositions. On the lines to the right, write the English translation of each preposition.

Spanish	English
Preposiciones __________ la ardilla	__________________
La ardilla va:	
__________ mi casa	__________________
__________ descanso	__________________
__________ el parque	__________________
__________ su hogar	__________________
__________ el árbol	__________________
_____ ______ _____ lago.	__________________
Llega __________ su nido	__________________
__________ una nuez	__________________
________ ______ correr	__________________
________ ______ comer.	__________________

Canto: Review of Pronouns (Chapter 6)

	Subject Pronouns	Direct-Object Pronouns	Indirect-Object Pronouns
1st-person singular	__________	__________	__________
2nd-person singular	__________	__________	__________
2nd-person formal	__________	__________	__________
3rd-person singular	__________	__________	__________
1st-person plural	__________	__________	__________
2nd-person plural	**vosotros/vosotras** (you all)	**os** (you all)	**os** (you all)
2nd-person plural formal (Latin American "you all")	__________	__________	__________
3rd-person plural	__________	__________	__________

La cuarta piedra:
Fourth Preterit Puzzle Piece

Yo-Form Irregulars

To find your next **piedra**, you need to master the **yo**-form spelling-change preterits. Some verbs have a preterit-tense spelling change only in the **yo** form. Here are three rules for **yo**-form spelling-change preterits.

1. Verbs that end in **-zar** change the ***z*** to a ***c*** in the preterit **yo** form.
   almorzar » **almorcé**

Now you try it. Fill in the missing letters.

empezar: **yo empe( )é** **tú empe___aste**

comenzar: **yo comen( )é** **él comen___ó**

abrazar: **yo abra( )é** **ellos abra___aron**

2. Verbs that end in **-gar** (such as **pagar**) change the ***g*** to a ***gu***.
   pagar » **pagué**

You can remember this one because without adding the *u*, the *e* would change the sound of the *g*. This would make the **yo**-form preterit of **pagar** sound like "paHAY" instead of "paGAY."

Here are some other verbs that would sound funny in the preterit without the *u*. Remember, you only add it in the **yo** form. Finish the conjugations to earn your **piedra**.

jugar: yo ju __ ( ) __, tú ju( ) __ __ __ __, él ju( ) __,

nosotros ju( ) __ __ __ __, ellos ju __ __ __ __ __

llegar: yo lle __ ( ) __, tú lle( ) __ __ __ __, él lle __ __,

nosotros lle( ) __ __ __ __, ellos lle __ __ __ __ __

apagar: yo apa __ ( ) __, tú apa __ __ __ __ __, él apa __ __,

nosotros apa __ __ __ __ __, ellos apa( ) __ __ __ __

3. Verbs that end in **-car** change the ***c*** to a ***qu***.

tocar » **toqué**

Now you try it. Conjugate the verbs to match the subjects provided.

buscar: yo __ __ __ __ ◯ __, **nosotros** __ __ __ ◯ __ __ __ __,

ellas __ __ __ ◯ __ __ __ __

explicar: yo __ __ __ __ __ __ ◯ __, **tú** __ __ __ __ __ ◯ __ __ __ __,

ustedes __ __ __ __ __ ◯ __ __ __ __

practicar: yo __ __ __ ◯ __ __ __ ◯ __, **él** __ __ __ ◯ __ __ ◯ __,

ellos __ __ __ __ __ __ ◯ __ __ __ __

Now earn your **piedra**. Count how many of each of these letters you wrote in the circled spaces.

Your next **piedra** is: ____ ____ ____

G C U

But wait—that doesn't mean anything! Use this decoder strip to turn your numbers into a word.

a	b	c	d	e	f	g	h	i	j	k	l	m
20	19	18	17	16	15	14	13	12	11	10	9	8

n	o	p	q	r	s	t	u	v	w	x	y	z
7	6	5	4	3	2	1	26	25	24	23	22	21

The image on your next **piedra** is an __ __ __.

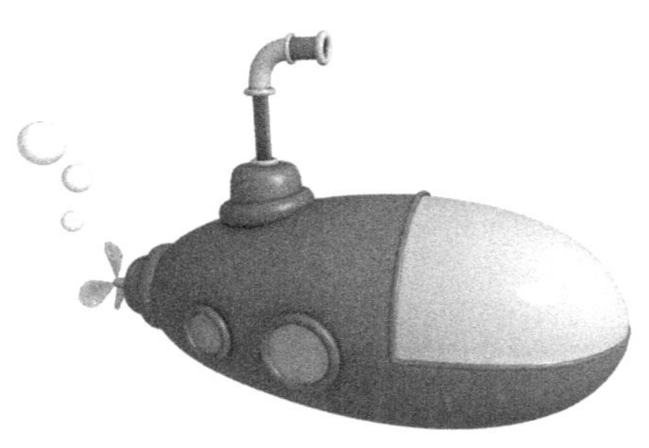

Frases:

Hay que hacer la cama:	*(Have to make the bed:*
Recoge del suelo	*Pick up from the floor*
almohada y manta.	*pillow and blanket.*
La sábana despliega,	*Unfold the sheet,*
la almohada arregla.	*straighten the pillow.*
Eso es tan bueno,	*This is so good,*
quiero dormir de nuevo.	*I want to sleep again.)*

Canto:

En mi casa hay un jardín.	*(At my house there is a yard.*
En el jardín hay un árbol.	*In the yard there is a tree.*
En el árbol hay un nido.	*In the tree there is a nest.*
En el nido hay un huevo.	*In the nest there is an egg.*
¿Qué hay en el huevo?	*What is there in the egg?*
¡Hay que esperar!	*You have to wait!)*

Vocabulario:

Vocabulario nuevo

Spanish	English
arreglar: arreglo, arreglé, arreglaré	to tidy: I tidy, I tidied, I will tidy
recoger: recojo, recogí, recogeré	to pick up: I pick up, I picked up, I will pick up
pasar: paso, pasé, pasaré	to pass: I pass, I passed, I will pass
pasar la aspiradora	to vacuum
la aspiradora	vacuum cleaner
el dormitorio	bedroom
la alfombra	rug
la almohada	pillow
la manta	blanket
el juguete	toy
el muñeco de peluche	stuffed animal
el huevo	egg

Vocabulario de repaso

Spanish	English
limpiar: limpio, limpié, limpiaré	to clean: I clean, I cleaned, I will clean
el jardín	garden, yard
el árbol	tree
el libro	book
la cama	bed
hacer la cama	to make the bed

You've already learned the word **hay**. It's pronounced just as you would say the English word "eye," and it means "there is" or "there are." Maybe you've tried using it a little bit, or maybe you've seen it other places. In this chapter, you're going to learn two main things: the proper way to form sentences using **hay** and a common expression that uses the verb **hay**. But first, I want to tell you **hay**'s secret story—you'll never guess what it is. Are you ready for it?

Hay's secret story is that it is a runaway verb! Officially, it's a present-tense form of the verb **haber**. But when you learn about **haber** later in this book, you'll memorize its six present-tense forms as your **canto**. When you memorize those forms, you're going to see that ***hay*** *isn't anywhere on the chart*! And guess what: It doesn't really have person or number! It's a little verb that breaks all the verb rules. **¡Qué loco!**

So how do you use this little grammatical troublemaker? It's **muy fácil**. You use **hay** just as you would use "there is" or "there are" in English. You don't have to worry about person. You don't have to worry about number. You just have to think about tense: **hay** is in the present tense. It's so easy that now *you* are going to provide some examples. Fill in the following blanks:

_______________ **tres árboles en mi jardín.** (There are three trees in my yard.)

_______________ **una estrella en el cielo esta noche.** (There is a star in the sky tonight.)

_______________ **siete personas en mi familia.** (There are seven people in my family.)

Muy fácil, ¿no? All you do is fill in the word **hay**.

¡Hay que estudiar!

Would you like to learn another fun way you can use the word **hay**? Look at the title of this section: **¡Hay que estudiar!** You might think, at a glance, that this could mean "you should study," but you already know that **hay** doesn't have person, so it can't mean "you," so "you should study" would not be correct. Instead, we would translate this sentence as "Everyone should study!" "People should study!" or even, "Studying is necessary!" Here's the way it works:

Hay + **que** + a verb in the infinitive = "It is necessary to _______________."

When you use this formula, you're saying that the action of the verb is necessary. Remember, though, you don't have to do any conjugating. This is a lot like saying **tienes que** (you have to), but it isn't directed at anyone in particular. Let's look at **hay** with some of our vocabulary words from this week.

Oh, no! Someone spilled cookie crumbs all over **la alfombra**!
<u>Hay que</u> pasar la aspiradora.

Someone left his or her shoes (**zapatos**) in the middle of the floor.
<u>Hay que</u> recoger los zapatos.

Oh, I know! It was Jorge!
Jorge <u>tiene que</u> recoger sus zapatos.

A. Translation:

1. **la manta**	____________	9. **hacer la cama**	____________
2. **el dormitorio**	____________	10. **limpiar**	____________
3. **el libro**	____________	11. **pasar la aspiradora**	____________
4. **el juguete**	____________	12. **arreglar**	____________
5. **el muñeco de peluche**	____________	13. **recoger**	____________
6. **la alfombra**	____________	14. **el jardín**	____________
7. **la almohada**	____________	15. **el árbol**	____________
8. **la cama**	____________	16. **el huevo**	____________

B. Canto:

Fill in the blanks of this week's **canto**.

En mi casa __________ **un** ________________.

En ______ ________________ **hay un** ________________.

En el ________________ **hay un nido.**

En el nido hay un ________________.

¿__________ __________ **en el huevo?**

¡__________ __________ ________________!

C. Grammar: **Hay**

Describe your room. Use **hay** and your vocabulary words, and be sure to add adjectives (especially color words) to tell what your **dormitorio** looks like. Here's an example: **En mi dormitorio, hay una cama grande. En la cama, hay una manta blanca y azul. En mi dormitorio hay muchos libros…** Go ahead, you try it!

En mi dormitorio, hay…

____

____

____

____

____

____

D. Grammar: **Hay que**

What do you have to do to take care of your **dormitorio**? Use **hay que** and some of your vocabulary phrases to tell how to keep your **dormitorio "bien arreglado."**

1. How do you have to clean **la alfombra**?

____

____

2. What do you have to do with your **muñecos de peluche**?

____

____

3. What do you have to do with your **cama** after you get up?

____

____

4. What else do you have to do?

____

____

A. New and Review Vocabulary:

Spanish	English
______________________	to tidy: I tidy, I tidied, I will tidy
______________________	to pick up: I pick up, I picked up, I will pick up
______________________	to pass: I pass, I passed, I will pass
______________________	to vacuum
______________________	vacuum cleaner
______________________	bedroom
______________________	rug
______________________	pillow
______________________	blanket
______________________	toy
______________________	stuffed animal
______________________	to clean: I clean, I cleaned, I will clean
______________________	garden, yard
______________________	tree
______________________	egg
______________________	book
______________________	bed
______________________	to make the bed

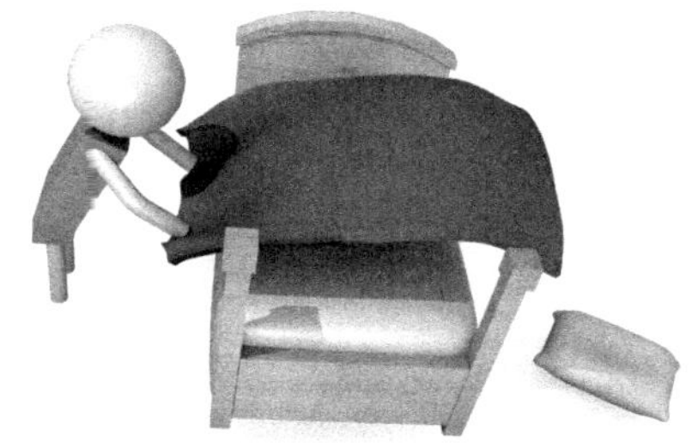

B. Canto:

Write out this week's **canto**. First, write it in Spanish:

____

____

____

____

____

____

Then, write the English translation:

____

____

____

____

____

____

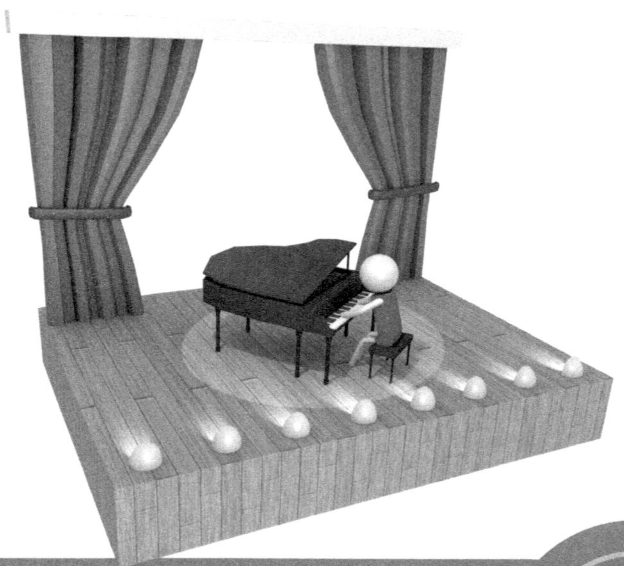

Frases:

¿Qué te gusta hacer? Para mí, pasar tiempo con los amigos es muy divertido. Cuando acabo con mi tarea, puedo jugar videojuegos o mirar la tele, pero prefiero salir y jugar con los niños que viven al lado. Nos gusta practicar los deportes e inventar historias interesantes. Mi sueño es ser escritora o jugadora de fútbol. Yo sueño también con tocar el piano en Carnegie Hall. Y tú, ¿qué es tu sueño?

(What do you like to do? For me, spending time with friends is really fun. When I finish my homework, I can play video games or watch TV. But I prefer to go out and play with the kids who live next door. We like to play sports and make up interesting stories. My dream is to be a writer or a soccer player. I also dream about playing the piano in Carnegie Hall. And you, what's your dream?)

Canto:

Leer es muy bueno;	*(Reading is very good;*
me gusta leer.	*I like to read.*
Para leer, necesito un libro.	*To read, I need a book.*
Y cuando yo quiero	*And when I want*
hablar de leer,	*to talk about reading,*
yo uso el infinitivo.	*I use the infinitive.)*

Vocabulario:

Vocabulario nuevo

Spanish	English
soñar con: sueño con, soñé con, soñaré con	to dream about: I dream about, I dreamed about, I will dream about
odiar: odio, odié, odiaré	to hate: I hate, I hated, I will hate
mirar la tele	to watch TV
tocar música	to play music (on a musical instrument)
tocar el piano	to play the piano
jugar videojuegos	to play video games
pasar tiempo con los amigos	to spend time with friends
practicar deportes	to play sports
jugar al fútbol	to play soccer
el sueño	dream

Vocabulario de repaso

Spanish	English
amar: amo, amé, amaré	to love: I love, I loved, I will love
salir: salgo, salí, saldré	to go out: I go out, I went out, I will go out
la tarea	homework
hacer la tarea	to do homework
el tiempo	time, weather

Infinitives:

You've spent a lot of time learning about **infinitives**. Do you remember what they are? That's right, **an infinitive is the basic form of a verb, without any endings to give it person, number, or tense**. But an infinitive can be so much more! In this chapter, we're going to look at how you can use them as (drumroll, please) . . . nouns. *Nouns?* That's right! Sometimes you can use the infinitive of a verb just as you would use a noun! You know that a noun is a person, place, thing, or sometimes an idea. At times, the *thing* that you're talking about is an action. Look at this sentence: **Yo quiero correr.** (I want to run.) What "thing" do I want? I want *to run*! Even though **correr** is a verb, it's the "thing" that I want, and a thing is a noun. Ta-da! We just turned our verb into a noun by keeping it in the infinitive form. In Spanish, whenever we talk about the action of a verb as a "thing," the verb is an infinitive. This is similar to English: We like *to dance*; we want *to eat*; we're afraid *to jump* into the deep end. Even if these verbs would end in an *-ing* in English, they're still infinitives in Spanish. Check it out:

Yo quiero bailar. (I want to dance.)

Yo odio cantar. (I hate to sing./I hate singing.)

Yo temo nadar. (I'm afraid to swim./I'm afraid of swimming.)

Look! There are two ways to say it in English, but only *one* way in Spanish!

We can flip that around, too, and **make the infinitive the subject of the sentence**:

Jugar me hace feliz. (Playing makes me happy./To play makes me happy.)

Leer es muy divertido. (Reading is really fun./To read is really fun.)

Look! There are two ways to say it in English, but only *one* way in Spanish!

Adding Prepositional Phrases

You can also get even fancier and add prepositions and prepositional phrases to sentences in which an infinitive serves as the (direct) object. Remember, a prepositional phrase is a group of words working together to act like a giant adverb or adjective.

Me gusta cantar en el coro. (I like to sing in the choir.)

En el coro has that preposition, **en**, which works as a team leader to help the other words act like an adverb. They all tell us *where* "I like to sing": in the choir—not in my garage, not in the shower—just in the choir. Take a look: No matter what is added to the sentence, **cantar** stays in the infinitive.

Various Examples

There are many ways you can use infinitives in sentences. Here are a few more!

After a Preposition

Remember your **canto** about the squirrel? We said the squirrel gets to its nest **después de correr, antes de comer** (before running and after eating). *Before* and *after* are both prepositions. **Any time you use a verb right after a preposition in Spanish, it will be in the infinitive form.**

Yo corro para estar sano. (I run to be healthy.)

Sueño con volar. (I dream about flying.)

Check out that second example. In Spanish, we don't say, "dream about"; we say, "dream *with*"! Remember, if you are **soñando con** (dreaming about) an action, that action will be in the infinitive form.

Infinitives with Other "Helping" Verbs

You already know about two tenses that use an infinitive plus a helping verb. Can you remember what they are? That's right, they're the near-future tense (**ir** + **a** + infinitive) and the near-past tense (**acabar** + **de** + infinitive). Here they are in sentences:

Voy a comer pizza. (I'm going to eat pizza.)

Acabo de comer pizza. (I just ate pizza.)

Can you think of other helping verbs that work with infinitives? How about **hay que** and **tener que**?

Hay que llevar zapatos en el invierno. (People have to wear shoes in the winter.)

Yo tengo que comprar zapatos nuevos. (I have to buy new shoes.)

A. Translation:

1. **to dream about**	________________	9. **I play football**	________________
2. **I hated**	________________	10. **dream**	________________
3. **mirar la tele**	________________	11. **amo**	________________
4. **tocar música**	________________	12. **I will go out**	________________
5. **tocar el piano**	________________	13. **la tarea**	________________
6. **to play video games**	________________	14. **to do homework**	________________
7. **pasar tiempo con los amigos**	________________	15. **time, weather**	________________
8. **to play sports**	________________		

B. Canto:

Fill in the blanks of this week's **canto**.

________________ **es muy bueno;**

me ________________ ________________ **.**

Para ________________**,** ________________ **un libro.**

Y cuando yo quiero

________________ **de** ________________**,**

yo uso ________________ ________________**.**

C. Build Your Own **Canto**:

Fill in the blanks of this week's **canto** again—but this time, choose your own verbs! Make sure you think of a noun to replace **libro** from the original **canto** that makes sense with the verb you choose.

_______________ es muy bueno;

me gusta _______________.

Para _______________, necesito un(a) _______________.

Y cuando yo quiero

hablar de _______________,

yo uso el infinitivo.

D. Grammar:

Use infinitive forms of any verbs you like to finish these sentences and tell about yourself! You might want to look up some extra words in a Spanish-English dictionary.

____________________ me hace feliz.

____________________ es mi sueño.

Yo sueño con ____________________.

No me gusta ____________________.

No quiero ____________________.

Yo amo ____________________.

Yo odio ____________________.

Para mí, ____________________ es muy difícil.

Para mí, ____________________ es muy divertido.

Tengo que ____________________.

Yo estudio para ____________________.

A. New and Review Vocabulary:

Spanish	English
____________________	**to dream about: I dream about, I dreamed about, I will dream about**
____________________	**to hate: I hate, I hated, I will hate**
____________________	**to watch TV**
____________________	**to play music (on a musical instrument)**
____________________	**to play the piano**
____________________	**to play video games**
____________________	**to spend time with friends**
____________________	**to play sports**
____________________	**to play soccer**
____________________	**dream**
____________________	**to love: I love, I loved, I will love**
____________________	**to go out: I go out, I went out, I will go out**
____________________	**homework**
____________________	**to do homework**
____________________	**time, weather**

B. Canto:

Go for it—write out this week's **canto**! First, write it in Spanish:

____

____

____

____

____

____

Then, write the English translation:

____

____

____

____

____

____

C. Grammar:

1. How could you translate the sentence, **Me gusta jugar**, into English? Circle one:
   a. I like to play.
   b. I like playing.
   c. Both
   d. Neither

2. An infinitive verb can be the subject of a sentence.
   Circle one: True False

Frases:

A las ocho de la mañana, tengo que hacer la cama y desayunar. Salgo de la casa a las ocho y media. La escuela comienza a las nueve, y ¡hay que llegar temprano! Paramos a la una para una siesta. Volvemos a casa y comemos con la familia. A las tres de la tarde, estamos en clase de nuevo. Acabamos el día escolar a las cinco. Cuando acabas el día escolar, ¿qué hora es?

(At eight in the morning, I have to make my bed and eat breakfast. I leave the house at eight thirty. School starts at nine, and you have to be early! We stop at one for a break. We go home and eat with our families. At three in the afternoon we're in class again. We finish our school day at five. When you finish your school day, what time is it?)

Canto:

Move your arms like hands on a clock while you say this **canto**:

Mediodía,	*(Noon,*
¡hora de la comida!	*time for food!*
Es la una.	*It's one o'clock.*
Son las dos.	*It's two o'clock.*
Son las tres en punto.	*It's three o'clock on the nose.*
Son las cuatro.	*It's four o'clock.*
Son las cinco.	*It's five o'clock.*
Son las seis y cuarto.	*It's six fifteen.*
Son las siete.	*It's seven o'clock.*
Son las ocho.	*It's eight o'clock.*
Son las ocho y media.	*It's eight thirty.*
Son las nueve.	*It's nine o'clock.*
Son las diez.	*It's ten o'clock.*
Son las once menos tres.	*It's three to eleven.*
Medianoche,	*Midnight,*
son las doce.	*it's twelve o'clock.)*

Vocabulario:

Vocabulario nuevo

Spanish	English
la hora	hour
¿Qué hora es?	What time is it?
Es hora de . . . (finish this sentence with an infinitive)	It's time to . . .
medio/a	half, middle
el cuarto	quarter, fourth, room
la medianoche	midnight
el mediodía	noon
la tarde	afternoon
menos	minus, less
el/la menos	the least
el sol	sun

Vocabulario de repaso

Spanish	English
comenzar: comienzo, comencé, comenzaré	to begin: I begin, I began, I will begin
hoy	today
la luna	the moon
la noche	night
el día	day
la mañana/mañana[1]	morning/tomorrow
el reloj	clock, watch

1. Note: The term **la mañana** means "morning," but without the definite article (**mañana** only), it means "tomorrow."

Time Is Feminine!

In this unit, we've been looking at a lot of sentences without the subject-verb structure you might be used to. Guess what: In this chapter, it's going to get even wackier! You're going to learn to tell time in Spanish, and you're going to be making some sentences that make you feel as though they're breaking all the rules you know about Spanish grammar.

Let's start with the question, "What time is it?" In Spanish, you say, **¿Qué hora es?** Instead of the word "time," you use the word **hora** (hour)—but other than that, it isn't very different from English.

Here's where it gets tricky: How do you answer that question in English? First of all, you can just say the number of the hour.

Q: What time is it?

A: Four.

In Spanish, you can't just say the number. You have to use an article.

Q: ¿Qué hora es?

A: Las cuatro.

All the articles for time are plural, except for the article for one o'clock. Also, they're all feminine! Why? It is because the word we use for time (**la hora**) is feminine.[2]

What About the "O'Clock"?

In English, you can say, "I ate dinner at seven" *or* "I ate dinner at seven o'clock." However, there is only *one* way to say this in Spanish:

Cené a las siete.

In other words, you don't write the word "o'clock" in Spanish; the "o'clock" is simply assumed. In fact, there is no way to say "o'clock" in Spanish, but we'll still use it in the English translations.

Time Is Plural (Except One O'Clock)!

Just saying the number isn't a very polite way to tell someone the time, is it? Instead, you'll probably want to use a whole sentence. When you tell time in English, you start your sentence with "it is," as seen in these examples:

It is one o'clock.

It is four fifty-three.

If we were to think about the person, number, and tense of "it is," we would say that it is a third-person singular verb form. In Spanish, the only time you say "it is" with a third-person singular verb, as you would in English, is when it's one o'clock. That's it!

Es la una.[3]

For all the other times, you use the third-person *plural* form of **ser**.

Son las dos. (It's two o'clock.)

Son las cuatro y media. (It's four thirty.)

Son las cinco. (It's five o'clock.)

You might be a little confused, because **ser** is usually the "being verb" we use for things that are permanent. Time is definitely not a "permanent" kind of thing, but we use the verb **ser** for it anyway.

When Did It Happen?

In English, we say things happen "at" certain times. For example, "I ate dinner today *at* seven o'clock," or "I will go to sleep *at* ten o'clock." It's exactly the same in Spanish. Do you remember how to say "at" in Spanish? That's right, **a**. Make sure you don't forget the articles that go with your time numbers.

Cené a las siete.

Duermo a las diez.

Subtraction

When it gets close to the next hour, Spanish speakers usually tell the time in this way:

Son las ocho menos cuarto. (It's eight minus a quarter. = It's quarter to eight.)

Son las ocho menos diez. (It's eight minus ten. = It's ten to eight.)

To tell someone the exact time, such as four fifty-six, you could still say this:

Son las cuatro y cincuenta y seis. (It's four fifty-six.)

But you'll hear more people say it this way:

Son las cinco menos cuatro. (It's five minus four. = It's four minutes to five.)

It's fun, isn't it? You get to do a bit of math.

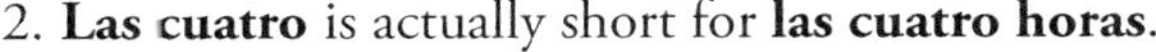

2. **Las cuatro** is actually short for **las cuatro horas**.
3. When you're telling time, you also use the feminine form of "one," which is **una**. You don't have to worry about gender with any other time numbers.

Halftime

If you were paying attention, you might have noticed that when we said, "It's four thirty," we actually used the word **media** (half) instead of the word **treinta** (thirty). In Spanish, you can use numbers as we do in English, but it's more common to use fraction words. Take a look at the clock below to learn how to tell time in Spanish.

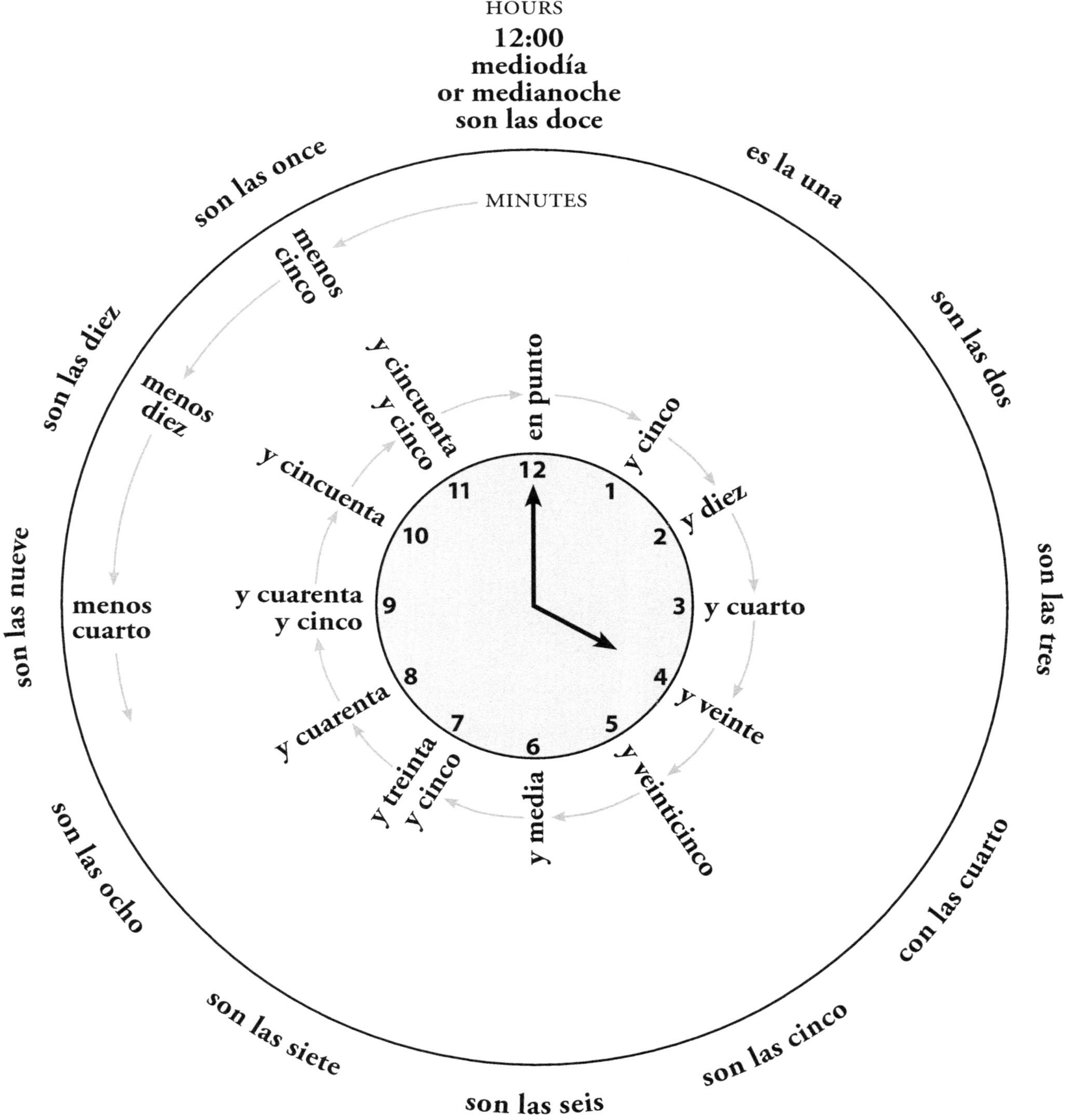

A. Translation:

1. **la hora**	________	11. **minus**	________
2. **What time is it?**	________	12. **el/la menos**	________
3. **It's time to . . .**	________	13. **sun**	________
4. **clock**	________	14. **comienzo**	________
5. **half**	________	15. **today**	________
6. **quarter**	________	16. **tomorrow**	________
7. **midnight**	________	17. **the moon**	________
8. **noon**	________	18. **night**	________
9. **afternoon**	________	19. **day**	________
10. **morning**	________		

Which one of this week's vocabulary words can be a synonym for **dormitorio**? ____________

B. Canto:

Fill in the blanks of this week's **canto**. Then write what time it is (in numbers) after each line.

Canto	Time
____________,	________
¡________ de la comida!	
___ **la** ________.	________
Son las dos.	________
Son las tres ___ ________.	________
________ **las cuatro.**	________
Son las cinco.	________
Son las seis ___ ________.	________

___ las __________. __________

Son las ocho. __________

Son las ocho ___ __________. __________

Son las nueve. __________

___ las diez. __________

Son las once __________ tres. __________

__________, __________

son las __________. __________

C. ¿Qué hora es?

Look at each of the following clocks and tell the time in Spanish. Then finish the sentence: Tell what it is time to do by filling in an infinitive.

1. 

¿Qué hora es? ______________________________

____

Es hora de ______________________________

2. 

¿Qué hora es? ______________________________

____

Es hora de ______________________________

3. 

¿Qué hora es? ______________________________

____

Es hora de ______________________________

4.

¿Qué hora es? ______________________________

____

Es hora de ______________________________

D. Extra Practice!

Practice on your own with a toy clock, or draw little clock faces for yourself. Move (or draw) the hands in different places, and see if you can tell the time in Spanish for any hour of the day.

E. Cognates:

This week's vocabulary words have quite a number of English cognates. Let's take a look.

1. The ______________ system is a group of planets that revolve around the sun. (**sol**)
2. When students graduate from high school, they have a ceremony called *commencement.* Do you think this ceremony celebrates the end of high school or the beginning of the rest of their lives? What Spanish word gives you a clue?

   ____

   ____

   ____

3. If you're between size "small" and size "large" in clothing, you might wear a size ________________ (**media**).

A. New and Review Vocabulary:

Spanish	English
____________________	hour
____________________	What time is it?
____________________	It's time to . . .
____________________	half, middle
____________________	quarter, fourth, room
____________________	midnight
____________________	noon
____________________	afternoon
____________________	minus, less
____________________	the least
____________________	sun
____________________	to begin: I begin, I began, I will begin
____________________	today
____________________	the moon
____________________	night
____________________	day
____________________	morning/tomorrow
____________________	clock, watch

B. Canto:

Write out this week's **canto** in Spanish. The **hora** for each line is listed as a guide.

12:00 ______________________________

12:00 ______________________________

1:00 ______________________________

2:00 ______________________________

3:00 ______________________________

4:00 ______________________________

5:00 ______________________________

6:15 ______________________________

7:00 ______________________________

8:00 ______________________________

8:30 ______________________________

9:00 ______________________________

10:00 ______________________________

10:57 ______________________________

12:00 ______________________________

12:00 ______________________________

C. Grammar:

1. What gender do you use when you are telling time? ______________________________

2. What verb do you use to tell what time it is? ______________________________

3. What is the only hour that isn't plural? ______________________________

4. You always use articles when you're telling time in Spanish.

   Circle one: True False

Chapter 11

Repaso de vocabulario

After completing chapters 8, 9, and 10, you're ready to review more vocabulary words! You know what to do here: Put a check mark next to the words you don't know.

Chapter 8

☐	1. **arreglar**	☐	6. **el dormitorio**	☐	11. **el muñeco de peluche**	☐	15. **el árbol**
☐	2. **recoger**	☐	7. **la alfombra**	☐	12. **el huevo**	☐	16. **el libro**
☐	3. **pasar**	☐	8. **la almohada**	☐	13. **limpiar**	☐	17. **la cama**
☐	4. **pasar la aspiradora**	☐	9. **la manta**	☐	14. **el jardín**	☐	18. **hacer la cama**
☐	5. **la aspiradora**	☐	10. **el juguete**				

Chapter 9

☐	19. **soñar con**	☐	23. **tocar el piano**	☐	27. **jugar al fútbol**	☐	31. **la tarea**
☐	20. **odiar**	☐	24. **jugar videojuegos**	☐	28. **el sueño**	☐	32. **hacer la tarea**
☐	21. **mirar la tele**	☐	25. **pasar tiempo con los amigos**	☐	29. **amar**	☐	33. **el tiempo**
☐	22. **tocar música**	☐	26. **practicar deportes**	☐	30. **salir**		

Chapter 10

☐	34. **la hora**	☐	39. **la medianoche**	☐	44. **el sol**	☐	48. **la noche**
☐	35. **¿Qué hora es?**	☐	40. **el mediodía**	☐	45. **comenzar**	☐	49. **el día**
☐	36. **Es hora de . . .**	☐	41. **la tarde**	☐	46. **hoy**	☐	50. **la mañana/ mañana**
☐	37. **medio/a**	☐	42. **menos**	☐	47. **la luna**	☐	51. **el reloj**
☐	38. **el cuarto**	☐	43. **el/la menos**				

Practicing Cantos

Now's the time to show your stuff! Write out your three **cantos** in Spanish here.

Chapter 8 **Canto: Hay**

Chapter 9 **Canto**: Infinitives

Chapter 10 **Canto**: Telling Time

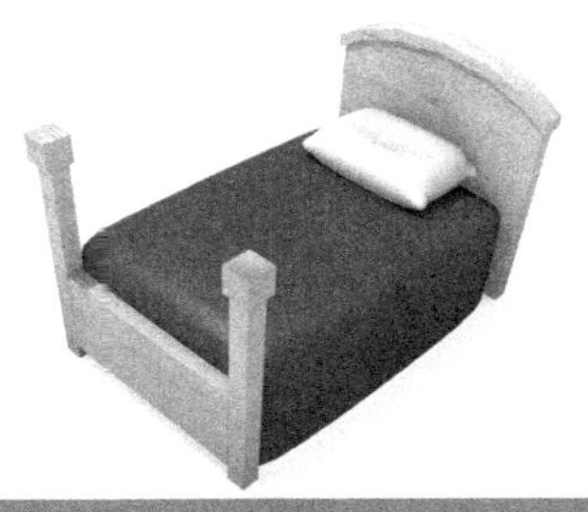

Telling Time

Practice with a buddy for some out-loud time-telling. (If you don't have a buddy nearby, grab a few stuffed animals, and use them as puppets having this conversation.) Take turns pointing to a clock and asking, **¿Qué hora es?** Once you've asked what time it is, your partner can answer you in Spanish (or you can answer for both yourself and your "partner," if your partner is a stuffed animal). When you're done with the whole exercise, go back and write down the time in numbers on the first line and in sentence form on the second and third lines.

Using **Hay**

Finish the following sentences by inserting **hay** or **hay que** into the blanks. Not sure which to choose? Look at chapter 8 again to refresh your memory.

1. **En la casa de mi abuela,** _________ **una piscina** (pool). **Si queremos nadar,** _________ _________ **pedir permiso.**
2. _________ **un nuevo estudiante en mi clase. No sé su nombre.** _________ _________ **preguntarle.**
3. _________ _________ **llevar un abrigo** (wear a coat) **si** _________ **mucho viento** (wind).
4. **Si** _________ _________ **usar huevos en esta receta** (recipe), _________ _________ **ir a la tienda** (store) **porque no** ______ **huevos en la casa.**
5. **¿** _________ **tarea?**

Using Infinitives

Here's another set of sentences to finish. Use the verb in parentheses to fill in each blank. Figure out from the rest of the sentence whether you should conjugate your verb or leave it in the infinitive form.

1. **Me gusta (*ir*) ________________ a la playa con mis amigos.**
2. (***jugar***) **________________al fútbol con mis amigos es muy divertido.**
3. **Yo (*jugar*) ________________al fútbol con mis amigos.**
4. **Estudiamos para (*aprender*) ________________ el español.**
5. **Sueño con (*ser*) ________________ astronauta.**
6. (***tener***) **________________ un perro o un gato es bueno para aprender la responsabilidad.**

Greetings (Earthling)

Now that you know how to tell what time of day it is, let's review different Spanish greetings you use at different times of day.

In the morning, you say, "**Buenos días.**"
In the afternoon, you say, "**Buenas tardes.**"
In the evening, you say, "**Buenas noches.**"

Now, let's hop into our time machine and time travel through the day. Each time we stop, I'll tell you (in Spanish) what time it is. You then have to stick your head out the window and shout a greeting in Spanish—make sure you use the right one for the time I told you. And look out—we might jump around in time a bit! Here we go.

¡Ponte el cinturón de seguridad! (Put your seatbelt on!)

Our first stop:
Me: **Son las nueve y media de la mañana.**
You: ____

Our second stop:
Me: **Son las once y media de la noche.**
You: ____

Our third stop:
Me: **Son las tres de la tarde.**
You: ____

Our fourth stop:
Me: **Es la hora de cenar.**
You: ____

And finally, our last stop:
Me: **Es la hora de desayunar.**
You: ____

Frases:

Había una vez un pájaro que amaba a una pájara. Vivían en un árbol y eran muy felices. Su árbol era muy grande y tenía muchas hojas. Los pájaros hablaban con las ardillas y jugaban con las mariposas. Había muchos animales en el bosque donde vivían.

que = *that* ***ardillas*** = *squirrels* ***el bosque*** = *the woods*
hojas = *leaves* ***mariposas*** = *butterflies* ***donde*** = *where*

Canto:

Imperfect-Tense Endings

-ar Verb Imperfect Endings

	Singular	Plural
1st person	**-aba**	**-ábamos**
2nd person	**-abas**	**-abais**
3rd person	**-aba**	**-aban**

-er and -ir Verb Imperfect-Tense Endings

	Singular	Plural
1st person	**-ía**	**-íamos**
2nd person	**-ías**	**-íais**
3rd person	**-ía**	**-ían**

Vocabulario:

Vocabulario nuevo

Spanish	English
proteger: protejo, protegí, protegeré	to protect: I protect, I protected, I will protect
continuar: continúo, continué, continuaré	to continue: I continue, I continued, I will continue
contar: cuento, conté, contaré	to count/tell: I count/tell, I counted/tell, I will count/tell
contar con	to count on
de repente	suddenly
había	there was, there were
había una vez . . .	once upon a time there was . . .
el pájaro	bird
nadie	no one, nobody
alguien	someone, somebody

Vocabulario de repaso

Spanish	English
trabajar: trabajo, trabajé, trabajaré	to work: I work, I worked, I will work
nacer: nazco, nací, naceré	to be born: I am born, I was born, I will be born
conseguir: consigo, conseguí, conseguiré	to get: I get, I got, I will get
deber: debo, debí, deberé	to owe/ought to: I owe/should, I owed/should have, I will owe/should
dejar: dejo, dejé, dejaré	to leave (something): I leave (something), I left (something), I will leave (something)

Imperfect Tense

Are you ready to learn one more tense? In this chapter, you're going to learn about the imperfect tense. **The *imperfect tense* is for actions that happened in the past.** "But wait," you're probably saying, "I already learned a past tense!" You're right; you learned the **preterit tense**, which is also for actions that happened in the past. But guess what: In Spanish, there is more than one past tense!

So, how are you going to know which past tense to use? There are some rules you will learn; but first, you're going to hear a story. To help you out, this story is also animated in the corner of your textbook. Flip the pages very quickly from front to back (you might want to hold the book shut with one hand and flip the pages at the corner with the other) to see the cartoon version of our tale.

El pájaro nació (The Bird Was Born)

Chapter 1
The bird watched her egg every day.

Chapter 2
The egg was smooth and round.

Chapter 3
The bird was watching her egg . . .

Chapter 4
. . . when suddenly, it hatched!

Chapter 5
The bird thought her baby was beautiful.

The Grammar Rules

Each chapter in our story about the bird and her egg tells us a different rule about how to use the imperfect and preterit tenses. Before we get to the rules, here's a general explanation of the difference between the preterit and the imperfect: **We use the preterit tense for actions that have a clear beginning and end, or for actions that happened once. We use the imperfect tense for actions that don't have a clear beginning and end, and for actions that were ongoing.** What does that mean? Let's look at our story more closely to find out.

Chapter 1: "Used To"

The bird watched her egg every day.

We could also phrase this sentence as this: "The bird *used to* watch her egg every day," or "The bird *would* watch her egg every day," right?[1] Watching the egg is an action in the past that happens over and over again. When something

1. That's not "would," as in "she would watch her egg if you paid her to do it"—rather, this is "would," as in "she would often (that is, she would habitually) watch her egg."

happens over and over again, the beginning and end of the action aren't really important to the story, are they? **So, for an action in the past that happens again and again, use the imperfect tense:**

La pájara <u>miraba</u> su huevo cada día. (The bird watched her egg every day.)

Now, let's examine the information given in chapter 2 of the story.

Chapter 2: What Things Are Like

The egg was smooth and round.

What kind of information does this sentence provide? It tells us what the egg was like. We call that a description. **In Spanish, past-tense descriptions are in the imperfect tense.** If you think about chapter 5 of the story, the mommy bird thought the baby bird was *beautiful.* That's a description, too: It tells you what the baby bird was like, so it should be in the imperfect tense.

Oftentimes in stories, descriptions tell you what is in the *background.* Look at the cartoon in the corner of the book again. The tree doesn't move, does it? The nest doesn't move either. That's because they're in the background. If something is part of the background, you describe it with the imperfect tense.

El huevo era liso y redondo. (The egg was smooth and round.)

(By the way, don't worry about **era**; it's the imperfect form of **ser**. It's an irregular, and we'll get to irregular forms in the next chapter.)

Let's look at chapter 3 of the story again:

Chapter 3: Don't Interrupt!

The bird was watching her egg . . .

A great way to tell which verbs should be in the preterit and which should be in the imperfect is this: **Preterit actions interrupt imperfect actions.** We know the bird's watching is going to get interrupted, because we've already read the next chapter. So, we'll put the watching in the imperfect:

La pájara miraba su huevo . . . (The bird was watching her egg . . .)

We're almost done with the story! Check out chapter 4:

Chapter 4: The Preterit

. . . when suddenly, it hatched!

How many times did the bird hatch? Once! And, in the story, we know that it *started* hatching and then it was *done* hatching. The act of hatching is a completed action in the past that has a clear beginning and end. It started, it happened, and then it was over, so we use the preterit tense. Here's another quick hint: When you see the word "suddenly," it is a big tip-off that you should use the preterit because actions in the imperfect don't happen suddenly.

. . . **cuando de repente, ¡<u>nació</u>!** (. . . when suddenly, it hatched!)

And now, let's read the end of the story again:

Chapter 5: Emotions and "Brain Actions"

The bird thought her baby was beautiful.

Here is the last rule about choosing between the preterit and imperfect tenses: Actions that are emotions or "brain actions"—things such as thinking, hoping, believing, and feeling—are usually in the imperfect tense. The bird didn't think her baby was beautiful only once. She didn't suddenly think he was beautiful and then suddenly stop thinking he was beautiful. So, we'll use the imperfect. **We use the imperfect tense for emotions and "brain-action" verbs.**

La pájara <u>creía</u> que su bebé <u>era</u> muy guapo. (The bird thought her baby was beautiful.[2])

How to Conjugate in the Imperfect Tense

Let's just look at how to do the basic imperfect conjugations. Here's how you conjugate verbs in the imperfect: **You find the stem, and then add the imperfect ending.** It's *so* easy! There are two sets of imperfect endings—one for **-ar** verbs, and another for **-er** and **-ir** verbs. To get you started, one verb for each type of ending has been conjugated for you:

Hablar Imperfect-Tense Forms

	Singular	Plural
1st person	**habl*aba***	**habl*ábamos***
2nd person	**habl*abas***	**habl*abais***
3rd person	**habl*aba***	**habl*aban***

The only **-ar** imperfect ending that gets an accent is the **nosotros** form. In Spanish, for words ending in a vowel or with an *n* or an *s*, we say the second-to-last syllable the loudest. Because the word **hablábamos** has more syllables than other imperfect forms of **hablar**, and since we want to keep the pronunciation similar to the other forms, we need to say its *third*-to-last syllable the loudest. That's why that little accent is there: It tells us how to pronounce it just right.

Comer Imperfect-Tense Forms

	Singular	Plural
1st person	**com*ía***	**com*íamos***
2nd person	**com*ías***	**com*íais***
3rd person	**com*ía***	**com*ían***

Vivir Imperfect-Tense Forms

Singular	Plural
viv*ía*	**viv*íamos***
viv*ías*	**viv*íais***
viv*ía*	**viv*ían***

2. You may note that the translation of **guapo** here as "beautiful" does not match what you've learned in the past. There are often other uses for many of the words you are learning, so you shouldn't be surprised when you come across alternate meanings or nuances.

A. Translation:

1. **protejo**	______	9. **once upon a time there was . . .**	______
2. **bird**	______	10. **debo**	______
3. **I will work**	______	11. **dejo**	______
4. **somebody**	______	12. **I will continue**	______
5. **I was born**	______	13. **I count/tell**	______
6. **I get**	______	14. **nobody**	______
7. **there was**	______	15. **to count on**	______
8. **there were**	______	16. **suddenly**	______

B. Canto:

Conjugate **hablar** and **comer** in the imperfect tense by filling in the missing verb endings.

Hablar Imperfect-Tense Forms

	Singular	Plural
1st person	**yo habl**______	**nosotros habl**______
2nd-person familiar	**tú habl**______	**vosotros hablabais**
2nd-person formal[3]	**usted habl**______	**ustedes habl**______
3rd person	**él, ella habl**______	**ellos habl**______

Comer Imperfect-Tense Forms

	Singular	Plural
1st person	**yo com**______	**nosotros com**______
2nd-person familiar	**tú com**______	**vosotros comíais**
2nd-person formal	**usted com**______	**ustedes com**______
3rd person	**él, ella com**______	**ellos com**______

3. Remember, the second-person formal uses the same ending as the third-peson.

C. Grammar:

List the four situations in which you'll use the imperfect tense.

1. ____

____

2. ____

____

3. ____

____

4. ____

____

Here are four sentences that use the imperfect tense. Next to each one, write the number of the rule (from the previous question) that says why we should use the imperfect in that situation.

____ **Cuando mi madre llegó, yo leía un libro.**

____ **Mi hermano era rubio** (blond) **cuando era niño.**

____ **Yo pensaba que debíamos ir al hospital.**

____ **En España, yo comía pan cada mañana.**

D. Conjugating Verbs in the Imperfect Tense:

Here's a list of verbs—see if you can put them in the imperfect tense. (None of them are irregular.) All you need to do is take off the last two letters and add the correct ending.

saber	**yo** ___________	**tú** ___________	**él** ___________	**nosotros** ___________	**ellos** ___________
pensar	**yo** ___________	**tú** ___________	**ella** ___________	**tú y yo** ___________	**ustedes** ___________
querer	**yo** ___________	**tú** ___________	**él** ___________	**nosotros** ___________	**ellas** ___________
tener	**yo** ___________	**tú** ___________	**usted** ___________	**él y yo** ___________	**ellos** ___________
poder	**yo** ___________	**tú** ___________	**mi amigo** ___________	**nosotros** ___________	**ustedes** ___________
creer	**yo** ___________	**tú** ___________	**él** ___________	**ella y yo** ___________	**ellos** ___________
estar	**yo** ___________	**tú** ___________	**ella** ___________	**nosotros** ___________	**ustedes** ___________
dormir	**yo** ___________	**tú** ___________	**él** ___________	**mi amigo y yo** ___________	**ellas** ___________
temer	**yo** ___________	**tú** ___________	**usted** ___________	**nosotros** ___________	**mis amigos** ___________
usar	**yo** ___________	**tú** ___________	**él** ___________	**nosotros** ___________	**ustedes** ___________

A. New and Review Vocabulary:

Spanish	English
______________________	**to protect: I protect, I protected, I will protect**
______________________	**to continue: I continue, I continued, I will continue**
______________________	**to count/tell: I count/tell, I counted/tell, I will count/tell**
______________________	**to count on**
______________________	**suddenly**
______________________	**there was, there were**
______________________	**once upon a time there was. . .**
______________________	**bird**
______________________	**nobody, no one**
______________________	**somebody, some one**
______________________	**to work: I work, I worked, I will work**
______________________	**to be born: I am born, I was born, I will be born**
______________________	**to get: I get, I got, I will get**
______________________	**to owe/ought to: I owe/should, I owed/should have, I will owe/should**
______________________	**to leave (something): I leave (something), I left (something), I will leave (something)**

B. Canto:

Fill in the imperfect-tense verb endings to conjugate the verbs **hablar** and **comer**.

Hablar Imperfect-Tense Forms

	Singular	Plural
1st person	**habl**__________	**habl**__________
2nd person	**habl**__________	**hablabais**
3rd person	**habl**__________	**habl**__________

Comer Imperfect-Tense Forms

	Singular	Plural
1st person	**com**__________	**com**__________
2nd person	**com**__________	**comíais**
3rd person	**com**__________	**com**__________

C. Grammar:

Next to each English sentence, write an *I* if you would use the imperfect tense and a *P* if you would use the preterit tense in Spanish.

____ My brother was born last week.

____ My dog always used to sleep in my bed when I was little.

____ My grandma was a great dancer.

____ My balloon popped!

____ My house was yellow.

____ At my old house, I knew my next-door neighbors.

____ I thought about soccer all the time.

____ Once, my family went on vacation to Puerto Rico.

Frases:

Yo iba a la escuela cuando, de repente, ¡vi un monstruo! El monstruo era muy grande y tenía dientes y garras muy grandes. Yo tenía mucho miedo. El monstruo gritó y corrió hacia mí, pero me di cuenta de que él lloraba. El monstruo se paró en frente de mí y miró tristemente mi lonchera. Le di mi sandwich y el monstruo volvió al bosque. ¡Qué susto!

dientes y garras = *teeth and claws*
tener miedo = *to be scared (to have fear)*
me di cuenta de que = *I noticed that*
lonchera = *lunchbox*
bosque = *woods*
¡Qué susto! = *How scary!*

Canto:

Ser, **Ir**, and **Ver** Imperfect-Tense Forms

Ser Imperfect-Tense Forms / Ir Imperfect-Tense Forms

	Ser Singular	Ser Plural	Ir Singular	Ir Plural
1st person	**era** (I was)	**éramos** (we were)	**iba** (I went)	**íbamos** (we went)
2nd person	**eras** (you were)	**erais** (you all were)	**ibas** (you went)	**ibais** (you all went)
3rd person	**era** (he/she/it was)	**eran** (they/you all were)	**iba** (he/she/it went)	**iban** (they/you all went)

Ver Imperfect-Tense Forms

	Singular	Plural
1st person	**veía** (I saw)	**veíamos** (we saw)
2nd person	**veías** (you saw)	**veíais** (you all saw)
3rd person	**veía** (he/she/it saw)	**veían** (they/you all saw)

Vocabulario:

Vocabulario nuevo

Spanish	English	Spanish	English
el juego	game	**la luz**	light
el lugar	place	**la llave**	key
el mar	sea	**la vez**	time (instance, occasion)
el hogar	home	**la fecha**	date (on a calendar)
el ejemplo	example	**la parte**	part

Vocabulario de repaso

Spanish	English
descansar: descanso, descansé, descansaré	to rest: I rest, I rested, I will rest
dibujar: dibujo, dibujé, dibujaré	to draw: I draw, I drew, I will draw
descubrir: descubro, descubrí, descubriré	to discover: I discover, I discovered, I will discover
encontrar: encuentro, encontré, encontraré	to find/meet: I find/meet, I found/met, I will find/meet

Imperfect Irregulars

In this chapter, we're going to tackle the irregulars in the imperfect tense. There aren't many. We did the preterit tense first because it's more difficult, so learning the imperfect form should be a piece of cake. Just memorize these verbs as your **canto** (I know it's a long one, but you can do it!), and you'll be set.

Imperfect **Ir** Forms

Our first irregular verb is **ir**. Do you remember the imperfect **ir** forms from the **canto** at the beginning of this chapter? OK, good—then *you* write the rest of this section:

Ir Imperfect-Tense Forms

	Singular	Plural
1st person	________	________
2nd person	________	**ibais**
3rd person	________	________

How did you do? If you had trouble writing out the forms of **ir**, *make sure you study your* ***canto*** *very diligently*! Now that you know how to conjugate **ir** in the imperfect tense, do you want to know something fun you can do with it?

Do you remember the **near-future tense**? It's for things that are about to happen, and you form it using **ir** (conjugated in the present tense), plus **a**, plus a verb in the infinitive. Here's the formula:

ir + **a** + infinitive = near-future tense

So, guess what: You can also use this little formula to do something *really cool* in the imperfect tense. **When you make the near-future tense but conjugate *ir* in the *imperfect tense*, it means "was going to."** Look:

Íbamos a correr, pero no teníamos zapatos.
(We were going to run, but we didn't have shoes.)

Miguel iba a comer un helado cuando su mamá le dijo que no.
(Miguel was going to eat ice cream when his mom said no.)

Imperfect **Ser** and **Ver** Forms

What will be written here about **ser** and **ver**? Believe it or not, nothing! Even so, be sure to memorize them for your **canto**. You'll need to know them.

Words with Changes in Meaning Between the Preterit and Imperfect

Now this is pretty interesting. There are a couple of verbs in Spanish whose meanings in the preterit are different from those in the imperfect! Here are two of them:

Saber (to know)

Imperfect = knew

Yo sabía que era su cumpleaños.

(I *knew* it was his birthday.)

Preterit = found out

Yo supe que él no tenía dinero.

(I *found out* he didn't have money.)

Conocer (to know)

Imperfect = to know (a person or a place)

Mi abuelo conocía muy bien Alemania.

(My grandfather *knew* Germany very well.)

Preterit = to meet a person for the first time

Mi amiga conoció al presidente.

(My friend *met* the president.)[1]

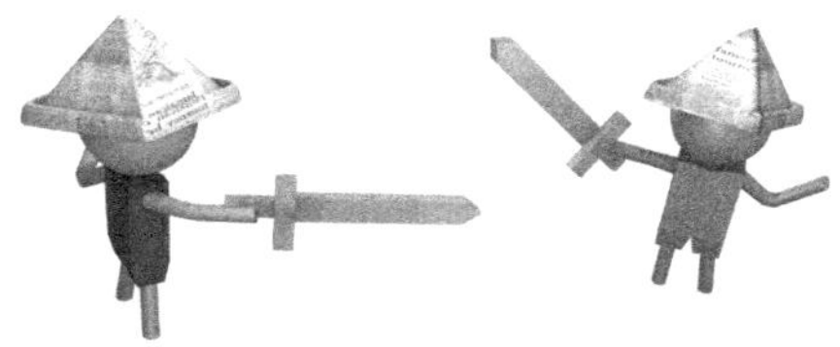

1. Why does the Spanish sentence say ***al* presidente** and not ***el* presidente**? Remember that **al** is a contraction of **a** + **el**. In this case, that's the personal **a** that you use before a direct object that is a person.

A. Translation:

1. **el lugar**	______	8. **dibujo**	______
2. **la llave**	______	9. **I discovered**	______
3. **time (instance, occasion)**	______	10. **encontrar**	______
4. **date (on a calendar)**	______	11. **sea**	______
5. **to rest**	______	12. **home**	______
6. **la parte**	______	13. **example**	______
7. **game**	______	14. **light**	______

B. Canto:

Fill in the boxes of this week's **canto**.

Ser Imperfect-Tense Forms

	Singular	Plural
1st person	______	______
2nd person	______	erais
3rd person	______	______

Ir Imperfect-Tense Forms

Singular	Plural
______	______
______	ibais
______	______

Ver Imperfect-Tense Forms

	Singular	Plural
1st person	______	______
2nd person	______	veíais
3rd person	______	______

C. Grammar:

Here are some sentences with the verbs left in the infinitive form. For each sentence, decide whether the verb should be in the imperfect or the preterit tense. Then, conjugate the verb to complete the sentence. If you're not sure which tense to use, review chapter 12.

1. **Yo (*ir*) ________________ a la escuela cuando vi un monstruo.**

2. **El monstruo (*ser*) ________________ muy grande.**

3. **Él (*tener*) ________________ dientes y garras** (teeth and claws)**.**

4. **De repente, el monstruo (*hacer*) ________________ un ruido.**

4. **Yo (*ir*) ________________ a correr pero me di cuenta de algo** (I realized something)**.**

5. **¡El monstruo (*estar*) ________________ llorando** (crying)**!**

6. **Él tenía hambre y (*querer*) ________________ algo para comer.**

7. **Le (*dar*) ________________ mi sandwich, y el monstruo desapareció** (disappeared)**.**

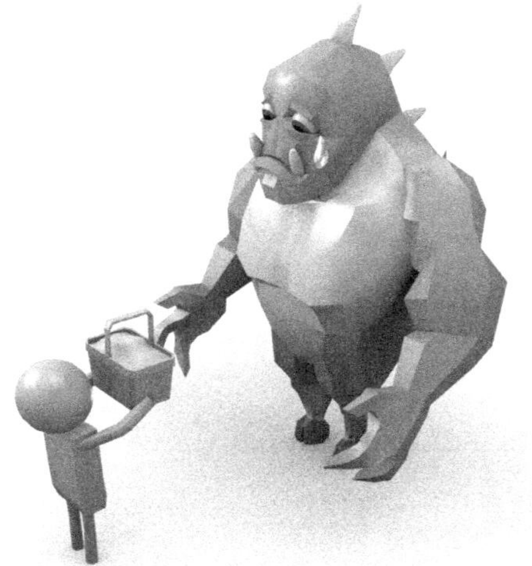

A. New and Review Vocabulary:

Spanish	English
________	**game**
________	**place**
________	**sea**
________	**home**
________	**example**
________	**light**
________	**key**
________	**time (instance, occasion)**
________	**date (on a calendar)**
________	**part**
________	**to rest: I rest, I rested, I will rest**
________	**to draw: I draw, I drew, I will draw**
________	**to discover: I discover, I discovered, I will discover**
________	**to find/meet: I find/meet, I found/met, I will find/meet**

B. Canto:

Fill in the boxes of this week's **canto**.

Ser Imperfect-Tense Forms

	Singular	Plural
1st person	________	________
2nd person	________	erais
3rd person	________	________

Ir Imperfect-Tense Forms

Singular	Plural
________	________
________	ibais
________	________

Ver Imperfect-Tense Forms

	Singular	Plural
1st person	________	________
2nd person	________	veíais
3rd person	________	________

Frases:

Al fin del día, yo estaba muy cansado. Cuando yo caminaba para mi casa, pasé por un restaurante. La puerta estaba abierta. Había gente sentada en las mesas y yo podía oler papas fritas y salchichas. Las mesas estaban cubiertas con comida, bebidas, y cosas buenas, hechas por la señora que trabajaba allí. Ella tenía su delantal puesto. Aunque ella estaba muy ocupada, ella sonreía y charlaba con los clientes. Cuando ella me vio, me dio una sonrisa y una canasta de salchichas y papas. Ella sabía que mis padres no tenían mucho.

fin = *end*
sentado/a/os/as = *seated*
papas = *potatoes*
salchichas = *sausages*
allí = *there*
delantal = *apron*
aunque = *although*
sonreír = *to smile*
charlar = *to chat*
clientes = *customers*
sonrisa = *smile*
canasta = *basket*

Canto y vocabulario nuevo:

Your job this week is to memorize this list of past participles. Here are a few useful regular past participles and also the most common irregular past participles.

Spanish	English	Spanish	English
cerrar: cerrado	to close: closed	**decir: dicho**	to say: said
cansar: cansado	to tire: tired	**hacer: hecho**	to make/do: made, done
abrir: abierto	to open: open (opened)	**ver: visto**	to see: seen
ocupar: ocupado	to occupy: busy, occupied	**poner: puesto**	to put/place: put, placed
cubrir: cubierto	to cover: covered	**morir: muerto**	to die: died, dead
escribir: escrito	to write: written	**romper: roto**	to break: broken
freír: frito	to fry: fried	**volver: vuelto**	to return: returned

Vocabulario de repaso

Spanish	English
nadar: nado, nadé, nadaré	to swim: I swim, I swam, I will swim
necesitar: necesito, necesité, necesitaré	to need: I need, I needed, I will need
olvidar: olvido, olvidé, olvidaré	to forget: I forget, I forgot, I will forget
pagar: pago, pagué, pagaré	to pay: I pay, I paid, I will pay
parar: paro, paré, pararé	to stop: I stop, I stopped, I will stop

Past Participles as Adjectives

By now, you're a pro at changing endings on verbs to show person, number, and tense. But in this chapter, you're going to put new endings on verbs to turn them into adjectives. Cool, huh? Let's do it in English first:

After I *vacuum* my room, my room is *vacuumed.* My mom says, "Look at this nice *vacuumed* room!" "Vacuum" was the action of the first part of the sentence. "Vacuumed" is the adjective that describes the room.

After I *brush* my hair, my hair is *brushed.* My grandma says, "*Brushed* hair is much neater than messy hair." "Brush" was the action in the first part of the sentence. "Brushed" is the adjective that describes the hair.

After I *lick* the lollipop, the lollipop is *licked.* My brother says, "I don't want a *licked* lollipop! Give me a new one!" What was the verb in the first part of the sentence? What adjective does it turn into?

In each sentence, a verb (vacuum, brush, lick) was turned into an adjective. Can you see what all of these adjectives have in common? They all end in *-ed.*[1] They are also all past participles. How do you make a past participle in Spanish? It's easy!

To make a past participle, you find the stem of your verb and add "ado" to an *-ar* verb or "ido" to an *-er* or *-ir* verb. Here's an example:

Step 1: **acabar** (to finish) – **-ar** = **acab-**

Step 2: **acab-** + **-ado** = **acabado** (finished)

Sometimes, there are irregular past participles, especially with verbs that change their stems. You're memorizing some of the most important ones for your **canto** this week. When you find yourself needing the use of past participles that you didn't learn in this book, you can always look them up in a Spanish conjugation guide or on the Internet.

Using Past Participles as Adjectives in Spanish

Using a past participle as an adjective is very easy. All you do is make a past participle and then use it as an adjective! Remember that **an adjective usually goes *after* a noun in Spanish**. We don't say **blanca casa** (white house); we say **casa blanca** (house white). And don't forget that **adjectives have to agree in gender and number with the nouns they**

1. In English, there are many adjectives that come from verbs and don't end in *-ed.* They're irregulars, which means they don't follow the regular rules. For now, don't worry about these.

describe! How do you think you change a past-participle adjective to make it agree with a noun? You do it the same way you would change any other adjective, of course! Take off the **-o**, and add the proper ending:

	Singular	Plural
Masculine	**-o**	**-os**
Feminine	**-a**	**-as**

Here's an example:

Let's use the verb **pintar** (to paint). The past participle of **pintar** is **pintado**. When we add it to a feminine adjective, we say:

casa pintada (painted house)

Or, if our adjective is plural, we say:

casas pintadas (painted houses)

Some "Famous" Past-Participle Adjectives

Here are some of the more regularly used past-participle adjectives and the verbs from which they come.

Past Participle	Means	Comes from the Verb	Which Means
cansado	tired	**cansar**	to tire
Example: **Estoy muy <u>cansado</u> a las diez de la noche.**			
aburrido	bored	**aburrir**	to bore
Example: **Tu estás muy <u>aburrido</u> en la clase.**			
mojado	wet	**mojar**	to wet
Example: **El piso** (floor) **está <u>mojado</u>.**			
querido	beloved, dear	**querer**	to want/to love
Example: **<u>Querida</u> mamá, he llegado a la casa de abuela.** (Dear Mom, I've arrived at Grandma's house.)			

Another word with an **-ado** ending that you'll see a lot is **cuidado**. It can be a past-participle adjective, and it means "careful." It can also be a noun, meaning "care" or "carefulness." You can also just say the word **¡cuidado!** by itself, and then it means "watch out!" Usually, when you see the word **cuidado**, it's used as a noun. People use it with the verb **tener**, and when you want to tell someone to "be careful," you tell him or her to "have care": **¡tenga cuidado!**[2]

2. Want to know why we conjugated **tener** differently? You'll find out in chapter 26!

A. Translation:

1. **to close**	____________	11. **romper**	____________
2. **cansar**	____________	12. **to write**	____________
3. **to occupy**	____________	13. **to fry**	____________
4. **to cover**	____________	14. **to say**	____________
5. **hacer**	____________	15. **necesitar**	____________
6. **to swim**	____________	16. **to return**	____________
7. **ver**	____________	17. **to pay**	____________
8. **to put/place**	____________	18.abrir	____________
9. **to forget**	____________	19. **to stop**	____________
10. **to die**	____________		

B. Canto:

Write out the past participles of each of these verbs. Then translate the **canto** into English.

Verb	Past Participle	Translation
cerrar	____________	____________
cansar	____________	____________
abrir	____________	____________
ocupar	____________	____________
cubrir	____________	____________
escribir	____________	____________
freír	____________	____________
decir	____________	____________
hacer	____________	____________
ver	____________	____________

Verb	Past Participle	Translation
poner	____________________	____________________
morir	____________________	____________________
romper	____________________	____________________
volver	____________________	____________________

C. Grammar:

Use your new skills (or your memory) to turn these verbs into past participles. Then, use them as adjectives to describe the nouns provided here. Finally, translate the phrases you've made into English.

1. **cerrar** (to close) = ____________________

   una puerta ____________________

   Translation: ____________________

2. **arreglar** (to tidy) = ____________________

   un dormitorio ____________________

   Translation: ____________________

3. **lavar** (to wash) = ____________________

   unos platos (plates) ____________________

   Translation: ____________________

4. **prestar** (to loan) = ____________________

   un CD ____________________

   Translation: ____________________

5. **compartir** (to share) = ____________________

   un helado ____________________

   Translation: ____________________

6. **vestir** (to dress) = ____________________

   unos perros ____________________ **de payasos** (like clowns)

   Translation: ____________________

A. New and Review Vocabulary:

Spanish	English
	to close: closed
	to tire: tired
	to open: open (opened)
	to occupy: busy, occupied
	to cover: covered
	to write: written
	to fry: fried
	to say: said
	to make/do: made, done
	to see: seen
	to put/place: put, placed
	to die: died, dead
	to break: broken
	to return: returned
	to swim: I swim, I swam, I will swim
	to need: I need, I needed, I will need
	to forget: I forget, I forgot, I will forget
	to pay: I pay, I paid, I will pay
	to stop: I stop, I stopped, I will stop

B. Grammar:

1. What are the past-participle endings for the following?

   -ar verbs: ______________________________

   -er and **-ir** verbs: ________________________

2. A past participle can act exactly like an adjective. Circle one: True False

3. When you use a past participle as an adjective, it doesn't need to match nouns in gender and number. Circle one: True False

C. **¡Ya está hecho!** (It's Already Done!)

You've been very busy completing all of your chores, and now there's nothing left to do. Your dad sees you sitting on the couch and asks you to do each chore. In each of the following sentences, fill in the past participle to tell him the job has already been done. How will you know which past participle to use? Use the verb underlined in each sentence.

1. **No puedo <u>cerrar</u> la puerta porque ya está** ______________________________ .

2. **No puedo <u>abrir</u> la ventana porque ya está** ______________________________ .

3. **No puedo <u>hacer</u> mi tarea porque ya está** ______________________________ .

4. **No puedo <u>freír</u> los huevos porque ya están** ______________________________ .

Repaso de vocabulario

In the last 14 chapters, you have learned more than 200 new words. That's quite a bit of new **vocabulario**! Let's see if you can remember them. If there are any that give you trouble, you can go back and practice them again.

Chapter 1

1. **desayunar**
2. **cortar**
3. **el lápiz**
4. **el bolígrafo**
5. **el papel**
6. **el cuaderno**
7. **las tijeras**
8. **la mochila**
9. **la palabra**
10. **la página**
11. **hablar**
12. **cantar**
13. bailar
14. correr
15. abrir
16. vivir

Chapter 2

17. **mostrar**
18. **bajar**
19. **venir**
20. **el almuerzo**
21. **el desayuno**
22. **la fiesta**
23. **la bebida**
24. **la fruta**
25. **las verduras**
26. **el postre**
27. **querer**
28. **tener**
29. **poder**
30. **poner**
31. **hacer**
32. **ver**

Chapter 3

33. **empezar**
34. **almorzar**
35. **conducir**
36. **reducir**
37. **creer**
38. **el aeropuerto**
39. **el avión**
40. **el autobús**
41. **el barco**
42. **la maleta**
43. **decir**
44. **saber**
45. **estar, ser**
46. **dormir**
47. **pedir**

Chapter 4

48. **limpio/a/os/as**
49. **sucio/a/os/as**
50. **feliz/felices**
51. **triste/es**
52. **divertido/a/os/as**
53. **aburrido/a/os/as**
54. **difícil/difíciles**
55. **fácil/fáciles**
56. **diferente/es**
57. **mismo/a/os/as**
58. **yo mismo/ yo misma**
59. **grande/es**
60. **pequeño/a/os/as**
61. **bueno/a/os/as**
62. **malo/a/os/as**

Chapter 5

63. **siempre**
64. **nunca**
65. **todavía**
66. **también**
67. **tarde**
68. **temprano**
69. **tampoco**
70. **sólo**
71. **solo/a/os/as**
72. **demasiado/a/os/as**
73. **demasiado**
74. **por**
75. **para**
76. **a**
77. **de**
78. **con**
79. **sin**

Chapter 6

80. **temer**
81. **escoger**
82. **enviar**
83. **las noticias**
84. **la flor**
85. **el parque**
86. **la carta**
87. **el problema**
88. **el idioma**
89. **el programa**
90. **el poema**
91. **gustar**
92. **tirar**
93. **usar**
94. **beber**
95. **recibir**

Chapter 8

96. **arreglar**
97. **recoger**
98. **pasar**
99. **pasar la aspiradora**
100. **la aspira-dora**
101. **el dormitorio**
102. **la alfombra**
103. **la almohada**
104. **la manta**
105. **el juguete**
106. **el muñeco de peluche**
107. **limpiar**
108. **el jardín**
109. **el árbol**
110. **el huevo**
111. **el libro**
112. **la cama**
113. **hacer la cama**

Chapter 9

114. **soñar con**
115. **odiar**
116. **mirar la tele**
117. **tocar música**
118. **tocar el piano**
119. **jugar videojuegos**
120. **pasar tiempo con los amigos**
121. **practicar deportes**
122. **jugar al fútbol**
123. **el sueño**
124. **amar**
125. **salir**
126. **la tarea**
127. **hacer la tarea**
128. **el tiempo**

Chapter 10

129. **la hora**
130. **¿Qué hora es?**
131. **Es hora de . . .**
132. **la mañana/ma-ñana**
133. **el reloj**
134. **medio/a**
135. **el cuarto**
136. **la medianoche**
137. **el mediodía**
138. **la tarde**
139. **menos**
140. **el/la menos**
141. **el sol**
142. **comenzar**
143. **hoy**
144. **la luna**
145. **la noche**
146. **el día**

Chapter 12

147. **proteger**	151. **de repente**	155. **nadie**	159. **conseguir**
148. **continuar**	152. **había**	156. **alguien**	160. **deber**
149. **contar**	153. **había una vez . . .**	157. **trabajar**	161. **dejar**
150. **contar con**	154. **el pájaro**	158. **nacer**	

Chapter 13

162. **el juego**	166. **el ejemplo**	170. **la fecha**	173. **dibujar**
163. **el lugar**	167. **la luz**	171. **la parte**	174. **descubrir**
164. **el mar**	168. **la llave**	172. **descansar**	175. **encontrar**
165. **el hogar**	169. **la vez**		

Chapter 14

176. **cerrar**	185. **cubierto**	193. **hecho**	201. **roto**
177. **cerrado**	186. **escribir**	194. **ver**	202. **volver**
178. **cansar**	187. **escrito**	195. **visto**	203. **vuelto**
179. **cansado**	188. **freír**	196. **poner**	204. **nadar**
180. **abrir**	189. **frito**	197. **puesto**	205. **necesitar**
181. **abierto**	190. **decir**	198. **morir**	206. **olvidar**
182. **ocupar**	191. **dicho**	199. **muerto**	207. **pagar**
183. **ocupado**	192. **hacer**	200. **romper**	208. **parar**
184. **cubrir**			

Cantos

Fill in the **cantos** from this unit.

Hablar Imperfect-Tense Forms (Chapter 12)

	Singular	Plural
1st person	**yo** ____________________	**nosotros** ________________
2nd person	**tú** ____________________	**vosotros hablabais**
3rd person	**él, ella** _________________	**ellos** ____________________

R

Comer Imperfect-Tense Forms (Chapter 12)

	Singular	Plural
1st person	**yo** ______________	**nosotros** ______________
2nd person	**tú** ______________	**vosotros comíais**
3rd person	**él, ella** ______________	**ellos** ______________

Ser Imperfect-Tense Forms (Chapter 13)

	Singular	Plural
1st person	______________	______________
2nd person	______________	**erais**
3rd person	______________	______________

Ir Imperfect-Tense Forms (Chapter 13)

	Singular	Plural
1st person	______________	______________
2nd person	______________	**ibais**
3rd person	______________	______________

Ver Imperfect-Tense Forms (Chapter 13)

	Singular	Plural
1st person	______________	______________
2nd person	______________	**veíais**
3rd person	______________	______________

Past Participles (Chapter 14)

Write out the past participles of each of these verbs. Then translate the **canto** into English.

Verb	Past Participle	Translation	Verb	Past Participle	Translation
cerrar	______________	______________	**decir**	______________	______________
cansar	______________	______________	**hacer**	______________	______________
abrir	______________	______________	**ver**	______________	______________
ocupar	______________	______________	**poner**	______________	______________
cubrir	______________	______________	**morir**	______________	______________
escribir	______________	______________	**romper**	______________	______________
freír	______________	______________	**volver**	______________	______________

A List of Words You're More Likely to Find in the Imperfect (Chapters 12 and 13)

Let's think about our "rules" for using the imperfect tense. We know that what someone looks like (a description) is usually in the imperfect, and so are "brain actions," such as thinking or believing. Because certain actions such as these tend to happen over a space of time instead of "once and done," you'll find that there are verbs that are usually in either the imperfect or the preterit. Here are some verbs that you'll usually use in the imperfect tense if you want to conjugate them in the past. Go ahead and practice your conjugations by putting them in the imperfect tense:

ser	**yo** ______________	**tú** ______________	**él** ______________	**nosotros** ______________	**ellos** ______________
pensar	**yo** ______________	**tú** ______________	**ella** ______________	**tú y yo** ______________	**ustedes** ______________
querer	**yo** ______________	**tú** ______________	**él** ______________	**nosotros** ______________	**ellas** ______________
tener	**yo** ______________	**tú** ______________	**usted** ______________	**él y yo** ______________	**ellos** ______________
poder	**yo** ______________	**tú** ______________	**mi amigo** ______________	**nosotros** ______________	**ustedes** ______________
creer	**yo** ______________	**tú** ______________	**él** ______________	**ella y yo** ______________	**ellos** ______________
desear	**yo** ______________	**tú** ______________	**usted** ______________	**nosotros** ______________	**ustedes** ______________

Preterit and Imperfect (Chapters 12 and 13)

Here are some sentences that use both the preterit and imperfect tenses. Imagine that each sentence is a little timeline. Verbs that are in the imperfect tense last a long time, so when you find them, draw a long horizontal line through them. Verbs that are in the preterit tense are "once-and-done" actions. Find the verbs in the preterit tense, and draw a vertical line through them, so they look like quick little events interrupting the long, drawn-out imperfect verbs.

1. **Cuando conocí a Gema, ella tenía un mono** (a monkey).

2. **Yo estaba comiendo mi pastel cuando perdí un diente** (I lost a tooth).

3. **Caminábamos a la escuela cada día, pero un día nuestro padre nos condujo** (drove us).

4. **Mi abuela hacía galletas cada domingo, y esta semana yo la ayudé.**

Describe Your Day

On a separate piece of paper, try writing a little story about events from yesterday. You can write it in either English or Spanish. Mark your verbs in the same manner that you did in the last exercise (using horizontal lines to indicate verbs in the imperfect tense and vertical lines to indicate verbs in the preterit tense), regardless of which language you choose.

Practicing Past Participles (Chapter 14)

You've spent a lot of time memorizing verbs, and with past participles you get some payoff for all your work. Since every verb has a past participle, and past participles can act like adjectives, you now know a "bonus" adjective for every verb you've learned! You've just doubled the number of words you know! So, let's have some fun with your new-and-improved vocabulary. Make a list of ten verbs you might want to use as adjectives. Then, figure out what their past participles are. In case any irregulars sneak in, check your work in a conjugation book or on a conjugation website.[1]

Verbs	Past Participles
______________	______________
______________	______________
______________	______________

1. The Internet has a number of conjugation guides—check the links on the author blog for this book (www.spanishforchildrenonline.com). You can also use the classic book *501 Spanish Verbs* by Christopher Kendris.

Verbs	Past Participles

Using Past Participles (Chapter 14)

Take the past participles you just listed, and rewrite them in the following chart. Then, choose ten nouns that could be described using your ten past participles. Finally, choose five of these past participle/noun combinations to write sentences that use the past participles and their corresponding nouns.

Past Participles	Nouns

1. ______________________________

2. ______________________________

3. ______________________________

4. ______________________________

5. ______________________________

¿Te gusta el imperfecto? (Chapters 12 and 13)

Do you remember learning about the verb **gustar** and his buddies, **encantar** and **importar**? These are all verbs that describe how someone feels about something, which falls under the "brain-action" category. That means you'll almost always use these verbs in the imperfect tense.

Me encantaban las vacaciones. (I loved the vacation.)

Me gustaba el payaso. (I liked the clown.)

No me importaban las arañas. (I didn't care about spiders.)

Remember, the verb is conjugated to match the thing you are liking (or loving, or not caring about) in person and number—the verb is *not* conjugated to match you!

Let's practice using these verbs in the imperfect tense. Use the imperfect tense of these verbs (**gustar**, **encantar**, and **importar**) to write a few sentences about things you liked, loved, didn't like, or didn't care about when you were younger. Make sure your nouns and your verbs have matching numbers!

La quinta piedra:

Fifth Preterit Puzzle Piece

Double-Vowel Verbs

To earn this **piedra**, you must learn the preterit forms of the verbs **creer**, **leer**, **oír**, and **caer**. All of these verbs have vowels right before their **-er** or **-ir** endings, so that means they get a "special treatment" when we add their preterit-tense endings. What's the special treatment? It's an accent! An accent mark allows these verbs to be spelled the same way they're pronounced. Take a look at **leer**. There is an accent on every ending except for the third-person plural form.

Leer, Preterit-Tense Forms

	Singular	Plural
1st person	**leí**	**leímos**
2nd person	**leíste**	leísteis
3rd person	**leyó**	**leyeron**

Accents — No accent

These verbs are irregular in another way. Did you see the third-person endings? The ***i*** has changed into a ***y***! The verbs **creer**, **caer**, and **oír** all get a ***y*** instead of an ***i*** in the third-person preterit form, too.

Can you do the job and find your next **piedra**? Complete this chart by adding the missing letters to their respective boxes.

	Creer	Leer	Caer	Oír
yo	c r e í	_ _ _	_ _ _	o í
tú	c r e í s t e	_ _ _ _ _ _	c a í s t e	_ _ _ _ _
él	_ _ _ _ _	_ _ _ _	_ _ _ _	o y _
nosotros	_ _ _ _ _ _ _	l e í m o s	_ _ _ _ _ _	_ _ _ _ _
ellos	c r e y e r o n	_ _ _ _ _ _ _	_ _ _ _ _ _ _	_ _ _ _ _ _

Are you ready to uncover the next **piedra**? Imagine you're brushing away the dirt from an artifact you've dug out of the ground—that's how carefully you'll have to unearth this **piedra**. Go back to the previous chart, and shade in every box that has one of the following letters:

- ***í***
- ***ó***
- ***c***

Now, using a marker, trace over *only* the dotted lines that connect shaded-in boxes.

You should see the image on the next **piedra** emerge out of the dust. What is it?

Es un _____ _____ _____.

Frases:

Mi hermana: No puedo decidir. Me gusta el tuyo, pero el que tiene Jorge parece muy bien también. El suyo es más grande . . . pero me gusta el color del tuyo. ¿Qué debo hacer? ¿Qué debo elegir? No puedo decidir . . . ¡vainilla! No, ¡chocolate! No, ¡vainilla! Necesito ayuda. ¿Puedo probar el tuyo? Mmm, gracias, es muy bueno. Jorge, ¿puedo probar tu helado? Mmmm . . . el tuyo también es muy bueno. ¡Ajá! Yo sé que hacer.

Jorge y yo: ¡Ay, no! ¡Son nuestros!

Mi hermana: Pues, ¡ahora son míos!

hermana = *sister*
decidir = *to decide*
lo que tiene Jorge = *what Jorge has*
parece muy bien = *looks really good*
¿Qué debo elegir? = *What should I choose?*
necesito ayuda = *I need help*
probar = *taste, try, test*
ahora = *now*

Canto:

Possessive Pronouns

	Singular	Plural
1st person	**mío/a/os/as** (mine)	**nuestro/a/os/as** (ours)
2nd-person familiar	**tuyo/a/os/as** (yours)	**vuestro/a/os/as** (yours)
2nd-person formal	**suyo/a/os/as** (yours)	**suyo/a/os/as** (yours)
3rd person	**suyo/a/os/a** (his/hers/its)	**suyo/a/os/as** (theirs)

Vocabulario:

Vocabulario nuevo	
Spanish	**English**
montar: monto, monté, montaré	to ride: I ride, I rode, I will ride
el patinete	scooter
la bicicleta	bicycle
la ropa	clothes
el casco	helmet
los pantalones	pants
la chaqueta	jacket
la falda	skirt
el vestido	dress
las gafas	glasses

Vocabulario de repaso	
Spanish	**English**
llevar: llevo, llevé, llevaré	to carry/wear: I carry/wear, I carried/wore, I will carry/wear
prestar: presto, presté, prestaré	to loan: I loan, I loaned, I will loan
la camisa	shirt
los zapatos	shoes
el abrigo	coat

Possessive Pronouns

Possessive pronouns, do those sound familiar to you? They might, because you've learned quite a bit about pronouns, and you've also learned about possessive adjectives. In *SFCA*, you learned that **possessive adjectives are words that modify a noun by telling you to whom it belongs**. So, what do you think a possessive pronoun is? You know that a pronoun is a word that replaces a noun in a sentence. Guess what: **A *possessive pronoun* is a mighty little guy—he doesn't just replace a noun. He's so strong, he can replace a noun *and* a possessive adjective at the same time.** Wow!

Do you want to know something else that's great about possessive pronouns? They work basically the same in Spanish as they do in English. So, let's start with some English possessive pronouns.

I read my math textbook, and you read your math textbook.

OK, this sentence isn't too bad. It's a little tough saying "math textbook" two times, but we aren't going crazy wishing we had a pronoun. But what about the following sentence?

I'll battle my evil, hypnotic space-robot enemy,
and you battle your evil, hypnotic space-robot enemy.

It would be so much easier to say this if there was just one word we could say instead of "your evil, hypnotic space-robot enemy." Why don't we replace the second use of this term with the word "yours"?

I'll battle my evil, hypnotic space-robot enemy, and you battle *yours*.

Did you see that? The word "yours" took the place of "your" plus the noun it modified (and all the extra adjectives attached).

Here are a few more examples, just so you can get the hang of it:

I hug my dog, and you hug your dog. = I hug my dog, and you hug *yours*.

He reads his book, and she reads her book. = He reads his book, and she reads *hers*.

Now Let's Do It in Spanish

Are you ready to play with some possessive pronouns in Spanish? There are just three rules.

Rule 1: *The pronoun has to agree with the noun.* A possessive pronoun in Spanish must agree in gender with the noun and possessive adjective it replaces. For example, **mi casa**: The term **casa** is feminine and singular, so we would say it's **la mía.**

Rule 2: *The pronoun needs a definite article.* A possessive pronoun in Spanish almost always has a definite article in front of it. Did you see the example above? We don't just say **mía**, we say it's **la mía.**

Rule 3: *The article has to agree, too.* The definite article has to agree in gender and number with the possessive pronoun. Since **casa** and **mía** are feminine and singular, which article did we use for both of these terms? We used **la**, the feminine singular article, of course!

Yo leo mi libro y tu lees *tu libro.*
tu libro » el tuyo[1]
Yo leo mi libro y tu lees *el tuyo.*

1. Check out that definite article. It follows the third rule.

Yo llevo mi chaqueta y ellos llevan *sus chaquetas.*
sus chaquetas » las suyas[2]
Yo llevo mi chaqueta y ellos llevan *las suyas.*

2. Do you see how **suyas** agrees in gender and number with **chaquetas**?

Yo abrazo a mi padre y tu abrazas *a tu padre.*
a tu padre » al tuyo[3]
Yo abrazo a mi padre y tu abrazas *al tuyo.*

3. Remember, **a** + **el** = **al**.

Take a Break from the Definite Article

Are you catching on? Great! Now, you are going to learn about **the only time you don't need a definite article with a possessive pronoun**. It's when the possessive pronoun comes right after the verb **ser**.

El perro es *mío.* (The dog is *mine.*)

Las casas eran *suyas.* (The houses were *theirs.*)

A. Translation:

1. **bicicleta**	____________	9. **el casco**	____________
2. **shoes**	____________	10. **glasses**	____________
3. **el abrigo**	____________	11. **I will carry/wear**	____________
4. **pants**	____________	12. **scooter**	____________
5. **jacket**	____________	13. **I loaned**	____________
6. **skirt**	____________	14. **la camisa**	____________
7. **montar**	____________	15. **el vestido**	____________
8. **clothes**	____________		

B. Canto:

Fill in the boxes of this week's **canto**.

Possessive Pronouns

	Singular	Plural
1st person	____________	____________
2nd-person familiar	____________	**vuestro/a/os/as**
2nd-person formal	____________	____________
3rd person	____________	____________

C. ¡Viajamos!

Let's pack to go on a trip. We're going to organize things by suitcases: one suitcase for me, one for you, one for both of us to share, and a few more suitcases. Each suitcase is labeled with a pronoun to tell you to whom it belongs. There are four nouns in each suitcase. Your job is to go through the labels and replace each noun with a possessive pronoun plus an article. How will you know which possessive pronoun to pick? Match the person and number of the owner of the object, and then match the gender and number of the object. The first one is done for you. Got it? Get packing!

yo

abrigo = el mío

camisa = ____________________

zapatos = ____________________

medias = ____________________

tú

chaqueta = ____________________

pantalones = ____________________

camisas = ____________________

nosostros

ropa = ____________________

gafas = ____________________

ellos

chaquetas = ____________________

pantalones = ____________________

ella

vestido = ____________________

faldas = ____________________

D. Solve Your Problems with Some Pronouns:

You go over to a friend's house to play, and you have some problems. Solve them by finishing these sentences with articles and possessive pronouns.

Hace frío (It's cold)**. Yo llevo mi abrigo. Tú llevas _____ ______________.**

No tengo mi patinete. ¿Puedo montar en _____ ______________?

No tengo mi casco. ¿Puedo llevar _____ ______________?

No me gusta mi camisa. ¿Puedes prestarme _____ ______________?

¿No quieres comar un helado? Yo puedo comer _____ ______________.

A. New and Review Vocabulary:

Spanish	English
____________________	to ride: I ride, I rode, I will ride
____________________	scooter
____________________	bicycle
____________________	clothes
____________________	helmet
____________________	pants
____________________	jacket
____________________	skirt
____________________	dress
____________________	glasses
____________________	to carry/wear: I carry/wear, I carried/wore, I will carry/wear
____________________	to loan: I loan, I loaned, I will loan
____________________	shirt
____________________	shoes
____________________	coat

B. Canto:

Fill in the boxes of this week's **canto**.

Possessive Pronouns

	Singular	Plural
1st person	______________	______________
2nd-person familiar	______________	**vuestro/a/os/as**
2nd-person formal	______________	______________
3rd person	______________	______________

C. Grammar:

1. A possessive pronoun has to agree in ______________ and ______________ with the noun it replaces.

2. What else do you have to think about when you choose a possessive pronoun?

____

____

3. *I like my dog more than I like John's dog, but not as much as I like yours.* Which word in this sentence is a possessive pronoun? Circle one:

   a. I

   b. my

   c. yours

   d. John's

4. Translate your answer from question number 3 into Spanish: ______________

Frases:

En el museo:

Andrés: ¡Mira, Ana! Me gusta aquella pintura.

Ana: Sí, aquella pintura es muy bonita, pero a mí me gusta más esta escultura.

Andrés: ¿Te gusta esta escultura? Pero, ¡se parece a una hamburguesa!

Ana: Sí. Yo tengo hambre.

Andrés: Pues, ¿te gusta ese dibujo? Es un dibujo de un frutero.

Ana: No, no me gusta ese dibujo. No tengo ganas de comer fruta. Prefiero este dibujo, aquí al lado.

Andrés: Pero, ¡es un dibujo de un edificio!

Ana: Sí, ¡puedo imaginar que el edificio es un restaurante!

museo = *museum*
pintura = *painting*
bonito/a/os/as = *pretty*
escultura = *sculpture*
dibujo = *drawing*
frutero = *fruit bowl*
No tengo ganas de comer = *I don't feel like eating*
aquí al lado = *here next to (it)*
edificio = *building*

Canto:

Demonstrative Adjectives

Something "Near You" (this, these)

	Singular	Plural
Masculine	este (this)	estos (these)
Feminine	esta (this)	estas (these)

Something "Farther from You" (that, those)

	Singular	Plural
Masculine	ese (that)	esos (those)
Feminine	esa (that)	esas (those)

Something "Over There" (that "over there," those "over there")

	Singular	Plural
Masculine	aquel (that over there)	aquellos (those over there)
Feminine	aquella (that over there)	aquellas (those over there)

Vocabulario:

Vocabulario nuevo

Spanish	English
este/esta	this
ese/esa	that
estos/estas	these
esos/esas	those
aquel/aquella	that over there
aquellos/aquellas	those over there
libre/libres	free
listo/a/os/as	ready, smart[1]
cada	each, every

Vocabulario de repaso

Spanish	English
ayudar: ayudo, ayudé, ayudaré	to help: I help, I helped, I will help
comprar: compro, compré, compraré	to buy: I buy, I bought, I will buy
compartir: comparto, compartí, compartiré	to share: I share, I shared, I will share
buscar: busco, busqué, buscaré	to look for: I look for, I looked for, I will look for
contestar: contesto, contesté, contestaré	to answer: I answer, I answered, I will answer
todo/a/os/as	all

1. Usually, **listo** means "ready." It only means "smart" when you use it with the verb **ser**, for example: **somos listos** (we're smart), **estamos listos** (we're ready).

Demonstrative Adjectives

In this chapter, you're going to learn about something called a **demonstrative adjective**. You should know what an adjective is by now, but what does the word "demonstrative" mean? Well, to *demonstrate* something means to show it. For example, when your mom asks which piece of cake you want, you could say, "the biggest one with the giant sugar rose on top," or you could just *demonstrate* which one you want by pointing to it with your finger. You could also say, "*that* one." **A *demonstrative* is a word that points something out**, such as "this," "that," "these," or "those."

The Rules

Demonstratives in Spanish have to agree in gender and number with the nouns they modify. Take a look:

Singular demonstratives: ***este* juguete** (*this* toy), ***ese* juguete** (*that* toy)
Plural demonstratives: ***estos* juguetes** (*these* toys), ***esos* juguetes** (*those* toys)

Masculine demonstratives: ***este* helado** (*this* ice cream), ***ese* helado** (*that* ice cream)
Feminine demonstratives: ***esta* casa** (*this* house), ***esa* casa** (*that* house)

If you look at your **canto**, you'll see that there are separate columns for Spanish **singular demonstratives** and **plural demonstratives**. The little charts in the **canto** are divided up by what you use the demonstratives for. "This" and "these" are in the first chart. **"This" and "these" are adjectives for things that are close to you. "That" and "those" are for things that are farther away from you.**

Esta bicicleta es mía; esa bicicleta es tuya.
(This bike is mine; that bike is yours.)

You can also use "this" and "these" to show how close something is to you **in time**.

Ese año yo no estudiaba mucho, pero este año, yo estudiaré cada día.
(That year I didn't study much, but this year I will study every day.)

That wasn't too difficult, right? But wait, there's an extra little chart! Those extra demonstratives are **aquel**, **aquella**, **aquellos**, and **aquellas**. They are generally used just as "that" and "those" are (things a little farther from the speaker), but **when people use *aquel, aquella, aquellos,* or *aquellas,* they want to *emphasize* the fact that the thing they are talking about is far away**. That's why we translate those demonstratives as "that *over there*," or "those *over there*."

Puedo correr hasta aquel árbol en tres segundos.
(I can run to that tree over there in three seconds.)

No quiero jugar con aquellos niños porque son malos.
(I don't want to play with those kids over there because they're mean.)

Trying It Out

So, how do you use demonstrative adjectives? It's easy! Think about it: Is the thing you're demonstrating close or far away? Is it a "this" or a "that"? Or is it a "that *over there*"? Once you've decided which kind of demonstrative adjective you want, just **pick the right one to match your noun in gender and number**. But watch out: **Unlike most masculine adjectives in Spanish, singular masculine demonstrative adjectives end in *-e* instead of *-o*.**

A. Translation:

1. **this**	______	9. **each, every**	______
2. **I looked for**	______	10. **that over there**	______
3. **that**	______	11. **those over there**	______
4. **to share**	______	12. **free**	______
5. **these**	______	13. **I will buy**	______
6. **I helped**	______	14. **ready**	______
7. **those**	______	15. **all**	______
8. **smart**	______		

B. Canto:

Fill in the boxes of this week's **canto**.

Something "Near You" (this, these)

	Singular	Plural
Masculine	______	______
Feminine	______	______

Something "Farther from You" (that, those)

	Singular	Plural
Masculine	______	______
Feminine	______	______

Something "Over There" (that "over there," those "over there")

	Singular	Plural
Masculine	____________	____________
Feminine	____________	____________

C. Grammar:

You and your brother go shopping, but he's too shy to talk to anyone but you. He'll tell you what he wants and whether it's the one that's near you, the one that's a little farther away, or the one that's "way over there." It's your job to tell the store employees what he wants. Remember to match your demonstrative adjective and your noun in gender and number.

1. **camisa** (near) = **Él quiere** ____________ **camisa.**
2. **zapatos** (way over there) = **Él quiere** ____________ **zapatos.**
3. **medias** (a little farther away) = **Él quiere** ____________ **medias.**
4. **bicicleta** (way over there) = **Él quiere** ____________ **bicicleta.**
5. **mochila** (a little farther away) = **Él quiere** ____________ **mochila.**
6. **pantalones** (near) = **Él quiere** ____________ **pantalones.**
7. **casco** (near) = **Él quiere** ____________ **casco.**

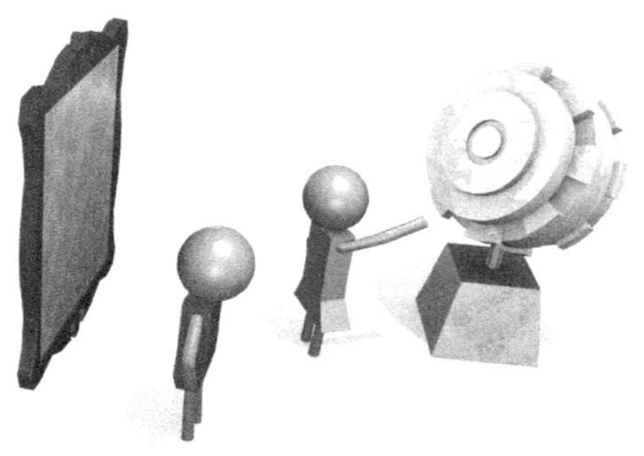

A. New and Review Vocabulary:

Spanish	English
______________________	**this**
______________________	**that**
______________________	**these**
______________________	**those**
______________________	**that over there**
______________________	**those over there**
______________________	**free**
______________________	**ready, smart**
______________________	**each, every**
______________________	**to help: I help, I helped, I will help**
______________________	**to buy: I buy, I bought, I will buy**
______________________	**to share: I share, I shared, I will share**
______________________	**to look for: I look for, I looked for, I will look for**
______________________	**to answer: I answer, I answered, I will answer**
______________________	**all**

B. Canto:

Fill in the boxes of this week's **canto**.

Something "Near You" (this, these)

	Singular	Plural
Masculine	______________	______________
Feminine	______________	______________

Something "Farther from You" (that, those)

	Singular	Plural
Masculine	______________	______________
Feminine	______________	______________

Something "Over There" (that "over there," those "over there")

	Singular	Plural
Masculine	______________	______________
Feminine	______________	______________

C. Grammar:

1. Number these three books to tell how close they are to you. Write a "1" over the book that is closest, a "2" over the book in the middle, and a "3" over the book that is farthest away.

ese libro **aquel libro** **este libro**

2. Draw lines between the demonstrative adjectives and their corresponding nouns:

Adjectives	Nouns
estos	**gafas** (near)
estas	**medias** (way over there)
aquel	**fiesta** (near)
este	**camisa** (a little farther away)
esa	**bolígrafo** (a little farther away)
ese	**aviones** (near)
esta	**jardín** (way over there)
aquellas	**reloj** (near)

Frases:

¿Qué es eso? *(What's that?)*

¿Qué es esto? *(What's this?)*

Canto:

Demonstrative Pronouns

Something "Near You" (this, these)

	Singular	Plural
Masculine	éste (this)	éstos (these)
Feminine	ésta (this)	éstas (these)
Neuter	esto (this)	N/A[1]

Something "Farther from You" (that, those)

Singular	Plural
ése (that)	ésos (those)
ésa (that)	ésas (those)
eso (that)	N/A

Something "Over There" (that "over there," those "over there")

	Singular	Plural
Masculine	aquél (that over there)	aquéllos (those over there)
Feminine	aquélla (that over there)	aquéllas (those over there)
Neuter	aquello (that over there)	N/A

Vocabulario:

Vocabulario nuevo

Spanish	English	Spanish	English
derecha	right	**lejos de**	far from
izquierda	left	**entre**	between
encima de	on top of	**fuera de**	out of
delante de	in front of	**dentro de**	inside of
detrás de	behind	**debajo de**	underneath
cerca de	near		

Gestures will be very helpful this week as you learn your vocabulary words.

Vocabulario de repaso

Spanish	English
cambiar: cambio, cambié, cambiaré	to change: I change, I changed, I will change
comprender: comprendo, comprendí, comprenderé	to understand: I understand, I understood, I will understand
cocinar: cocino, cociné, cocinaré	to cook: I cook, I cooked, I will cook
la gente	people
la cosa	thing

1 Did you notice that there are no neuter plural forms in the tables? That's because there is no special form for these. This will be discussed later in the chapter.

Demonstrative Pronouns

Are you ready for something easy? If a possessive pronoun takes the place of a possessive adjective plus a noun, what do you think a demonstrative pronoun takes the place of? That's right—**a *demonstrative pronoun* takes the place of a demonstrative adjective plus a noun**. Take a look:

***Esta* fiesta es muy divertida.** (This party is really fun.)
***Ésta* es muy divertida.** (This is really fun.)

***Aquel* libro es muy interesante.** (That book over there is very interesting.)
***Aquél* es muy interesante.** (That one[2] over there is very interesting.)

¡Ten cuidado! (Be careful!): There's only one difference in spelling between a demonstrative adjective and a demonstrative pronoun. It's very tiny: The pronoun gets an accent on the first ***e***. Think of it this way: If the noun isn't there, it's disguised as an accent mark hiding in the pronoun's hair.

Don't Break the Rules!

You probably don't need this reminder, since you've heard it so many times, but remember the following: **Demonstrative pronouns have to agree in gender and number with the nouns they modify.**

But What About the Neuter Pronouns?

You can break the rules just this once. In the bottom row of each section of the **canto**, you'll find **neuter pronouns**. These don't have gender! *What?* Why not? Well, because sometimes you need to say "this" or "that," and you have no idea what the thing is that you are talking about. If you don't know what something is, how could you know its grammatical gender? So, in those special cases, you get to use the special **neuter demonstrative pronouns**, ***esto***, ***eso***, and ***aquello***. (They don't have accents.) Just to prepare you for these demonstrative pronouns, here are two common phrases using them:

¿Qué es esto? (What's this?)

¿Qué es eso? (What's that?)

You can also use the neuter pronouns to talk about something that isn't specific enough to have gender. For instance, imagine you find out that your favorite team lost every game and that the government just outlawed recess. You might say, "**¡Esto es horrible!**" ("This is horrible!"). Or imagine that your school is going to install a roller coaster on the playground. You could say, "**¡Eso es fenomenal!**" ("That's great!") How do you figure out the gender of "the facts that my team lost and the government is outlawing recess" or "the fact that we're getting a new roller coaster"? Don't worry about it. Just use neuter pronouns.

2. In English, we sometimes add "one" to our demonstrative pronouns and say "this one" or "that one." You don't have to do that in Spanish.

A. Translation:

1. **to change**	__________	9. **in front of**	__________
2. **I understand**	__________	10. **near**	__________
3. **behind**	__________	11. **far from**	__________
4. **people**	__________	12. **between**	__________
5. **thing**	__________	13. **out of**	__________
6. **right**	__________	14. **I will cook**	__________
7. **left**	__________	15. **inside of**	__________
8. **on top of**	__________	16. **underneath**	__________

B. **Canto**: Demonstrative Pronouns

Fill in the boxes of this week's **canto**.

Something "Near You" (this, these)

	Singular	Plural
Masculine	__________	__________
Feminine	__________	__________
Neuter	__________	N/A

Something "Farther from You" (that, those)

	Singular	Plural
Masculine	__________	__________
Feminine	__________	__________
Neuter	__________	N/A

Something "Over There" (that "over there," those "over there")

	Singular	Plural
Masculine	______________	______________
Feminine	______________	______________
Neuter	______________	N/A

C. Grammar:

1. A demonstrative pronoun takes the place of a ____________________

____________________ and a ________________________.

2. Can a demonstrative pronoun be the subject of a sentence? ___________

3. Neuter pronouns don't have (circle one):
   a. Number
   b. Gender
   c. Friends

4. When would you use a neuter pronoun? ____

____

____

5. The only spelling difference between demonstrative adjectives and demonstrative pronouns is that the pronouns have ____________________ and the adjectives don't.

D. Focus on **Vocabulario**:

Here, we've got an **árbol** with letters all over it. We also have some sentences that use the vocabulary words. Finish each sentence by filling in the corresponding letter.

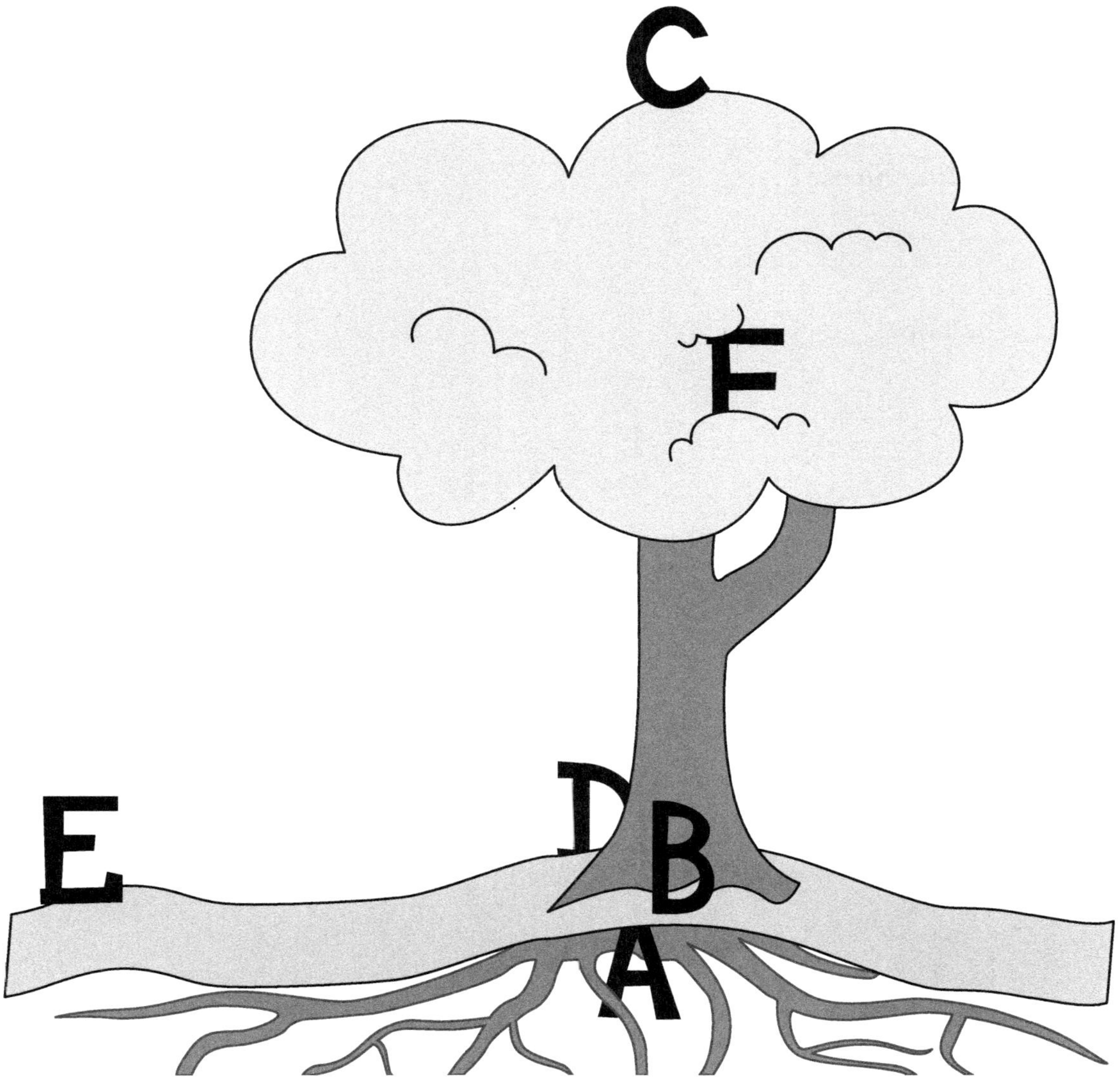

1. **Letra _____ está delante del árbol.**

2. **Letra _____ está detrás del árbol.**

3. **Letra _____ está adentro del árbol.**

4. **Letra _____ está debajo del árbol.**

5. **Letra _____ está lejos del árbol.**

6. **Letra _____ está encima del árbol.**

E. Let's Do Some Demonstrating:

Here we go: Each sentence has a noun and a demonstrative adjective. You're going to replace them both with a demonstrative pronoun. Then, for each sentence, put a check in the box to indicate whether the noun is near, a little bit farther away, or very far away.

	Near	Little Bit Farther	Very Far
1. **Yo conocía a aquellos chicos.** **Yo conocía a ____________________.**			
2. **Me gustaba ese helado.** **Me gustaba ____________________.**			
3. **Yo leí este libro.** **Yo leí ____________________.**			
4. **Yo vi aquel árbol.** **Yo vi ____________________.**			
5. **Yo llevaré aquellas medias.** **Yo llevaré ____________________.**			

A. New and Review Vocabulary:

Spanish	English
______________________	right
______________________	left
______________________	on top of
______________________	in front of
______________________	behind
______________________	near
______________________	far from
______________________	between
______________________	out of
______________________	inside of
______________________	underneath
______________________	to change: I change, I changed, I will change
______________________	to understand: I understand, I understood, I will understand
______________________	to cook: I cook, I cooked, I will cook
______________________	people
______________________	thing

B. Canto:

Fill in the boxes of this week's **canto**.

Something "Near You" (this, these)

	Singular	Plural
Masculine	______________	______________
Feminine	______________	______________
Neuter	______________	N/A

Something "Farther from You" (that, those)

	Singular	Plural
Masculine	______________	______________
Feminine	______________	______________
Neuter	______________	N/A

Something "Over There" (that "over there," those "over there")

	Singular	Plural
Masculine	______________	______________
Feminine	______________	______________
Neuter	______________	N/A

C. Grammar:

Fill a demonstrative pronoun into each Spanish sentence.

1. Let's go look at that butterfly (**mariposa**).
   Vamos para mirar ______________________.

2. Would you like to ride this bicicle (**bicicleta**)?
   ¿Quieres montar en ______________________?

3. If so, you'd better wear that helmet (**casco**) over there!
   Si es así, debes llevar ______________________.

Frases:

No necesitas frases esta semana. ¡El canto es bastante grande!
semana = *week*
bastante = *enough*

Canto:

Yo soy más alto que mi madre
y menos alto que mi padre.
Ya que yo nací más temprano,
yo soy mayor que mi hermano.
Pero aunque a su lado salto,
mi hermanito es más alto.
Yo soy menor que mi prima,
y aquí concluyo la rima.

ya que = *since, because*
aunque = *even though*
a su lado = *at his side*
aunque a su lado salto = *even though at his side I jump*
(The words are a bit mixed up to make it rhyme!)
hermanito = *little brother*
prima = *girl cousin*
concluyo = *I conclude, I finish, I end*
la rima = *the rhyme*

Vocabulario:

Vocabulario nuevo

Spanish	English
mejorar: mejoro, mejoré, mejoraré	to improve (something): I improve (something), I improved (something), I will improve (something)
añadir: añado, añadí, añadiré	to add: I add, I added, I will add
mejor	better
el/la mejor	the best
peor	worse
el/la peor	the worst
más	more
más que	more than
menos que	less than
menor/es	younger
mayor/es	older

Vocabulario de repaso

Spanish	English
mover: muevo, moví, moveré	to move: I move, I moved, I will move
morir: muero, morí, moriré	to die: I die, I died, I will die
morder: muerdo, mordí, morderé	to bite: I bite, I bit, I will bite
molestar: molesto, molesté, molestaré	to bother: I bother, I bothered, I will bother
menos	minus, less

Making Comparisons

Did you like the last chapter? This one is going to be even *better*! Or maybe it will be *worse*. Either way, by the end of this chapter, you'll be able to say in Spanish that things are *better* or *worse* than other things. You'll be learning to use comparatives.

What are comparatives? Here are two examples in English—the comparative words are in bold: "This car's bumper is **bigger** than that car's bumper," and "My dog is **dirtier** than your dog!"

In these two sentences, **you see that we are *comparing* two ideas** (first, the size of bumper 1 and the size of bumper 2, and second, the dirtiness of my dog and the dirtiness of your dog), **which is why we call these words *comparatives*.**

In English, words you use to compare things often look like this:

dirty (This is just an *adjective*. It's not making a comparison.)
dirti***er*** (This is a *comparative adjective*. This means it is more dirty than the thing to which it is being compared.)
clean (Adjective)
clean***er*** (Comparative adjective)

Do you see how we just change the ending of "dirty" or "clean" to show what kind of comparison we're making? Guess what: We don't do that in Spanish. Instead of changing the endings of adjectives when we're making comparisons in Spanish, we use other words to help our adjectives. It looks like this:

English	Spanish
dirty	**sucio**
dirtier	***más*** **sucio**
intelligent	**inteligente**
more intelligent	***más*** **inteligente**

For the idea of "dirtier," why is there the extra word **más** in Spanish? Look hard at the rest of the chart. Maybe you figured out from looking at the term **más inteligente** that **más** just means "more." **Más sucio** literally means "more dirty," which, of course, we don't say in English.[1]

Now, how could you say the whole sentence "My dog is dirtier than your dog!" in Spanish?

Mi	**perro**	**está**	**más sucio**	**que**	**tu**	**perro.**
↓	↓	↓	↘ ↙	↓	↓	↓
My	dog	is	dirtier	than	your	dog.

1. You may be tempted to complain, "But saying 'dirtier' with one word is so much easier than saying **más sucio** with two words. You have to do so much more work in Spanish!" But think about this: In English, do you say something is "funner" or "more fun" than something else? You can usually just add the *-er* ending in English, but with some words, such as "fun," there's a different rule. English can get tricky, huh? Well, in Spanish you don't have to remember when to use an **-er** ending (as you do in English) and when to say "**más** + adjective"—you just say **más** all of the time!

On the other hand, if you want to say your dog is "less dirty" than my dog, we have to use two words to do that in English. This is closer to Spanish (which, as you now know, likes to use two words with comparatives):

English	Spanish
dirty	**sucio**
less dirty	***menos* sucio**
intelligent	**inteligente**
less intelligent	***menos* inteligente**

Did you spot the key Spanish word? It's **menos**, which means "less." So then, a sentence such as "Your dog is less intelligent than my dog" would be:

Tu	**perro**	**es**	**menos**	**inteligente**	**que**	**mi**	**perro.**
↓	↓	↓	↓	↓	↓	↓	↓
Your	dog	is	less	intelligent	than	my	dog.

"More Than" and "Less Than"

Now that you know some good comparison words, let's focus on how you put them into sentences. Here's a little formula you can use:

más	+	?	+	**que**
more	+	?	+	than

What's the "?" going to be? We said previously that **más** and **menos** can be used with almost any adjective. Let's give it a try:

Yo estoy más *enojada* que tú. (I'm more *angry* than you.)
El libro es menos *aburrido* que la película. (The book is less *boring* than the movie.)

That was pretty easy, right? It's simple since it's basically the same formula that we use in English. And guess what: Just as in English, you can also use this formula with other parts of speech, not just adjectives. Sometimes you can even drop the extra word altogether! Take a look:

A noun:
Yo tengo más *dinero* que tú. (I have more *money* than you.)
Yo tengo más que tú. (I have more than you.)

An adverb:
Tú lees menos *rápidamente* que ella. (You read less *quickly* than she does.)

No extra word at all:
Yo corro menos que tú. (I run less than you.)

Extra Vocabulary

You've been learning to use the words **más** and **menos** in combination with other words to make comparisons. But there are a few adjectives that don't follow this pattern. You still use them in sentences just as you would use other comparison words. Take a look:

English	Spanish
good	**bueno**
better	**mejor**
bad	**mal**
worse	**peor**

Esteban estuvo enfermo, pero ahora él está *mejor*. (Esteban was sick, but now he's *better*.)
Alicia estudió, pero ¡su español es *peor*! (Alicia studied, but her Spanish is *worse*!)

Here's another set of comparison adjectives that don't follow the usual rule.

English	Spanish
old	**viejo**
older	**mayor**
young	**joven**
younger	**menor**

Esteban es mi hermano *menor*. (Esteban is my *younger* brother.)
Esteban es viejo, pero yo soy *mayor*. (Esteban is old, but I'm *older*.)

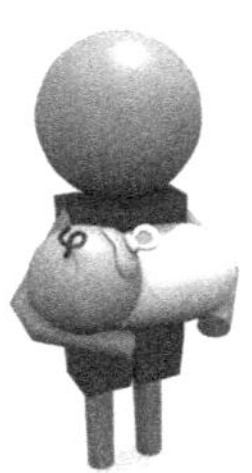

A. Translation:

1. **I move**	______________	9. **el/la mejor**	______________
2. **I die**	______________	10. **peor**	______________
3. **I bite**	______________	11. **el/la peor**	______________
4. **to bother**	______________	12. **more**	______________
5. **minus, less**	______________	13. **more than**	______________
6. **mejorar**	______________	14. **less than**	______________
7. **añadiré**	______________	15. **mayor/es**	______________
8. **mejor**	______________	16. **menor/es**	______________

B. Canto:

Fill in the blanks to complete this week's **canto**.

Yo soy _______ _________ _______ **mi madre,**

y _________ ________ ______ **mi padre.**

Ya que yo nací ______ _______________,

yo ______ _________ ______ **mi hermano.**

Pero aunque a su lado salto,

mi hermanito _____ ______ ________.

Yo soy _________ ______ **mi prima,**

y aquí concluyo la rima.

C. Grammar:

1. What's the English word ending that means "more than"? Circle one:
   a. *-ed*
   b. *-er*
   c. *-ing*
   d. *-able*

2. In Spanish, to make a word mean "more than," we add a special ending to the word.

   Circle one: True False

3. In Spanish, change the word "sad" (**triste**) to "sadder." ______________________

4. Now change **triste** to "*less* sad." ______________________

5. What is a comparative? ______________________

   ____

D. Have You Been Paying Attention?

1. Answer this question: **¿Por qué no hay *frases* esta semana?** (**esta semana** = this week)

   ____

   ____

E. Making Comparisons

There are twins in your Spanish class, and you're trying to explain to your friends how you can tell them apart. Sentences about the twins (**los gemelos**) will be provided in English, and you will use the adjectives—shown in bold italics in parentheses to the right of the sentences—to describe them in new sentences. With those adjectives, complete the new sentences using **más . . . que** or **menos . . . que** to tell your friends about the twins. The first one is done for you as an example.

1. Miguel is five feet tall; Rafael is four feet tall. (**alto**, tall)
   Miguel es más alto que Rafael.

2. Miguel is pudgy; Rafael is skinny. (**flaco**, skinny)

   Rafael es ______________________.

3. Rafael is always smiling; Miguel only smiles sometimes. (**feliz**, happy)

   Miguel es ______________________.

4. Miguel loves to play sports; Rafael would rather play his **guitarra**. (**atlético**, athletic)

   Rafael es ______________________.

5. Rafael loves to tell jokes; Miguel is very serious. (**cómico**, funny)

   Rafael es ______________________.

A. New and Review Vocabulary:

Spanish	English
______________________	to improve (something): I improve (something), I improved (something), I will improve (something)
______________________	to add: I add, I added, I will add
______________________	better
______________________	the best
______________________	worse
______________________	the worst
______________________	more
______________________	more than
______________________	less than
______________________	younger
______________________	older
______________________	to move: I move, I moved, I will move
______________________	to die: I die, I died, I will die
______________________	to bite: I bite, I bit, I will bite
______________________	to bother: I bother, I bothered, I will bother
______________________	minus, less

B. Canto:

Fill in the blanks to complete this week's **canto**.

Yo soy ________ ___________ ________ mi madre,

y ___________ __________ ________ mi padre.

Ya que yo nací ________ ____________________,

yo ________ ___________ ________ mi hermano.

Pero aunque a su lado salto,

mi hermanito _______ ________ __________.

Yo soy ___________ ________ mi prima,

y aquí concluyo la rima.

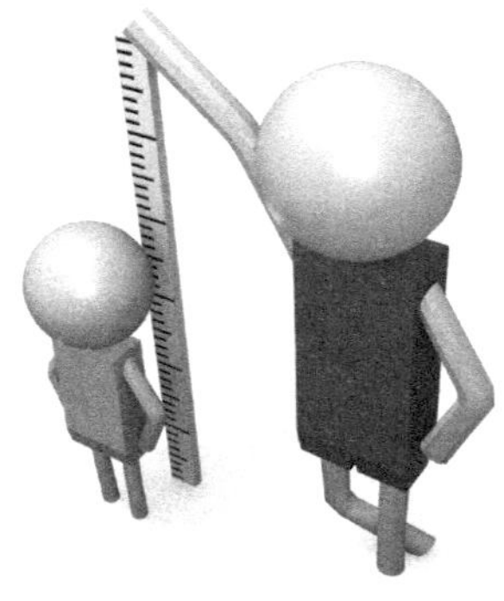

Frases:

Mi hermanita es mi mejor amiga del mundo, y yo la trato muy bien. Ella es más joven y no puede hacer muchas cosas. Yo soy más fuerte que ella y cuando ella necesita algo, yo la ayudo. Ella me quiere mucho y jugamos juntos todo el tiempo. Yo soy muy cómico, pero ella es la más cómica de toda la familia. Ella siempre me hace reír.

hermanita = *little sister*
juntos = *together*
me hace reír = *makes me laugh*

Canto:

¡Nuestro equipo es el mejor!
Sí, ¡sí, señor!
Tenemos los jugadores más rápidos.
(¡Los jugadores son los más rápidos!)
Las jugadoras son las menos lentas.
(¡Son las menos lentas!)
¡Nuestro equipo es el mejor!
Sí, ¡sí, señor!

nuestro equipo = *our team*
jugadores = *players*
jugadoras = *female players*

Vocabulario:

Vocabulario nuevo

Spanish	English
probar: pruebo, probé, probaré	to try/taste: I try/taste, I tried/tasted, I will try/taste
tratar de: trato de, traté de, trataré de	to try to: I try to, I tried to, I will try to
tratar: trato, traté, trataré	to treat: I treat, I treated, I will treat
empujar: empujo, empujé, empujaré	to push: I push, I pushed, I will push
caro/a/os/as	expensive
barato/a/os/as	inexpensive
rápido/a/os/as	fast
lento/a/os/as	slow
fuerte/es	strong
cómico/a/os/as	funny
el mundo	world
el joven, la joven	young man, young woman

Take a look at the first two words on this week's vocabulary list: **probar** and **tratar**. They both mean "to try"—but they don't mean the same thing! How is that possible? Check it out: **Probar** means to try something new, to taste or test something, or to prove something. **Tratar** + **de** means to try to do something. Instead of saying "to try *to*," in Spanish we use the word **de**: **Yo trato de leer** (I'm trying to read). **Tratar** without **de** means "to treat," as in, "I treat my family well" (**Yo les trato bien a mi familia**).

Vocabulario de repaso

Spanish	English
inteligente/es	intelligent, smart
alto/a/os/as	tall, high
bajo/a/os/as	short, low
joven/jóvenes	young

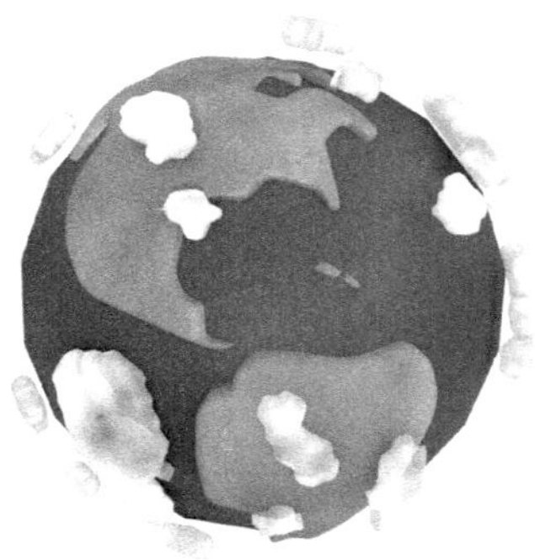

Superlatives

In the last chapter, we talked about your dirty dog. We learned how to say that he's dirtier than someone else's dog (**Mi perro es más sucio que tu perro**). But if your dog is so dirty that he could win a dirty-dog contest without even trying, you might need to use some stronger words to talk about him. You might need to use a **superlative**.

When you use a superlative, you're comparing something to a whole group of other things, and you're saying that it is "the most." So, you could say something such as "My dog is the dirtiest dog ever" or "My dog is the most dirty." Now, he's not just more dirty than something else. He's more dirty than everything else!

English	Spanish
dirty	**sucio**
the *most* dirty (the dirti*est*)	**el *más* sucio**

Or, if you want to talk about the cleanest dogs:

English	Spanish
dirty	**sucio**
the *least* dirty	**el *menos* sucio**

In English, we can either say that something is "the most dirty" or "the dirti*est*." In Spanish, there's no *-est* ending, so you'll always say something is "the most ________" when you want to use a superlative.

Yo soy el más alto de mi clase.
(I'm the most tall/tallest in my class.)

Isabel es la más inteligente de su familia.
(Isabel is the smartest/most smart in her family.)

Estas manzanas son las más ricas.
(These apples are the most rich/the most yummy.)

Here's the formula:
definite article + **más/menos** + adjective = superlative

You're using the words you learned in the last chapter, **más** and **menos**, but now you're adding the articles **el**, **la**, **los**, and **las**. Since you've got articles and adjectives hanging around with your noun, you need to **make sure they all agree in gender and number**. You might want to re-read the example sentence about the apples just to see how many words end up in their feminine-plural forms.

Here's one more little thing to note: In English, we say, "I'm the tallest *in* the class," but in Spanish you say, "I'm the tallest of the class." Here's another example of using *of* instead of *in* in Spanish:

Él es mi mejor amigo del mundo. (He's my best friend *of* the world.)

Some Extra Vocabulary

Remember those extra comparison words you learned in the last chapter? Here they are again:

English	Spanish
good	**bueno**
better	**mejor**
bad	**mal**
worse	**peor**
old	**viejo**
older	**mayor**
young	**joven**
younger	**menor**

When you want to turn "better" and "worse" into "the best" and "the worst," you just add an article:

The best: **el mejor/la mejor/los mejores/las mejores**
The worst: **el peor/la peor/los peores/las peores**
The oldest: **el mayor/la mayor/los mayores/las mayores**
The youngest: **el menor/la menor/los menores/las menores**

Mi madre es *la mejor* cocinera.
(My mom is *the best* cook.)

Mis padres son *los mejores* padres del mundo.
(My parents are *the best* parents in the world.)

¡Esta película es *la peor* película de todo el mundo!
(This movie is *the worst* movie in the whole world!)

Mi abuelo es *el mayor* de todo mi familia.
(My grandfather is *the oldest* in my whole family.)

Mi hermanito es *el menor* de su clase.
(My little brother is *the youngest* in his class.)

A. Translation:

1. **smart**	__________	11. **barato**	__________
2. **tall**	__________	12. **young man**	__________
3. **low**	__________	13. **fast**	__________
4. **young**	__________	14. **slow**	__________
5. **young woman**	__________	15. **fuerte**	__________
6. **to taste**	__________	16. **short**	__________
7. **to treat**	__________	17. **funny**	__________
8. **empujaré**	__________	18. **el mundo**	__________
9. **caro**	__________	19. **to try to**	__________
10. **high**	__________		

B. Canto:

Fill in the blanks of this week's **canto**.

¡ __________ equipo es _____ ________ !

Sí, ¡sí, señor!

__________ los __________ ______ rápidos,

(¡Los jugadores son _____ _____ __________ !)

Las __________ son _____ ________ ________ ,

(¡Son _____ ________ ________ !)

¡Nuestro equipo _____ _____ ________ !

Sí, ¡sí, señor!

C. Grammar:

Draw lines between the incomplete sentences on the left and their corresponding sentence endings on the right. Make sure you watch for gender and number, and choose sentences that make sense!

A mi amigo David le gusta correr. Él es	**la más cara.**
La camisa cuesta (costs) **más que las otras. Es**	**los menos rápidos.**
Nuestro equipo no gana ningunas carreras (doesn't win any races)**. Somos**	**la menos cara.**
Todas las bicicletas cuestan (cost) **100 dólares, pero ésta cuesta 50. Ésta es**	**el más rápido.**

D. Brain Challenge:

These grammar questions are a little more difficult than usual. See if you can rise to the challenge!

1. What does "superlative" mean?

____

____

2. What's the difference between making a comparative and a superlative in Spanish? There are two ways you can answer this—explain both of them.

   a. Explain the difference in *meaning*:

   ____

   ____

   b. Explain the difference in *the words you use*:

   ____

   ____

A. New and Review Vocabulary:

Spanish	English
____________	to try/taste: I try/taste, I tried/tasted, I will try/taste
____________	to try to: I try to, I tried to, I will try to
____________	to treat: I treat, I treated, I will treat
____________	to push: I push, I pushed, I will push
____________	expensive
____________	inexpensive
____________	fast
____________	slow
____________	strong
____________	funny
____________	world
____________	young man, young woman
____________	intelligent, smart
____________	tall, high
____________	short, low
____________	young

B. Canto:

Fill in the blanks of this week's **canto**.

¡ __________________ equipo es _____ _____________ !

Sí, ¡sí, señor!

____________________ los ___________________ _______ rápidos,

(¡Los jugadores son ______ ______ _________________ !)

Las ___________________ son ______ ____________ ____________,

(¡Son ______ ____________ ____________ !)

¡Nuestro equipo _____ _____ _____________ !

Sí, ¡sí, señor!

C. Grammar:

The difference in Spanish between comparatives (e.g., "my dog is dirtier") and superlatives (e.g., "my dog is the dirtiest") is just one little part of speech. What is it? Circle one:

a. An adjective

b. An article

c. A noun

d. An adverb

Repaso de vocabulario

Another unit, another set of review vocabulary words—let's see how well you did at memorizing them!

Chapter 16

- ☐ 1. **montar**
- ☐ 2. **el patinete**
- ☐ 3. **la bicicleta**
- ☐ 4. **la ropa**
- ☐ 5. **el casco**
- ☐ 6. **los pantalones**
- ☐ 7. **la chaqueta**
- ☐ 8. **la falda**
- ☐ 9. **el vestido**
- ☐ 10. **las gafas**
- ☐ 11. **llevar**
- ☐ 12. **prestar**
- ☐ 13. **la camisa**
- ☐ 14. **los zapatos**
- ☐ 15. **el abrigo**

Chapter 17

- ☐ 16. **este/esta**
- ☐ 17. **ese/esa**
- ☐ 18. **estos/estas**
- ☐ 19. **esos/esas**
- ☐ 20. **aquel/aquella**
- ☐ 21. **aquellos/aquellas**
- ☐ 22. **libre/es**
- ☐ 23. **listo/a/os/as**
- ☐ 24. **todo/a/os/as**
- ☐ 25. **cada**
- ☐ 26. **ayudar**
- ☐ 27. **comprar**
- ☐ 28. **compartir**
- ☐ 29. **buscar**
- ☐ 30. **contestar**

Chapter 18

- ☐ 31. **derecha**
- ☐ 32. **izquierda**
- ☐ 33. **encima de**
- ☐ 34. **delante de**
- ☐ 35. **detrás de**
- ☐ 36. **cerca de**
- ☐ 37. **lejos de**
- ☐ 38. **entre**
- ☐ 39. **fuera de**
- ☐ 40. **dentro de**
- ☐ 41. **debajo de**
- ☐ 42. **cambiar**
- ☐ 43. **comprender**
- ☐ 44. **cocinar**
- ☐ 45. **la gente**
- ☐ 46. **la cosa**

Chapter 19

- ☐ 47. **mejorar**
- ☐ 48. **añadir**
- ☐ 49. **mejor**
- ☐ 50. **el/la mejor**
- ☐ 51. **peor**
- ☐ 52. **el/la peor**
- ☐ 53. **más**
- ☐ 54. **más que**
- ☐ 55. **menos que**
- ☐ 56. **menor/es**
- ☐ 57. **mayor/es**
- ☐ 58. **mover**
- ☐ 59. **morir**
- ☐ 60. **morder**
- ☐ 61. **molestar**
- ☐ 62. **menos**

Chapter 20

☐	63. **probar**	☐	67. **caro/a/os/as**	☐	71. **fuerte/es**	☐	75. **inteligente/es**
☐	64. **tratar de**	☐	68. **barato/a/os/as**	☐	72. **cómico/a/os/as**	☐	76. **alto/a/os/as**
☐	65. **tratar**	☐	69. **rápido/a/os/as**	☐	73. **el mundo**	☐	77. **bajo/a/os/as**
☐	66. **empujar**	☐	70. **lento/a/os/as**	☐	74. **el joven, la joven**	☐	78. **joven/jóvenes**

Cantos

You know what to do! Show these **cantos** who's boss.

Possessive Pronouns (Chapter 16)

	Singular	Plural
1st person	______________	______________
2nd-person familiar	______________	**vuestro/a/os/as**
2nd-person formal	______________	______________
3rd person	______________	______________

Demonstrative Adjectives (Chapter 17)

Something "Near You" (this, these)

	Singular	Plural
Masculine	______________	______________
Feminine	______________	______________

Something "Farther from You" (that, those)

	Singular	Plural
Masculine	______________	______________
Feminine	______________	______________

Something "Over There" (that "over there," those "over there")

	Singular	Plural
Masculine	______________	______________
Feminine	______________	______________

Demonstrative Pronouns (Chapter 18)

Something "Near You" (this, these)

	Singular	Plural
Masculine	________________	________________
Feminine	________________	________________
Neuter	________________	N/A

Something "Farther from You" (that, those)

	Singular	Plural
Masculine	________________	________________
Feminine	________________	________________
Neuter	________________	N/A

Something "Over There" (that "over there," those "over there")

	Singular	Plural
Masculine	________________	________________
Feminine	________________	________________
Neuter	________________	N/A

Comparisons (Chapter 19)

Yo soy _______ _________ _______ mi madre,

y __________ _________ _______ mi padre.

Ya que yo nací _______ temprano,

yo _______ __________ _______ mi hermano.

Pero aunque a su lado salto,

mi hermanito es _______ _________.

Yo soy __________ _______ mi prima,

y aquí concluyo la rima.

Superlatives (Chapter 20)

¡Nuestro equipo es _____ ____________ !

Sí, ¡sí, señor!

Tenemos los jugadores ______ rápidos,

(¡Los jugadores son ______ ______ _______________ !)

Las jugadores son ______ ___________ ___________,

(¡Son ______ ___________ ___________ !)

¡Nuestro equipo _____ _____ ____________ !

Sí, ¡sí, señor!

Treasure Map

Draw **un mapa** (a map) of your room. Label **el mapa** in Spanish to show where your things are. (If you need a few extra vocabulary words, check a Spanish dictionary—otherwise, you should know enough words to label most things in your bedroom.) Then choose one of the following activities:

1. Make a list of all the things labeled on your **mapa**. Cut up the list so each word is on its own piece of paper. Turn the papers over, and mix them up. Pick up two papers, turn them over, and then write (on a separate piece of paper) or say a sentence to tell where those two things are in relation to each other.

   Example:
   Your two pieces of paper: **alfombra**, **cama**
   You write: **La alfombra está debajo de la cama.**

   Keep drawing pieces of paper until you've used each word at least once. Try to use each describing word you've learned, too. Here's a hint: See the list of descriptive words in chapter 18, such as **encima de** (on top of), **delante de** (in front of), etc.

   Here's an extra challenge: Try writing or saying your sentences in the past tense. You're describing where things usually were, so you'll use the imperfect tense.

2. Make a list of the items labeled on your **mapa**, and cut up the list of terms into separate pieces of paper as described in the first activity. This time, however, the game will change slightly. Play with a partner by asking each other where things are located in your room.

   Pick an item in the room, and ask your partner a question about it. For example, you ask:

   ¿Dónde estaba la alfombra?

Then, your friend picks up one of the pieces of paper before responding. He or she will tell you where the **alfombra** is in relation to the item listed on the piece of paper:

La alfombra estaba debajo de la cama.

Be sure to take turns! For the next turn, your friend would pick an item in the room and ask you a question, and then you would pick up a piece of paper and respond based on the item listed on that paper, and so on. Continue in this manner until all of the pieces of paper have been used. For an extra challenge, you could also use the imperfect tense in your questions and answers.

Grammar Rules

1. Circle the words on this list that *can't* change to reflect gender and number:

   más **listo** **bueno** **menos** **rápido** **este** **esto** **mío**

2. How do you say "happier" in Spanish? ______________________________

3. How do you say "the happiest" in Spanish? ______________________________

4. How do you say "the least happy" in Spanish? ______________________________

5. What is the special case when you would use a neuter pronoun? ______________

   ____

   ____

   ____

6. What is the spelling difference between demonstrative adjectives and demonstrative pronouns? ____

   ____

7. What's the difference between **ese** and **aquel**? ______________________________

   ____

8. What's the difference between **ese** and **eso**? ______________________________

   ____

9. What's the difference between **esta** and **esa**? ______________________________

   ____

Possessive Pronouns

Here we go—it's time to practice those possessive pronouns. The following is a list of nouns, and beside each noun there is an indicator telling to whom it belongs (italicized in parentheses). Write down which possessive pronoun you'd use in the noun's place. Don't forget that extra little word! The first one is done for you as an example.

1. **lápiz** (us) <u>el</u> <u>nuestro</u>
2. **bolígrafos** (him) _____ __________
3. **papel** (you all) _____ __________
4. **mochila** (me) _____ __________
5. **bebida** (her) _____ __________
6. **postre** (you) _____ __________
7. **maletas (usted)** _____ __________
8. **flores** (them) _____ __________
9. **poemas** (me) _____ __________
10. **cama** (her) _____ __________
11. **patinete** (us) _____ __________
12. **ropa (usted)** _____ __________

You Be the Judge

You've learned how to make comparisons and how to tell which thing is "the best" and which is "the worst." Now you're going to work as a judge at the local farmers' association. Your job is to check out each of the following sets of things (see the drawings) and indicate which one is the best. Or, if a group really stinks, you could say that one is the worst. You decide; you're the judge!

But wait—how will we know which one you're talking about? Here's a helpful note to keep in mind as you do this exercise: You're standing on the *left*, so the item on the left is the closest to you, and the item on the right is the farthest away. Still need a hint? Try some demonstrative adjectives. First try explaining out loud which is best (or the worst), and then write out your sentences for some extra practice.

5. **los huevos**   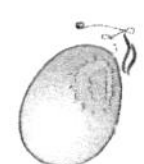

____

Logic Puzzle

You need to put together relay race teams based on how quickly your friends can run. Using the information from races they have run before, put everyone's name in order from the fastest (**más rápido**) to the slowest (**menos rápido**).

Paloma es más rápida que Rafael.
Victoria es más rápida que Sebastiano.
Paloma es menos rápida que Victoria.
Rafael es menos rápido que Sebastiano.
Sebastiano es más rápido que Paloma.

List:
más rápido
1. ____________
2. ____________
3. ____________
4. ____________

menos rápido

Equal Comparisons: It's All the Same to Me

You've probably gotten really good at comparing things . . . but what if they're exactly the same? You might need *this* little phrase: **tan** + ? + **como**. When you say, "**Lidia era *tan* cómica *como* Sara**," it means, "Lidia was *as* funny *as* Sara." The little **tan** + ? + **como** formula works the same way as **más** + ? + **que** and **menos** + ? + **que**. Take a look:

David era *más* alto *que* Josué.
David era *menos* alto *que* Josué.
David era *tan* alto *como* Josué. (David was as tall as Josh.)

You try it! Rewrite each sentence using the **tan** + ? + **como** formula. We'll use the imperfect tense and not the preterit, since we're describing what people were like.

1. **Lea y Juana eran rápidas.**

   Lea era ______________________________.

2. **Ricardo y Daniel eran fuertes.**

   Ricardo era ______________________________.

3. **Flor y Lucía eran felices.**

   Flor era ______________________________.

4. **Esteban y Martín eran inteligentes.**

   Esteban era ______________________________.

La sexta piedra:

Sixth Preterit Puzzle Piece

U-Group Irregulars

There are some verbs that change their stems in the preterit form so much that you almost wouldn't recognize them. You're going to learn them in three groups: the "U group," the "I group," and the "J group." Learning about each group will earn you another **piedra**—your last three. Are you ready to begin? To find this **piedra**, you've got to master the U group.

Here's a chart of some U-group verbs and their new stems. Take a look: There are a lot of *U*s.

U-Group Verb	Poder	Poner	Saber	Andar	Estar	Tener
New Stem	**pud-**	**pus-**	**sup-**	**anduv-**	**estuv-**	**tuv-**

Half of the U group could even be called the "UV group" because for many of these verbs, the last two letters in the stems are ***uv***. Here's a way to remember which ones they are: If you're *walking* (**andar**), and you *are* (**estar**) in the sun, you *have* (**tener**) to put on sunscreen because of those "**UV**" rays! Try making up your own silly sentence to remember the rest of the U-group verbs.

Now that you know the new preterit stems for the U group, all you have to do is add their endings to conjugate them. But wait—the "group" verbs have their own set of preterit endings! It may sound a little scary, but it's not so bad. Here are the endings:

UI-Group Irregular Preterit Endings

	Singular	Plural
1st person	**-e**	**-imos**
2nd person	**-iste**	**-isteis**
3rd person	**-o**	**-ieron**

What's different about these endings? There are no accents. And it looks like we're mixing **-ar** verb endings with **-er** and **-ir** verb endings, doesn't it? Don't worry about whether a U-group verb has an **-ar**, **-er**, or **-ir** ending in the infinitive; just learn their new preterit stems, and use their special preterit endings.

Are you ready to find the **piedra**? Fill in the missing **yo** and **tú** forms in the following charts.

U-Group Verb New Stem	Andar anduv-	Estar estuv-	Tener tuv-
yo form	_ _ _ _ _ ◯	_ _ _ _ _ _ _ _	_ _ _ _ _
tú form	_ _ _ _ _ _ _ _ _ _ _ _ _	_ _ _ _ _ _ _ _ _ _ _ _ _	_ _ _ _ _ _ _ _ _ _
él form	_ _ _ _ _ _ _ _	_ _ ◯ _ _ _	_ _ _ _ _
nosotros form	_ _ _ _ _ _ _ _ _ _ _ _ _	_ _ _ _ _ _ _ _ _ _ _ _ _	_ _ _ _ _ _ _ _ _ _
ellos form	◯ _ _ _ _ _ _ _ _ _ _ _ _ _	_ _ _ _ _ _ _ _ _ _ _ _ _ _ _	_ _ _ _ _ _ _ _ _ _ _ _

U-Group Verb New Stem	Poder pud-	Poner pus-	Saber sup-
yo form	_ _ ◯ _	_ _ _ _	_ _ _ _
tú form	_ _ _ _ _ _ _	**pusiste**	_ _ _ _ _ _ _
usted form	_ _ _ _	_ _ _ _	_ _ _ _
nosotros form	_ _ _ ◯ _ _ _	_ _ _ _ _ _ _	_ _ _ _ _ _ _
ustedes form	_ _ _ _ _ _ _ _ _	_ _ _ _ _ _ _ _ _	_ _ ◯ _ _ _ _ _ _

You know how to do the next step: Write out the circled letters, keeping them in order by reading across the columns (starting with the yo form).

_ _ _ _ _ _ _

Next, use the decoder strip to discover the picture on the next **piedra**.

a	b	c	d	e	f	g	h	i	j	k	l	m
l	m	n	o	p	q	r	s	t	u	v	w	x

n	o	p	q	r	s	t	u	v	w	x	y	z
y	z	a	b	c	d	e	f	g	h	i	j	k

This **piedra** has the image of a _ _ _ _ _ _ _.

La séptima piedra:

Seventh Preterit Puzzle Piece

I-Group Irregulars

Now that you've learned about the U-group irregular verbs, the I-group verbs should be a breeze. Use the special UI-group preterit endings with the I-group preterit stems. Here they are:

I-Group Verb	Hacer	Querer	Venir
New Stem	**hic-**	**quis-**	**vin-**

Here are the special UI-group endings again:

UI-Group Irregular Preterit Endings

	Singular	Plural
1st person	**-e**	**-imos**
2nd person	**-iste**	**-isteis**
3rd person	**-o**	**-ieron**

Be careful—there's one little trap. The stem for **hacer** is **hic-**, except for the third-person singular (**él**) form—then it's **hiz-**! Here are a few examples: **Yo hi<u>c</u>e**, **tu hi<u>c</u>iste**, **él hi<u>z</u>o**. Think about the "c" sounds you can make in Spanish, and you'll be able to figure out why it changes.

Ready to earn the next **piedra**? Finish the sentences by inserting the correct form of the verb, found in parentheses, on the dashed line. Then, write out the sentence in English on the lines provided.

Mis primos (*venir*) _ _ _ _ _ _ _ _ el verano pasado.

____

Mi hermano (*querer*)◯_ _ _ _ pegarme pero mi mamá lo vi.

____

Ellos (*querer*) _◯_ _ _ _ _ _ _ comprar un carro pero no lo (*poder*) _ _ _ _◯_ _ _.

____

Hoy yo (*tener*)◯_ _ _ una piedra en mi zapato.

____

Mi hermana (*hacer*) _ _◯_ la tarea en diez minutos.

____

Use the letters from the circles to finish the following word.

_ _ _ _ _ **a l**

Frases:

Teresa: ¿Cómo se dice "libro" en inglés?
Ana: Se dice "book."
Teresa: ¿Dónde se venden libros?
Ana: Se venden libros en la librería.
Teresa: ¿Cómo se hace un libro?
Ana: Se hace un libro con papel, un bolígrafo, y unas buenas ideas.

inglés = *English*
librería = *bookstore*

Canto:

Aquí se habla español;
aquí se juega voleibol.
Allí se habla chino;
suena muy fino.

aquí = *here*
voleibol = *volleyball*
allí = *there*
chino = *Chinese*
sonar = *to sound*
fino = *refined*

Vocabulario:

Vocabulario nuevo

Spanish	English
cubrir: cubro, cubrí, cubriré	to cover: I cover, I covered, I will cover
el país	country
la vida	life
la salud	health
el dibujo	drawing
el cambio	change
la razón	reason
tener razón	to be right
el chiste	joke

Vocabulario de repaso

Spanish	English
vender: vendo, vendí, venderé	to sell: I sell, I sold, I will sell
sonreír: sonrío, sonreí, sonreiré	to smile: I smile, I smiled, I will smile
seguir: sigo, seguí, seguiré	to follow: I follow, I followed, I will follow
saltar: salto, salté, saltaré	to jump: I jump, I jumped, I will jump
volver: vuelvo, volví, volveré	to return: I return, I returned, I will return

Passive Voice with **Se**

By now, you're used to perfect little sentences that each have a neat and orderly subject and verb. But sometimes, in the real world, it's not always that easy. Sometimes, you don't know who the subject of your sentence should be; you don't know who is doing the action you're describing. In English, there are two ways you can make a sentence without knowing exactly who is doing the action: using an indefinite pronoun or using the passive voice.

Indefinite Pronouns

The first way to create a sentence in English without knowing the subject is to use something called an **indefinite pronoun**. "Indefinite" means "not completely explained." Here are some sentences with indefinite pronouns:

One swims in the pool, not in the street.
They sell awesome toys here.
People say I'm smarter than a rock.

Who swims in the pool? *Who* sells the toys? *Who* says I'm smarter than a rock? It doesn't really matter. *You* are probably smarter than a rock, and so you've probably realized that "people" is not really a pronoun. That's right: "people" isn't really a pronoun, but we're using it like one here. All these words—"one," "they," and "people"—are words we can use like pronouns to take the place of the subject when we don't want to say exactly *who* swims in the pool, sells the toys, or says someone is smarter than a rock.

Passive Voice

The second way to make a sentence in English when you're not really sure who is doing the action is to use the **passive voice**. "Passive" means "not doing an action," and "voice" is a word we use in grammar to talk about the style or sound of a sentence. So, these are sentences that sound a little bit like *no one* is doing the action. How? Look at this:

They sell awesome toys here. ➔ Awesome toys are sold here.

José fixes cars at the garage. ➔ Cars are fixed at the garage.

Sra. López reads books at the library. ➔ Books are read at the library.

One buys vegetables at the market. ➔ Vegetables are bought at the market.

In each of the first sentences, we either know who is doing the action (José or Sra. López), or we have an indefinite pronoun to take the place of the subject ("they" or "one"). In all of the second sentences, what has happened? Our subjects have disappeared! In their places are the things that were the objects before: the toys, the cars, the books, and the vegetables. Who is doing the action in each of the second sentences? We don't really know. Instead of having good, strong action words ("sell," "fix," "read," and "buy"), we just have the being verb "are." We know that toys are sold, cars are fixed, books are read, and vegetables are bought, but we don't know who does any of those actions. That's why we call this the passive voice.

Let's Put It into Spanish with **Se**

In Spanish, we have one way of taking care of both of these situations: We use the pronoun se.

With Indefinite Pronouns:

Do you remember the indefinite pronouns we just used in the example sentences at the beginning of the chapter? We can use **se** for all of them! **Se** is our indefinite pronoun:

One swims in the pool, not in the street.
***Se nada* en la piscina, no en la calle.**

They say sunscreen is good for your health.
***Se dice* que la crema solar es buena para la salud.**

People say I'm smarter than a rock.
***Se dice* que yo soy más listo que una piedra.**

With the Passive Voice:

You also use **se** to make the passive voice in Spanish:

Amazing *hot chocolate is sold* in this hot chocolate shop.
***Se vende chocolate* fenomenal en esta chocolatería.**

Spelling is taught in elementary school.
***Se enseña la ortografía* en la escuela primaria.**

Singular or Plural?

How do you conjugate a verb used with the indefinite pronoun **se**? You always use a third-person form, **but *se* can be either singular or plural**. How do you know which it is? If **se** is followed by a singular noun (or no noun at all), then the verb gets a singular ending. If **se** is followed by a plural noun, then the verb gets a plural ending.

One awesome *toy* is sold here.	**Se vende *un juguete* fenomenal aquí.**
Awesome *toys* are sold here.	**Se venden *juguetes* fenomenales aquí.**
One car is fixed at the garage.	**Se arregla *un carro* en el garaje.**
Cars are fixed at the garage.	**Se arreglan *carros* en el garaje.**
One book is read at the library.	**Se lee *un libro* en la biblioteca.**
Books are read at the library.	**Se leen *libros* en la biblioteca.**
One vegetable is bought at the market.	**Se vende *una verdura* en el mercado.**
Vegetables are bought at the market.	**Se venden *verduras* en el mercado.**

Where You'll See It

"Questions? Comments?" Pick up a box of cereal or a can of soup and look for the information to contact the company. If it's a major brand, you'll probably see the words "**Se habla español**" somewhere near the company's phone number.

Here's another great example of **se** being used as an indefinite pronoun:

¿Cómo se dice __________ en español? (How do you say __________ in Spanish?)

A. Translation:

1. **I covered**	________________	8. **I return**	________________
2. **el dibujo**	________________	9. **reason**	________________
3. **change**	________________	10. **to be right**	________________
4. **I will sell**	________________	11. **joke**	________________
5. **health**	________________	12. **I smiled**	________________
6. **I follow**	________________	13. **el país**	________________
7. **to jump**	________________	14. **life**	________________

B. Canto:

Fill in the blanks of this week's **canto**.

Aquí ______________________ **español;**

aquí ______________________ **voleibol.**

Allí ______________________ **chino;**

______________________ **muy fino.**

C. Grammar:

1. What does "indefinite" mean when we're talking about pronouns?

____

____

2. When you see the indefinite pronoun **se**, for whom does it stand? Circle one:
   a. The person mentioned in the sentence before
   b. The speaker of the sentence
   c. **Usted**
   d. We don't know, and it doesn't really matter.

3. In a sentence with the passive voice, who is doing the action? Circle one:
   a. The person mentioned in the sentence before
   b. The speaker of the sentence
   c. **Usted**
   d. We don't know, and it doesn't really matter.

4. When you're using **se** to make a passive-voice sentence, how do you know if the verb should be in a singular or plural form?

____

____

D. Se estudia gramática:

Here's a list of sentences, each written with a regular subject. Imagine that we don't know who was doing the action and rewrite the sentences using the indefinite pronoun **se**.

1. **Lidia vende libros.**

____

2. **La gente dice que España es un país muy bonito.**

____

3. **Los estudiantes estudian el latín en una escuela clásica.**

____

4. **Todo el mundo debe llevar un casco en una bicicleta.**

____

5. **Los médicos** (doctors) **dicen que las verduras son buenas para la salud.**

____

6. **Aquí la gente habla español.**

____

A. New and Review Vocabulary:

Spanish	English
______________	to cover: I cover, I covered, I will cover
______________	country
______________	life
______________	health
______________	drawing
______________	change
______________	reason
______________	to be right
______________	joke
______________	to sell: I sell, I sold, I will sell
______________	to smile: I smile, I smiled, I will smile
______________	to follow: I follow, I followed, I will follow
______________	to jump: I jump, I jumped, I will jump
______________	to return: I return, I returned, I will return

B. **Canto**:

Fill in the blanks of this week's **canto**.

Aquí ______________________ español;

aquí ______________________ voleibol.

Allí ______________________ chino;

______________________ muy fino.

C. Grammar:

Translate these sentences into Spanish.

1. People study at school.

____

2. Hamburgers are eaten here.

____

3. Somebody says dessert is bad for your health.

____

4. Books are sold at a bookstore (**librería**).

____

Chapter 23

Frases:

Cada mañana, me levanto a las siete. Me baño y me cepillo los dientes. Me peino y me visto de uniforme. Pongo la mesa y desayuno con mis hermanos. Voy a la escuela donde aprendo mucho. Cuando vuelvo a casa, juego con mis hermanos y ceno a las ocho con mi familia. Me acuesto después de cenar.

uniforme = *uniform*

Canto:

Reflexive Pronouns

	Singular	Plural
1st person	**me**	**nos**
2nd-person familiar	**te**	os
2nd-person formal	**se**	**se**
3rd person	**se**	**se**

Bañarse (to take a bath) Present-Tense Forms

	Singular	Plural
1st person	**yo me baño**	**nosotros nos bañamos**
2nd-person familiar	**tú te bañas**	vosotros os bañáis
2nd-person formal	**usted se baña**	**ustedes se bañan**
3rd person	**él/ella se baña**	**ellos se bañan**

Vocabulario:

Vocabulario nuevo

Spanish	English
bañarse: me baño, me bañé, me bañaré	to take a bath: I take a bath, I took a bath, I will take a bath
vestirse: me visto, me vestí, me vestiré	to get dressed: I get dressed, I got dressed, I will get dressed
levantarse: me levanto, me levanté, me levantaré	to get up: I get up, I got up, I will get up
acostarse: me acuesto, me acosté, me acostaré	to go to bed: I go to bed, I went to bed, I will go to bed
peinarse: me peino, me peiné, me peinaré	to comb one's hair: I comb my hair, I combed my hair, I will comb my hair
el peine	comb
el cepillo	brush
los dientes	teeth
el cuerpo	body
la cara	face
el vestido	dress

Vocabulario de repaso

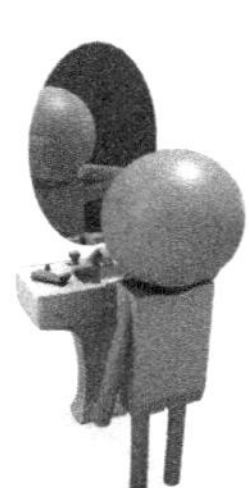

Spanish	English
lavar: lavo, lavé, lavaré	to wash: I wash, I washed, I will wash
la mano	hand
el baño	bathroom
el pelo	hair

Reflexives Part I

Here is a story about **mi amiga Lucía**:

Lucía siempre está sucia y huele mal. Sometimes she has bits of last night's dinner sticking in her hair, and her **uñas** (fingernails) are **siempre asquerosas** (gross).

One time, she came over to **mi casa** to play, and my mother asked her, "Don't you ever bathe?"

"Of course," Lucía said. "I bathe every day."

My mother's mouth fell open in shock. We knew Lucía had french fries last Thursday because she ate them at our house, and she still had ketchup on her chin.

My mom wouldn't have been confused if she had asked Lucía a very important question: *Whom* do you bathe? Lucía probably hasn't had a bath since she learned to walk, but every day after school, she and her big brother go down to the animal shelter and help bathe the dogs. So Lucía *is* bathing every day—just not herself. Although, she does get licked a lot.

The Grammar Part: What Are Reflexive Verbs?

OK, you probably know that story is made up (there's most likely a law against kids being that dirty). But it shows you a really important difference between Spanish and English. In English, you can say, "I bathe," and everyone will just assume that you are bathing yourself. But in Spanish, you have to say, "I bathe myself." That doesn't sound *too* weird, does it? But take a look at this:

In Spanish, you can't say:	*Instead, you say:*
I get dressed.	I dress myself.
I shave.	I shave myself.

Do you remember learning about direct and indirect objects? A direct object is the thing that receives the action of the verb—the thing to which the action of the sentence happens. Our example sentence in *SFCA* was "I throw the ball." What am I throwing? I'm throwing *the ball*. The ball is the direct object. In the sentence "I bathe myself," the word "myself" is the direct object. **When the subject of the verb does the action to itself, we say that the verb is *reflexive*.** (This isn't the only kind of reflexive verb, but we're going to start here.) Why do we call these verbs *reflexive*? It is because the verb acts like a mirror to show the subject its reflection!

We have a special set of pronouns that we use with reflexive verbs. They're called **reflexive pronouns**, and you're memorizing them this week as your **canto**. **We use these reflexive pronouns even in cases in which we might not feel like we need to say words such as "myself," "yourself," or "himself" in English.**

Check it out:

I bathe after dinner.	***Me* baño despúes de la cena.**
You dress in a hurry.	***Te* vistes de prisa.**

He shaves with a razor. — ***Se* afeita con navaja.**
We get dressed in the morning. — ***Nos* vestimos por la mañana.**
You guys take baths a lot. — **Ustedes *se* bañan mucho.**

In English, we understand that the people are doing these actions to themselves. We don't have to say anything extra to show it. **In Spanish, however, these verbs *require* that you use a reflexive pronoun if you're using the verb in a reflexive sense.**

Do you remember the story about Lucía and her dogs? Well, she was bathing the dogs, right? So, in the sentence "Lucía bathes the dogs," is that reflexive? No, it's not, because the subject of the verb (Lucía) and the object of the verb (the dogs) are not the same (although they probably smell a lot alike). That means we can say, "**Lucía baña a los perros**" (Lucía gives a bath to the dogs), without needing to use a reflexive pronoun.

Where Does the Reflexive Pronoun Go?

This question is an easy one to answer. **The reflexive pronoun goes right before the verb, unless the verb is staying in its infinitive form.** Check this out in the following examples:

Pronoun *before* verb:

***Yo me visto* de astronauta.** (I dress like an astronaut.)
***Él se viste* de pijama.** (He dresses in pajamas.)

Pronoun *at the end* of the verb (in infinitive form):

Yo quiero vestir*me* de astronauta. (I want to dress like an astronaut.)
Nosotros vamos a vestir*nos* como gemelos. (We're going to dress like twins.)

Let's summarize what we've learned in this chapter so far:

1. Sometimes the subject of the verb does the action to itself.
2. When that happens, we call it a reflexive.
3. In Spanish, if we have a reflexive verb, we have to use a reflexive pronoun, too.
4. A reflexive pronoun goes right before a conjugated verb, or it gets connected to the end of a verb in the infinitive form.

The Tough Part

Do you remember that there is another kind of reflexive verb? Well, we're going to learn about it now. **In Spanish, there are verbs that we use with reflexive pronouns even when we wouldn't use any reflexive words (such as "myself," "yourself," "herself," or "themselves") in English.** Are you ready? Here we go!

Lots of Reflexives!

You have seen a few examples of reflexive verbs in Spanish that you can easily translate into English. But in Spanish, there are *tons* of verbs that we use as reflexive verbs, even though you might not always (or ever) use them that way in English. Look over the following list. Do any seem familiar?

(Note: All the verbs marked with a single asterisk* are **e » ie** stem-change verbs: **despertarse = me desp*ie*rto**. The verb with the double asterisk** is an **o » ue** stem-change verb: **acostarse = me acuesto**.)

llamarse (to call oneself)
Esta chica *se llama* Inés.
(This girl is called Inés.)

levantarse (to get up)
Inés *se levanta* a las seis de la mañana.
(Inés gets up at 6:00 a.m.)

***despertarse** (to wake up)
A ella le gusta *despertarse* con el sol.
(She likes to wake up with the sun.)

quejarse (to complain)
¡Tú *te quejas* cuando tienes que *despertarte* temprano!
(You complain when you have to wake up early!)

ducharse (to take a shower)
Ella *se ducha* en una cascada.
(She takes a shower in a waterfall.)

acostumbrarse (to get used to)
Ella *se acostumbra* al agua fría.
(She gets used to the cold water.)

***sentarse** (to sit)
Luego ella *se viste y se sienta* en una roca para cantar.
(Later she gets dressed and sits on a rock to sing.)

***divertirse** (to have fun)
Inés *se divierte* de jugar con las sirenas.
(Inés has fun playing with the mermaids.)

casarse (to get married to)
Ella quiere *casarse* con el rey de las sirenas.
(She wants to get married to the king of the mermaids.)

preocuparse (to worry)
Ella no *se preocupa* por aprender a respirar debajo del agua.
(She doesn't worry about learning to breathe underwater.)

****acostarse** (to go to bed)
Inés *se acuesta* cuando salen las estrellas.
(Inés goes to bed when the stars come out.)

One More Thing . . .

Here's a funny question: When you wash your hands, who is getting washed? An English speaker might say, "your hands." A Spanish speaker would say, "you!" In each of the following cases, the subject is doing the action to himself, even though in English we might say he's doing the action to his hands, hair, or teeth.

lavarse las manos (wash [yourself] your hands)
***Me lavo las manos* antes de comer.** (I wash my hands before eating.)

cepillarse el pelo (brush [yourself] your hair)
***Te cepillas el pelo* con un cepillo.** (You brush your hair with a brush.)

cepillarse los dientes (brush [yourself] your teeth)
Raúl *se cepilla los dientes* cada día. (Raúl brushes his teeth each day.)

Or, as they say in Spain:
lavarse los dientes (wash [yourself] your teeth)
¡*Me lavo los dientes* cuando estoy en España! (I "wash" my teeth when I'm in Spain!)

A. Translation:

1. **I took a bath**	______________	9. **hair**	______________
2. **I got dressed**	______________	10. **lavarse**	______________
3. **body**	______________	11. **teeth**	______________
4. **to comb one's hair**	______________	12. **la cara**	______________
5. **comb**	______________	13. **lavar**	______________
6. **brush**	______________	14. **el vestido**	______________
7. **hand**	______________	15. **I will get up**	______________
8. **bathroom**	______________	16. **I go to bed**	______________

B. Canto:

Fill in the boxes of this week's **canto**.

Reflexive Pronouns

	Singular	Plural
1st person	______________	______________
2nd-person familiar	______________	**os**
2nd-person formal	______________	______________
3rd person	______________	______________

Bañarse (to take a bath) Present-Tense Forms

	Singular	Plural
1st person	______________	______________
2nd-person familiar	______________	**vosotros os bañáis**
2nd-person formal	______________	______________
3rd person	______________	______________

C. Grammar Out Loud!

For each of these reflexive verbs, say that you are doing the action. Once you've practiced them out loud, write a sentence with **yo** as the subject for each one.

1. **lavarse las manos** ______________________________

2. **cepillarse los dientes** ______________________________

3. **querer acostarse a las once** ______________________________

4. **peinarse** ______________________________

5. **levantarse a las siete** ______________________________

6. **querer llamarse Batman** ______________________________

A. New and Review Vocabulary:

Spanish	English
______________________	to take a bath: I take a bath, I took a bath, I will take a bath
______________________	to get dressed: I get dressed, I got dressed, I will get dressed
______________________	to get up: I get up, I got up, I will get up
______________________	to go to bed: I go to bed, I went to bed, I will go to bed
______________________	to comb one's hair: I comb my hair, I combed my hair, I will comb my hair
______________________	comb
______________________	brush
______________________	teeth
______________________	body
______________________	face
______________________	to wash: I wash, I washed, I will wash
______________________	hand
______________________	bathroom
______________________	hair
______________________	dress

B. Canto:

Fill in the boxes of this week's **canto**.

Reflexive Pronouns

	Singular	Plural
1st person	______	______
2nd-person familiar	______	os
2nd-person formal	______	______
3rd person	______	______

Bañarse (to take a bath) Present-Tense Forms

	Singular	Plural
1st person	______	______
2nd-person familiar	______	**vosotros os bañáis**
2nd-person formal	______	______
3rd person	______	______

C. Grammar:

1. What is a reflexive verb? Circle one:
   a. A verb that has good reflexes
   b. A verb that can mean more than one thing
   c. A verb that has the same subject and object
   d. A verb that always has a reflexive pronoun
   e. Both c and d
2. Where is the reflexive pronoun placed if the verb is conjugated?

   ____

3. Where is the reflexive pronoun placed if the verb is in the infinitive form?

   ____

4. You *only* use a reflexive pronoun in Spanish when you would say the word "myself" in English. Circle one: True False

Frases:

Esta chica se llama Inés. Inés se levanta a las seis de la mañana. A ella le gusta despertarse con el sol. ¡Tú te quejas cuando tienes que despertarte temprano! Inés se baña en una cascada. Ella se acostumbra al agua fría. Luego ella se viste y se sienta en una roca para cantar. Inés se divierte de jugar con las sirenas. Ella quiere casarse con el rey de las sirenas. No se preocupa por aprender a respirar debajo del agua. Inés se acuesta cuando salen las estrellas.

despertarse = *to wake up*
el sol = *the sun*
quejarse = *to complain*
cascada = *waterfall*
acostumbrarse = *to get used to*
fría = *cold*
sentarse = *sit*
sirenas = *mermaids*
casarse con = *to get married to*
rey = *king*
respirar = *breathe*
estrellas = *stars*

Canto:

Irse (to leave) Present-Tense Forms

	Singular	Plural
1st person	yo me voy (I leave)	nosotros nos vamos (we leave)
2nd-person familiar	tú te vas (you leave)	**vosotros os vais** (you all leave)
2nd-person formal	usted se va (you leave)	ustedes se van (you all leave)
3rd person	él/ella se va (he/she leaves)	ellos se van (they leave)

Vocabulario:

Vocabulario nuevo

Spanish	English
sentirse: me siento	to feel: I feel
divertirse: me divierto	to have fun: I have fun
despertarse: me despierto	to wake up: I wake up
preocuparse (por): me preocupo	to worry (about): I worry
sentarse: me siento	to sit: I sit
quejarse (de): me quejo	to complain (about): I complain
casarse (con): me caso	to get married (to): I get married
quitarse: me quito	to take off: I take off
apresurarse: me apresuro	to hurry: I hurry
enamorarse (de): me enamoro	to fall in love (with): I fall in love
irse: me voy	to leave: I leave

Vocabulario de repaso

Spanish	English
imaginar: imagino, imaginé, imaginaré	to imagine: I imagine, I imagined, I will imagine
incluir: incluyo, incluí, incluiré	to include: I include, I included, I will include
guardar: guardo, guardé, guardaré	to keep: I keep, I kept, I will keep
gritar: grito, grité, gritaré	to yell: I yell, I yelled, I will yell
ganar: gano, gané, ganaré	to win/earn: I win/earn, I won/earned, I will win/earn

Reflexives Part II

Tú te diviertes (are you having fun) with reflexives so far? Once you learn the patterns of reflexive verbs, they make a lot of sense, don't they? This week, we're going to learn one more kind of reflexive verb. Hopefully, you'll really enjoy using these. The verbs you'll see this week are **verbs that change their meaning when used with a reflexive pronoun**. Are you ready to see how it works? Look at this:

> ***Duermo* en mi cama cada noche.** (I *sleep* in my bed each night)
>
> ***Me duermo* cuando mi mamá canta una canción de cuna.** (I *fall asleep* when my mom sings a lullaby.)

You've seen the verb **dormir**, and you know it means "to sleep." Being as smart as you are, you probably have a feeling that "I sleep myself" wouldn't make any sense. So, in this case, when you add the reflexive pronoun to **dormir**, it doesn't necessarily mean you're doing the action to yourself. It just changes the meaning of the verb a little bit. Do you want to see another example? Take a look at **irse**:

> **Yo *voy* al parque con mis amigos.** (I'm *going* to the park with my friends.)
>
> ***Me voy* de esta fiesta aburrida.** (I'm *leaving* this boring party.)

When you make **ir** (to go) reflexive, it doesn't mean "to go yourself." It means to leave—to "get yourself outta there"!

How to Learn These Guys

So, how do you know when changing a verb to its reflexive form changes its meaning a little? First of all, when you're seeing a new word for the first time, the Spanish-English dictionary will tell you if a word is different when it's reflexive.[1] Then, once you know which words have that kind of meaning change, you can memorize them. Here's a head start: The following is a list of a few verbs that mean something slightly different when they become reflexive.

A Verb with No Reflexive Pronoun:	What It Means in English:	The Same Verb with a Reflexive Pronoun:	What It Means in English Now:
levantar	to lift/raise	**levantarse**	to get up
Levanto la mano cuando quiero hablar. (I raise my hand when I want to speak.)		Me levanto a las seis cada mañana. (I get up at six every morning.)	
hacer	to make/do	**hacerse**	to "get"/make yourself
Hago la tarea. (I do the homework.)		Me hago fuerte por ejercitar. (I get strong by exercising.)	
poner	to put/place	**ponerse**	to become/put something on
Pongo mis libros en mi mochila. (I put my books in my backpack.)		Me pongo un abrigo. Hace frío y ¡no quiero ponerme enfermo! (I put on a coat. It's cold, and I don't want to get sick!)	

1. A verb is listed in a dictionary in its infinitive form, such as **hablar**. When you see a reflexive verb, it will be listed in the infinitive, with the pronoun **se** added to the end, such as **divertirse**.

A Verb with No Reflexive Pronoun:	What It Means in English:	The Same Verb with a Reflexive Pronoun:	What It Means in English Now:
dormir	to sleep	**dormirse**	to fall asleep
Yo quiero dormir. (I want to sleep.)		**No quiero dormirme cuando me hablas.** (I don't want to fall asleep while you're talking to me.)	
ir	to go	**irse**	to leave
Tengo que ir al dentista. (I have to go to the dentist.)		**Tengo que irme temprano.** (I have to leave early.)	

One More Great Way to Use Reflexives

There's one more way a reflexive pronoun can be useful. Take a look at this sentence:

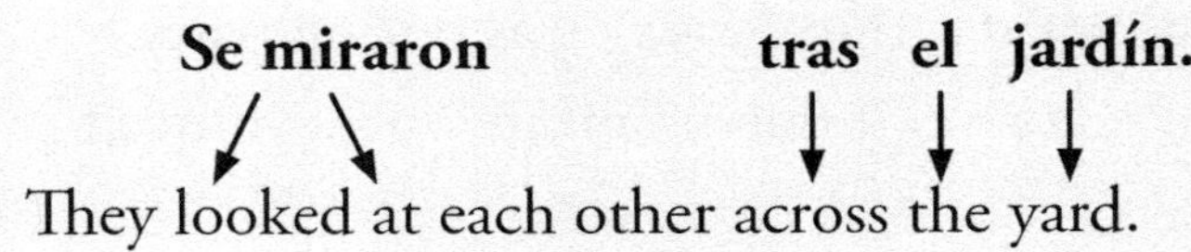

Let's compare those two sentences word for word. The phrases "**tras el jardín**" and "across the yard" mean the same thing, word for word. But the English sentence has a whole extra phrase that the Spanish sentence doesn't need: "at each other." In Spanish, instead of saying "at each other," we just use a reflexive pronoun. Here are some more examples:

Mi abuela y yo *nos* abrazamos cuando *nos* vemos.
(My grandma and I hug *each other* when we see *each other*.)

¡*Nos* vemos!
(Literally, "We see *each other*." It's similar to saying, "See ya!")

Mis amigos *se* pegan pero en plan de broma.
(My friends hit *each other*, but as a joke.)

Be On the Lookout

Were you surprised to see **sentirse** on the vocabulary list this week? You already memorized the verb **sentir** ("to feel") in *SFCA*. **Sentir** is one of those verbs that is sometimes reflexive and sometimes not, and an English speaker might not notice a big difference in meaning between the two.

Sentir*se* (reflexive) is used to describe *how* you are feeling:

No me siento bien. (I don't feel well.)

Sentir without a reflexive pronoun is usually used to say *what* you are feeling:

Siento mucho dolor en el estómago. (I feel a lot of pain in my stomach.)

So, how will you know if a verb has little changes of meaning such as this? A dictionary will help you, and so will paying attention to the way words are used.

A. Translation:

1. **I feel**	______________	9. **me enamoro (de)**	______________
2. **I have fun**	______________	10. **I leave**	______________
3. **I include**	______________	11. **imagino**	______________
4. **guardo**	______________	12. **I win/earn**	______________
5. **I yell**	______________	13. **I worry**	______________
6. **me despierto**	______________	14. **I sit**	______________
7. **I take off**	______________	15. **me quejo**	______________
8. **I hurry**	______________	16. **me caso**	______________

B. Canto:

Fill in the blanks of this week's **canto.**

Irse (to leave) Present-Tense Forms

	Singular	Plural
1st person	______________	______________
2nd-person familiar	______________	**vosotros os vais** (you all leave)
2nd-person formal	______________	______________
3rd person	______________	______________

C. Grammar:

1. Adding a reflexive pronoun to a regular verb never changes its meaning.

   Circle one: True False

2. When you have a sentence such as "**Nos abrazamos**," the reflexive pronoun means (circle one):

   a. We do the action of the sentence to ourselves.

   b. We do the action of the sentence to someone else who is not there.

   c. We do the action of the sentence to each other.

   d. None of these

   e. Both a and c

D. Let's Get It Right:

Here are some sentences written in Spanish. Choose whether each of these verbs should be reflexive or not by circling the best word or words to complete each sentence.

1. **Yo (*quejo, me quejo*) cuando tengo demasiado tarea.**

2. **Yo (*me levanto, levanto*) la mano cuando quiero hablar en clase.**

3. **Tú (*te quitas, quitas*) los zapatos.**

4. **Usted (*se levanta, levanta*) a las seis de la mañana.**

5. **Yo (*me voy, voy*) de la casa a las ocho. Llego a la escuela a las ocho y cuarto.**

A. New and Review Vocabulary:

Spanish	English
______________________	to feel: I feel
______________________	to have fun: I have fun
______________________	to wake up: I wake up
______________________	to worry (about): I worry
______________________	to sit: I sit
______________________	to complain (about): I complain
______________________	to get married (to): I get married
______________________	to take off: I take off
______________________	to hurry: I hurry
______________________	to fall in love (with): I fall in love
______________________	to leave: I leave
______________________	to imagine: I imagine, I imagined, I will imagine
______________________	to include: I include, I included, I will include
______________________	to keep: I keep, I kept, I will keep
______________________	to yell: I yell, I yelled, I will yell
______________________	to win/earn: I win/earn, I won/earned, I will win/earn

B. Canto:

Fill in the blanks of this week's **canto**.

Irse (to leave) Present-Tense Forms

	Singular	Plural
1st person	______________	______________
2nd-person familiar	______________	**vosotros os vais** (you all leave)
2nd-person formal	______________	______________
3rd person	______________	______________

Repaso de vocabulario

Here's another set of review vocabulary words. Did you memorize them all? You know what to do!

Chapter 22

☐	1. **to cover**	☐	5. **drawing**	☐	9. **joke**	☐	12. **to follow**
☐	2. **country**	☐	6. **change**	☐	10. **to sell**	☐	13. **to jump**
☐	3. **life**	☐	7. **reason**	☐	11. **to smile**	☐	14. **to return**
☐	4. **health**	☐	8. **to be right**				

Chapter 23

☐	15. **to take a bath**	☐	19. **to comb one's hair**	☐	23. **body**	☐	27. **bathroom**
☐	16. **to get dressed**	☐	20. **comb**	☐	24. **face**	☐	28. **hair**
☐	17. **to get up**	☐	21. **brush**	☐	25. **dress**	☐	29. **to wash**
☐	18. **to go to bed**	☐	22. **teeth**	☐	26. **hand**		

Chapter 24

☐	30. **to feel**	☐	34. **to sit**	☐	38. **to hurry**	☐	42. **to include**
☐	31. **to have fun**	☐	35. **to complain (about)**	☐	39. **to fall in love (with)**	☐	43. **to keep**
☐	32. **to wake up**	☐	36. **to get married (to)**	☐	40. **to leave**	☐	44. **to yell**
☐	33. **to worry**	☐	37. **to take off**	☐	41. **to imagine**	☐	45. **to win/earn**

It Wasn't Me!

"The baseball went through the window!" "The vase fell off the table!" "My backpack was left at school!" How do you talk about a problem without saying that it was someone's fault? In Spanish, you can use reflexive pronouns. Instead of saying, "I broke the window," you can say, "The window broke itself." That makes the window the subject of the sentence.

Imagine that it was a very bad day because your little brother did everything wrong while your mom was away. When your mom returns and asks what happened, you don't want to sound like a tattletale. The following are sentences that describe what happened during the day. Rewrite each sentence by using reflexive pronouns to explain to your mom what happened without blaming your brother. The first two sentences are done for you as examples.

Mi hermano rompió la ventana. **La ventana se rompió.**

Mi hermano no lavó los platos. **Los platos no se lavaron.**

Mi hermano no hizo la cama. ______

Mi hermano no pasó la aspiradora. ______

Mi hermano no arregló el dormitorio. ______

Conjugating Reflexive Verbs

Practice conjugating these reflexive verbs. A verb will be provided, as well as the tense and who is doing the action. Then, conjugate the verb, and add the reflexive pronoun. The first one has been completed for you.

Infinitive Verb	Person, Number, Tense	Conjugated Verb
bañarse	**él**/imperfect	**él se bañaba**
vestirse	**ustedes**/future	
levantarse	**yo**/preterit	
acostarse	**nosotros**/imperfect	
apresurarse	**tú**/future	
divertirse	**usted**/imperfect	
preocuparse	**yo**/future	
sentarse	**nosotros**/imperfect	
irse	**tú**/preterit	
imaginarse	**ellas**/present	

Bienvenido a mi pueblo (Welcome to My Town)

The Indefinite Pronoun **Se**

What do people do in your town? Imagine you have a visitor from another country (or perhaps another planet). Imagine that you show the visitor around your town and explain what people do. For the following exercise, use the indefinite pronoun **se** (since you're not saying exactly who does each thing) to create sentences

describing what people do in your town. Verbs and nouns have been provided for you to use in the sentences. First, try the exercise out loud with a friend (or stuffed animal). Then, write out the sentences that you created. The first one has been completed for you.

nadar/la piscina For example, you could say, "**Se nada en la piscina**" (People swim in the pool).

comer/el restaurante ____________________

aprender/la escuela ____________________

leer/la biblioteca (library) ____________________

jugar/el parque ____________________

viajar/el tren ____________________

Grammar Rules

Let's see how well you've mastered these new pronouns.

1. Draw lines between the sentences on the left and their corresponding subjects on the right.

El perro se baña.	I
Baño el perro.	You
Tú bañas el perro.	The dog

2. Go back to question 1, and circle the sentence that was reflexive.

3. A reflexive pronoun always goes after the verb. Circle one: True False

4. A reflexive pronoun always goes before the verb. Circle one: True False

5. Where is the reflexive pronoun placed if the verb is conjugated?

____

6. Where is the reflexive pronoun placed if the verb is in the infinitive form?

____

7. Either a verb is always reflexive, or it is never reflexive—no exceptions.

   Circle one: True False

8. What is the indefinite pronoun in Spanish? When do you use it?

____

____

9. What is "passive voice"?
   a. The speaker is talking softly.
   b. The speaker is not telling what really happened.
   c. The sentence is written so that you don't know who really did the action of the sentence.
   d. Nobody does the action in the sentence.
10. When you're using **se** to make a passive-voice sentence, how do you know if the verb should be in a singular or plural form?

____

____

Cantos

Fill in the blanks of the **canto** from chapter 22:

Aquí ____________________ **español;**

aquí ____________________ **voleibol.**

Allí ____________________ **chino;**

____________________ **muy fino.**

You know what to do! Fill in the boxes:

Reflexive Pronouns (Chapter 23)

	Singular	Plural
1st person	________	________
2nd-person familiar	________	os
2nd-person formal	________	________
3rd person	________	________

Bañarse (to take a bath) Present-Tense Forms (Chapter 23)

	Singular	Plural
1st person	________	________
2nd-person familiar	________	vosotros os bañáis
2nd-person formal	________	________
3rd person	________	________

Irse (to leave) Present-Tense Forms (Chapter 24)

	Singular	Plural
1st person	__________	__________
2nd-person familiar	__________	**vosotros os vais** (you all leave)
2nd-person formal	__________	__________
3rd person	__________	__________

La octava piedra:

Eighth (and Final) Preterit Puzzle Piece

J-Group Irregulars

You've almost done it! You're down to the last **piedra**. Won't it be satisfying to set the final stone on the ledge and watch the secret door swing open? But don't start daydreaming about piles of treasure or giant spiders or scary mummies that might be hidden away behind the door. You still have one more **piedra** to find. And here's how you'll do it: Learn the J-group irregulars.

These verbs have their own set of endings, but the J-group endings are different from the UI-group endings by only one letter. Here are the J-group endings. See if you can spot the difference between these and the UI-group endings.[1]

J-Group Irregular Preterit Endings

	Singular	Plural
1st person	**-e**	**-imos**
2nd person	**-iste**	**-isteis**
3rd person	**-o**	**-eron**

Now all you need in order to uncover your **piedra** are the J-group stems. Here they are:

J-Group Verb	Conducir	Decir	Reducir	Traer
New Stem	**conduj-**	**dij-**	**reduj-**	**traj-**

1. Did you figure out what the difference is? It's the third-person plural ending. The J-group **ellos** ending is missing the *i*.

Are you ready to dig up one last **piedra**? Write out the forms of each verb.

conducir: **yo** __ __ __ __ ◯ __ __, **tú condujiste**, **él** __ __ __ __ __ __ __,

nosotros __ __ __ __ __ __ __ __ __ __

traer: **yo** __ __ ◯ __ __, **tú** __ __ __ __ __ __ __ __ __, **ella** __ __ ◯ __ __, **nosotros**

trajimos

reducir: **yo** __ __ __ __ __ __, **ustedes** ◯ __ __ __ __ __ __ __ __

decir: **yo** __ __ __ __, **tú** __ __ ◯ __ __ __ __ __, **ellos** __ __ __ __ __ __ __

Write out all the circled letters:

__ __ __ __ __

Add a *g* to the group of letters. Finally, unscramble the letters to find the image on your last **piedra**:

__ __ __ __ __ __

You've done it! You've solved the last puzzle and found the last **piedra**. Now head to the maze, and look for each of your **piedras** in the order in which you found them. The map at the back of this book should help. Can you make it to the treasure and solve the mystery? **¡Vamos a ver!**

Frases:

Tenga cuidado; ¡las moscas pican!

No tenga miedo; no pican mucho.

moscas = *flies*

Canto:

Usted and Ustedes Command Endings

	-ar Endings	-er and -ir Endings
usted command form	**-e**	**-a**
ustedes command form	**-en**	**-an**

Commands: **Pensar** and **Tener**

	-ar Endings	-er and -ir Endings
usted command form	**piense**	**tenga**
ustedes command form	**piensen**	**tengan**

Vocabulario:

Vocabulario nuevo

Spanish	English
mandar: mando, mandé, mandaré	to command/send: I command/send, I commanded/sent, I will command/send
picar: pico, piqué, picaré	to sting/bite: I sting/bite, I stung/bit, I will sting/bite
tener cuidado: tengo cuidado	to be careful: I am careful
tener miedo: tengo miedo	to be scared: I am scared
tener razón: tengo razón	to be right: I am right
estar de acuerdo: estoy de acuerdo	to agree: I agree
el peligro	danger
peligroso/a/os/as	dangerous
caliente/es	hot
frío/a/os/as	cold

Vocabulario de repaso

Spanish	English
hace calor	it's hot
hace frío	it's cold
tengo once años	I'm eleven years old
tengo frío	I'm cold
tengo calor	I'm hot

Commands

Listen up! Pay attention! Do a silly dance! We're going to spend this entire unit learning how to tell people to do things—**how to give commands**. First, let's talk about how, in English, you **command** someone to do something.

You stop eating ice cream when you're full.
Stop eating my ice cream!

What's the difference between these two sentences? The first one just states a fact. The second one tells someone to do something. How do we know that? Look very closely at the second sentence, and see if you can find the subject. Where is it? It isn't there! When we want to tell someone to do something in English, instead of just saying that he or she *does* do it, we erase the word "you."

You stop eating my ice cream (because you decide you don't like chocolate).
(You) Stop eating my ice cream (or I'll tell Dad)!

That was pretty easy, right? Now, let's see how we do this in Spanish . . .

How We Do It in Spanish

We create commands a little differently in Spanish. Instead of fiddling around with the subject of a sentence, **when we want to give a command, we put a special "command ending" on a verb**. That doesn't seem too hard, right?

How to Make **Usted** and **Ustedes** Command Forms

When you conjugate a verb, usually you do this: Take the infinitive form of the verb; chop off the **-ar**, **-er**, or **-ir** ending; then add the new ending that shows person, number, and tense. With command forms, you do something a little different. We call it the "**yo**-chop-switch."

Yo Find the **yo** (first-person singular) form of the verb.

Chop Chop off the **-o** ending.

Switch Put on the new ending. We use the word "switch" because there's a little switcheroo. See if you can figure out what it is by looking at this chart:

	-ar Endings	-er and -ir Endings
usted command form	**-e**	**-a**
ustedes command form	**-en**	**-an**

Did you figure out what the switcheroo is? Usually you see **-e** or **-en** at the end of an **-er** or **-ir** verb, and **-a** or **-an** at the end of an **-ar** verb. With command form, it's actually the other way around. Watch out; it's getting tricky now!

Quick question: Why do you think it's important to find the **yo** form of a verb, instead of just using the stem of the infinitive? Well, do you remember stem-change (boot) verbs and **yo**-form irregulars? These are verbs that change their stems when you conjugate them. They change their stems in the command form, too. That's why you use the **yo** form as the base for conjugating commands; it shows you the stem change. Plus, you have all the **yo** forms memorized anyway. Aren't you glad you memorized all of your vocabulary words?

Usted and **Ustedes**

Do you remember what **usted** means? It's the polite form of "you" that you use with adults, teachers, and people you don't know. **Even though you're speaking to a "second person" when you use *usted*, we use third-person singular verbs with it.** It's just the way Spanish speakers show respect. It might seem a little funny to think of giving an adult a command when you're a kid, but we're starting with this form because it's the one in which you can most clearly see the rules.

Ustedes is the plural form of **usted**. It's considered the "formal" way to address a group of people in Spain, because in Spain, there's also an *informal* way to address a big group (**vosotros**). In most of the Spanish-speaking world, however, **ustedes** simply means "you all," and you don't have to worry about "formal or informal" when you use it. So, let's give some orders! Here's how we do it:

We start with our verb, or our phrase:
tener cuidado (to be careful)

We find the **yo** form of the verb:
tengo

We chop off the **-o** ending:
teng-

Then, we add the new ending:
teng*a*

And finally, we put the verb back in the sentence:
¡Tenga cuidado! (Be careful!)

If you want to put the pronoun **usted** (abbreviated: **Ud.**[1]) into the sentence, it goes right after the verb:

¡Tenga Ud. cuidado! ("Be careful, *sir*!" or "Be careful, *ma'am*!")

Can you go back and do all those steps, but this time conjugate your command for **ustedes** instead of **usted**? Here's a hint: The abbreviation for **ustedes** is **Uds.**[2] You still say "**ustedes**" when you read it, in the same way that you say "mister" when you see the abbreviation "Mr."

No, Don't!

Sometimes, you don't want to tell someone *to* do something; rather, you want to tell him *not* to do something. So, how do we do that in Spanish? Just add a **no** before the verb.

***No* tenga cuidado.** (Don't be careful.)
***No* tenga miedo.** (Don't be scared.)

When you tell someone *not* to do something, you are giving a **negative command**. When you tell someone *to* do something, you are giving an **affirmative command**.

Lots of Commands

Here's a chart with lots of verbs turning into commands:

Infinitive	Yo Form	Ud. Command Form	Affirmative Command	Negative Command
hablar	**hablo**	**hable**	**Hable más lento, por favor.** (Speak more slowly, please.)	**No hable rápido.** (Don't speak quickly.)
pensar	**pienso**	**piense**	**Piense en esto.** (Think about this.)	**No piense en esto.** (Don't think about this.)
hacer	**hago**	**haga**	**Haga un favor.** (Do a favor.)	**No haga esas tonterías.** (Don't do those dumb things.)
decir	**digo**	**diga**	**Diga.** (Go ahead and talk.)	**¡No diga eso!** (Don't say that!)
venir	**vengo**	**venga**	**Venga aquí, por favor.** (Please come here.)	**No venga conmigo.** (Don't come with me.)

1. Watch out: The term **usted** isn't capitalized unless it's the first word of the sentence or a quotation (just as you would in English), but the abbreviation **Ud.** is *always* capitalized.
2. Did you end up with "**Tengan Uds. cuidado**"? Good job!

A. Translation:

1. **danger**	______	9. **I am careful**	______
2. **dangerous**	______	10. **I am scared**	______
3. **hot**	______	11. **I am right**	______
4. **cold**	______	12. **I'm eleven years old**	______
5. **it's hot**	______	13. **I agree**	______
6. **it's cold**	______	14. **I command**	______
7. **I'm cold**	______	15. **I sting**	______
8. **I'm hot**	______		

B. Canto:

Fill in the boxes of this week's **canto**.

Command Endings

	-ar Endings	-er and -ir Endings
usted command form	______	______
ustedes command form	______	______

Commands: Pensar and Tener

	-ar Endings	-er and -ir Endings
usted command form	______	______
ustedes command form	______	______

C. Grammar:

1. Which one of these is a command? Circle one:
   a. **Hable usted menos rápido.**
   b. **Usted fue a la tienda** (the store)**.**
   c. **¿Cómo se llama usted?**
   d. **¿Tiene usted miedo?**

2. What is an *affirmative* command?

____

3. What is a *negative* command?

____

4. Write out the steps to turning an **infinitive** into a command:

____

____

____

5. How do you make a negative command?

____

6. What are the **usted** command endings?

____

____

7. What are the **ustedes** command endings?

____

____

D. Mamá Manda:

Imagine you're **la madre** and you need to tell your **niños** to do **las tareas de la casa** (chores). Fill in the blanks of the following chart to turn infinitive verbs into **ustedes** commands:

Infinitive	Yo Form	Affirmative Ustedes Command	Negative Ustedes Command
pasar la aspiradora	________	________	________
jugar videojuegos	________	________	________
hacer la cama	________	________	________
lavar la ropa	________	________	________
limpiar el baño	________	________	________
montar en bicicleta	________	________	________

Now pick three verbs from the previous chart and make full sentences telling your kids what to do—or what not to do! To help you get started, here are a few options for you to choose from to make complete sentences: **porque está sucio**, **en la casa**, and **todo el día**.

E. ¡Practiquen!

Here are some situations in which you might need to tell someone what to do. It's up to you to decide what to tell them. Choose the best response from these phrases—**tenga cuidado**, **no tenga miedo**, and **no haga eso**—and make them either affirmative or negative commands, depending on the situation. First, have a partner act out the different situations and practice using these commands in these pretend scenarios. Imagine that your partner is someone you don't know very well, since you'll be using **usted** commands. When you've finished acting out the situations, write down which command you chose to give in each one.

Your partner is afraid to go on a roller-coaster ride.

Your partner keeps poking you in the stomach.

Your partner thinks there's a spider on his or her head.

Your partner is about to trip.

Your partner is picking his or her nose.

Your partner is about to step into the street without looking both ways.

You are in a restaurant. Your partner doesn't see the giant **piso mojado** (wet floor) sign and is carrying a tray full of food.

A. New and Review Vocabulary:

Spanish	English
______________________	to command/send: I command/send, I commanded/sent, I will command/send
______________________	to sting/bite: I sting/bite, I stung/bit, I will sting/bite
______________________	to be careful: I am careful
______________________	to be scared: I am scared
______________________	to be right: I am right
______________________	to agree: I agree
______________________	danger
______________________	dangerous
______________________	hot
______________________	cold
______________________	it's hot
______________________	it's cold
______________________	I'm eleven years old
______________________	I'm cold
______________________	I'm hot

B. Canto:

Fill in the boxes of this week's **canto**.

Command Endings

	-ar Endings	-er and -ir Endings
usted command form	________	________
ustedes command form	________	________

Commands: Pensar and Tener

	-ar Endings	-er and -ir Endings
usted command form	________	________
ustedes command form	________	________

C. Grammar:

1. What are the steps to making an affirmative command?

____

____

2. What are the steps to making a negative command?

____

3. Use the verb **hablar**, and show the steps to make both an affirmative command and a negative command.

____

____

4. With whom do you use the **usted** form?

____

5. With whom do you use the **ustedes** form?

____

____

____

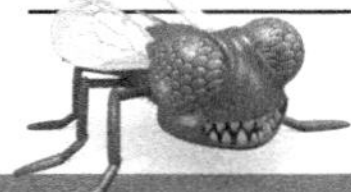

Frases:

Jaime: Discúlpeme, señor. ¿Quiere usted comprar unos chocolates?

El señor: No me interesan mucho los chocolates.

Jaime: Pruébelos, señor. Son muy buenos.

El señor: ¡Ay! Perdóname, pero ¡esos chocolates son terribles! Dime, muchacho, ¿por qué los vendes?

Jaime: Para recaudar dinero para la investigación sobre el cáncer.

El señor: Bueno, pues, en ese caso compro todos los chocolates. No son tan terribles.

Jaime: ¡Gracias, señor!

recaudar dinero = *to raise money*

caso = *case*

Dígame,
¡dígamelo!
No me diga,
¡no me lo diga!

Vocabulario nuevo

Spanish	English
discúlpeme	excuse me
perdóneme	pardon me
dígame	talk to me (a way to answer the phone)
bello/a/os/as, hermoso/a/os/as	beautiful
simpático/a/os/as	nice
contento/a/os/as, alegre/es	happy
tranquilo/a/os/as	calm, relaxed
pobre/es	poor
rico/a/os/as	rich
igual/es	equal

Vocabulario de repaso

Spanish	English
feliz/felices	happy
guapo/a/os/as	good-looking
amable/amables	nice
feo/a/os/as	ugly
lo siento	I'm sorry

Commands and Pronouns

Are you having fun learning how to tell people what to do? In this chapter, you're going to learn a very important part of how to be bossy in Spanish: pronouns. Remember, a pronoun is a word that takes the place of a noun in a sentence. Why do you think pronouns are so important when you're giving commands? Because when you say phrases such as "give me," "tell her," or "listen to him," you're using pronouns every time. Plus, with pronouns you can make your sentences shorter. Instead of saying, "Please wash the car," with the use of a pronoun you can say this: "Wash *it*!"

Know Your Pronouns

There's no way you can use pronouns with commands if you don't remember what pronouns are. (Well, you could probably try, but you might end up accidentally saying some crazy things.) If you have any questions about direct- and indirect-object pronouns, go back to chapter 6, and take another look. If you have any trouble with reflexive pronouns, revisit chapters 23 and 24.

Get Ready for Accents

When we add pronouns, you'll see that sometimes we stick them right onto the ends of the verbs. **Sometimes, when we stick on pronouns, an accent mark appears.** What a cool trick! See if you can spot where new accents are placed as you read along. You'll be given the rule later in the chapter.

Know Your Command

When you're giving a command, you're either telling someone *to* do something or telling someone *not* to do something:

Clean your room! (That's telling someone *to* do something.)
Don't sit on the cat! (That's telling someone *not* to do something.)

Do you remember what we call these different commands? (Hint: To refresh your memory, check out chapter 26.) When you tell someone *to* do something, you are giving an affirmative command. "Affirmative" is a really fancy way of saying "yes," so you're telling the person, "Yes, I want you to do this!" When you tell someone *not* to do something, you are giving a negative command. "Negative" is a fancy way of saying "no," so you're saying, "No! Don't do that!" In Spanish, negative commands always have the word ***no*** in them. Take a look:

Affirmative command: **Tenga cuidado.** (Be careful.)
Negative command: ***No* tenga cuidado.** (Don't be careful.)

You will need to know whether you're giving an affirmative or negative command before you'll know where to put your pronouns.

Affirmative Commands and Pronouns: Direct-Object Pronouns

Let's give a command with a direct-object pronoun.

1. We'll start with the sentence "**Tire la pelota** (Throw the ball)." The Spanish word for "to throw" is **tirar**, so we added our command ending to get **tire. La pelota** is our direct object, since it's the thing being thrown.
2. Then, let's put in our direct-object pronoun. How do you know which direct-object pronoun to use? Remember, the pronouns have to match the nouns in gender and number. If you're throwing **la pelota**, which pronoun do you use? You guessed it: **la. When you're giving an affirmative command, pronouns go on the end of the verb.**
3. Finally, let's put it all together. So, what will your whole command look like? Here it is: **¡Tírela!**

Quick Quiz 1: Here's a command with a direct object. Take out the direct object, and make a command sentence using a direct-object pronoun.

Coma las verduras. (Eat the vegetables.) ______________________________

Indirect-Object Pronouns

OK, learning how to use direct-object pronouns appears to be no problem. But what about using indirect-object pronouns? Don't worry—they do exactly the same thing. Let's give a command with an indirect-object pronoun, for example, "Throw *me* the ball." We start with **tire** again, our command form of **tirar**. This time, however, we're going to add a first-person indirect-object pronoun: **me**.

¡Tíreme la pelota!

Now, let's say you want to give a command using a reflexive verb. It will look just like any other kind of affirmative command with a pronoun. Check out **dormirse** (go to sleep). Let's see, that would be . . . **duerma**. Then, we add on our reflexive pronoun: **¡Duérmase!**

Quick Quiz 2: When you're giving an affirmative command, and you want to use a pronoun, where do you put the pronoun?

____

What to Do with More Than One Pronoun

Do you remember the rules for using more than one pronoun? **An indirect-object pronoun comes first, then a direct-object pronoun.**

Yo te envío la carta. (I send the letter to you.)
Yo *te la* envío. (I send you it.)

If they're both in the third person, the indirect-object pronoun will turn into **se** so your tongue doesn't have to say too many *l* sounds. Here's what it looks like in an indicative sentence (a sentence that is just stating information and is not a command):

Yo le envío la carta a mi madre. (I send the letter to my mom.)

Yo *se la* envío. (I send you it.)

When you are sticking pronouns onto the ends of command-form verbs, they go in the same order. Here's our basic sentence: **Tire la pelota a mí** (Throw the ball to me).

Tire la pelota a mí.

But wait—that isn't correct. If you have an indirect object (**a mí**), you need to have an indirect-object pronoun, too.

Tire*me* la pelota a mí.

That's better. Now, we don't really need the **a mí**—let's just get rid of it.

Tíre*me* la pelota. (Throw *me* the ball.)

Now let's put a direct-object pronoun in for **la pelota**. It goes after the indirect-object pronoun:

Tíre*mela*. (Throw *me it*.)

Quick Quiz 3: When you're using two object pronouns, which one comes first?

____

Quick Quiz 4: Rewrite the following sentence using a pronoun for **el libro**:

Léame el libro. (Read me the book.) ______________________________

What about reflexive pronouns? Sometimes you'll see a command with a reflexive pronoun and a direct object. Here's an example: **¡Lávese las manos!** (Wash your hands!) Let's put in a pronoun for **las manos**:

¡Lávaselas!

So, where do we put a reflexive pronoun? We place it in the same place we would have put an indirect-object pronoun: after the command-form verb and before the direct-object pronoun.

Negative Commands and Pronouns

You've just learned quite a bit about affirmative commands and pronouns. Now it's time to tackle negative commands and pronouns. Don't worry—it's not difficult! Here's the rule: **For any kind of negative command, put all your pronouns in front of the verb**. A negative command with pronouns will look just like any other kind of conjugated verb with pronouns.

Direct-object pronoun in front of a verb:

¡No *lo* coma! (Don't eat *it*!)

Indirect-object pronoun in front of a verb:

¡No *me* diga! (Don't tell *me*! You can use this expression when you're surprised by something someone is telling you, in the same manner as the English phrases, "You don't say!" or "No way!")

Double pronouns in front of a verb:
¡No *me la* tire! (Don't throw *me it*!)

Reflexive pronouns in front of verbs:
No *se* preocupe. (Don't worry [*yourself*]. **Preocuparse**, "to worry," is a reflexive verb.)
No *se* despierte. (Don't wake up [*yourself*].)

Quick Quiz 5: Where does the pronoun go when you're making a negative command?

____

The Rule for Accents

As you've been reading this chapter, did you figure out on your own what the rule is for accents? Here's what you probably figured out:

1. *Before* you add any pronouns to the end of an affirmative command, count the syllables in the command. **Diga** is pronounced in this manner: **di-ga** (two syllables).
2. Pick the syllable that's second to last.
   ***di*-ga** (second-to-last syllable = **di**)
3. Give the vowel in that syllable an accent mark when you add any pronouns.
   d*í*ga*me* (note the accent on the ***i*** and the addition of the pronoun ending, **-me**)
4. If you take all the pronouns away, take away the accent mark, too. Remember, if there are no pronouns stuck onto the end of a verb, it doesn't need an accent mark.
   diga (note there is no accent on the ***i***)

Using **Ustedes**

All of the examples you've seen have been using **usted** commands, but these rules work for all the other forms, too. Let's see some of our example sentences again, using **ustedes** command forms this time.

Direct-object pronouns:
¡Cóm*an*lo! (Eat it!)
¡No lo com*an*! (Don't eat it!)

Indirect-object pronouns:
¡Díg*an*me! (Tell me!)
¡No me dig*an*! (Don't tell me!)

Double pronouns in front of a verb:
¡Tír*en*mela! (Throw me it!)
¡No me la tir*en*! (Don't throw me it!)

Reflexive pronouns in front of verbs:
Preocúp*en*se. (Worry [yourselves].)
No se preocup*en*. (Don't worry [yourselves].)

Despiért*en*se. (Wake up [yourselves].)
No se despiert*en*. (Don't wake up [yourselves].)

A. Translation:

1. **happy (three words)** ______________________
2. **talk to me** ______________________
3. **rich** ______________________
4. **equal** ______________________
5. **beautiful (two words)** ______________________
6. **calm** ______________________
7. **relaxed** ______________________
8. **pardon me** ______________________
9. **poor** ______________________
10. **good-looking** ______________________
11. **nice (two words)** ______________________
12. **ugly** ______________________
13. **I'm sorry** ______________________
14. **excuse me** ______________________

B. Canto:

Write out this week's **canto**. Write the Spanish on the left and the English translation on the right.

Spanish	English
______________________	______________________
______________________	______________________
______________________	______________________
______________________	______________________

C. Grammar:

First of all, let's make sure you know your pronouns.

1. Fill in as many blanks as you can in the following chart to see if there are any pronouns you need to study more.

Subject Pronoun	Direct-Object Pronoun	Indirect-Object Pronoun	Reflexive Pronoun
yo	______	______	______
tú	______	______	______
usted	______	______	______
él, ella	______	______	______
nosotros, nosotras	______	______	______
vosotros, vosotras	**os**	**os**	**os**
ustedes	______	______	______
ellos, ellas	______	______	______

2. For the following, draw an "X" to show where the pronouns go in each case. Add accent marks if any are needed.
   a. Reflexive pronouns with an affirmative command:

      ___ **bañe** ___

   b. Indirect-object pronouns with an affirmative command:

      ___ **envíe** ___

   c. Direct-object pronouns with an affirmative command:

      ___ **envíe** ___

   d. Reflexive pronouns with a negative command:

      ___ **no** ___ **bañe** ___

   e. Direct- and/or indirect-object pronouns with a negative command:

      ___ **no** ___ **envíe** ___

3. When you're using both an indirect-object pronoun and a direct-object pronoun, which one comes first?

____

A. New and Review Vocabulary:

Spanish	English
______________________	**excuse me**
______________________	**pardon me**
______________________	**talk to me (a way to answer the phone)**
______________________	**beautiful**
______________________	**nice**
______________________	**happy**
______________________	**calm, relaxed**
______________________	**poor**
______________________	**rich**
______________________	**equal**
______________________	**happy**
______________________	**good-looking**
______________________	**nice**
______________________	**ugly**
______________________	**I'm sorry**

B. **Canto**:

Write out this week's **canto**. Write the Spanish on the left and the English translation on the right.

Spanish	English
______________________	______________________
______________________	______________________
______________________	______________________
______________________	______________________

C. Grammar:

Let's put it all together and practice making commands *and* adding pronouns. Translate these sentences into Spanish. The person being "commanded" in each one is someone with whom you would use **usted**.

1. Send me the letter (**la carta**). Send me it.

   ____

2. Tell him the truth (**la verdad**). Tell him it.

   ____

3. Go to bed.

   ____

4. Don't go to bed.

   ____

5. Don't send them the present (**el regalo**). Don't send them it.

   ____

Frases:

Duérmete mi niño,
duérmete mi amor,
duérmete pedazo
de mi corazón.
(Canción de cuna tradicional)

amor = *love*
pedazo = *little piece*
corazón = *heart*
cuna = *cradle*
canción de cuna = *lullaby*

Tú Command Endings

	-ar Endings	-er and -ir Endings
tú command form: affirmative command	**-a**	**-e**
tú command form: negative command	**-es**	**-as**

Commands: **Pensar and Comer**

	-ar Endings	-er and -ir Endings
tú command form: affirmative command	**piensa**	**come**
tú command form: negative command	**no pienses**	**no comas**

Vocabulario:

Vocabulario nuevo

Spanish	English
pasear: paseo, paseé, pasearé	to go for a walk: I go for a walk, I went for a walk, I will go for a walk.
pegar: pego, pegué, pegaré	to stick/hit: I stick/hit, I stuck/hit, I will stick/hit
pedir perdón: pido perdón	to ask forgiveness: I ask forgiveness
último/a/os/as	last
pasado/a/os/as	past
próximo/a/os/as	next, near
desde	since
durante	during
anoche	last night

Vocabulario de repaso

Spanish	English
recordar: recuerdo, recordé, recordaré	to remember: I remember, I remembered, I will remember
preguntar: pregunto, pregunté, preguntaré	to ask: I ask, I asked, I will ask
parecer: parezco, parecí, pareceré	to seem: I seem, I seemed, I will seem
preparar: preparo, preparé, prepararé	to prepare: I prepare, I prepared, I will prepare
pasar: paso, pasé, pasaré	to pass: I pass, I passed, I will pass
hasta	until

Informal Commands

Do you want to know what's really crazy about commands in the **tú** form? The verb endings are different depending on whether you're telling someone *to* do something or *not* to do something. Remember, a command *to* do something is an affirmative command. A command *not* to do something is a negative command.

Do Something!

When you want to give a command to a **tú** kind of person (a buddy or someone younger than you), and you want to make an affirmative command ("Yes, do this!"), you just use the regular old present-tense **usted** form. That's the third-person singular form, in case you were wondering. So, what does that mean? It means **you don't need to start with the *yo* form when you make affirmative *tú* commands**.

	Present-Tense Third-Person Singular Endings	Infinitive Verb	Usted Present-Tense Form	Tú Affirmative-Command Form
-ar verbs	**-a**	**hablar**	**habla**	**habla**
-er verbs	**-e**	**comer**	**come**	**come**
-ir verbs	**-e**	**pedir**	**pide**	**pide**

The following is a conversation example. The verbs in the command form are underlined.

Chico: Mamá, puedo salir con mis amigos? (Mom, can I go out with my friends?)
Madre: <u>Habla</u> con tu padre. (Talk to your father.)

Chico: Mamá, puedo tomar un helado? (Mom, can I eat an ice cream?)
Madre: Ahora no. <u>Come</u> tus verduras. (Not right now. Eat your veggies.)

Chico: Mamá, me das dinero? (Mom, can you give me money?)
Madre: <u>Píde</u>selo de tu padre. (Ask your father for it.)

Don't Do Something!

When you want to tell someone *not* to do something, you have some ending-swapping to do. That means you have to **go back and find the *yo* form, chop off the *-o* ending, and then add the negative *tú* command ending**. Don't worry—the endings are pretty easy.

	Negative Tú Endings	A Verb in the Yo Form	Chop Off the -o Ending	Tú Negative-Command Form
-ar verbs	**-es**	**hablo**	**habl-**	**no hables**
-er verbs	**-as**	**como**	**com-**	**no comas**
-ir verbs	**-as**	**pido**	**pid-**	**no pidas**

Remember, with commands it's really important that you find the stem of the **yo** form instead of the stem of the infinitive. Otherwise, you'd miss some of the stem changes in verbs such as **pedir**. Here are some example sentences. Let's hope this brother and sister realize that loving each other is more important than ice cream; but in the meantime, take a look at all the verbs in the command form. They're all underlined, and only one is an affirmative command. See if you can figure out which one is affirmative, and circle it.

Chico: ¡Hola, hermana!

Chica: <u>No hables</u> conmigo.

Chico: ¿Por qué no? (Why not?)

Chica: ¿Por qué no? La próxima vez, (Why not? Next time,) **¡<u>no comas</u> mi helado!**

Chico: ¡Lo siento! ¡<u>Discúlpame</u>! (I'm sorry! Forgive me!)

Chica: <u>No me pidas</u> perdón. ¡Tú eres un monstruo! (Don't ask for my forgiveness! You're a monster!)

A. Translation:

1. **I went for a walk**	______________	9. **until**	______________
2. **I passed**	______________	10. **I ask forgiveness**	______________
3. **I stuck**	______________	11. **last**	______________
4. **last night**	______________	12. **past**	______________
5. **I remember**	______________	13. **next**	______________
6. **I asked**	______________	14. **since**	______________
7. **I seem**	______________	15. **during**	______________
8. **to prepare**	______________		

B. Canto:

Fill in the boxes of this week's **canto**.

Tú Command Endings

	-ar Endings	-er and -ir Endings
tú command form: positive command	______________	______________
tú command form: negative command	______________	______________

Commands: Pensar and Comer

	-ar Endings	-er and -ir Endings
tú command form: positive command	______________	______________
tú command form: negative command	______________	______________

C. Grammar:

Let's make some commands in the **tú** form. The verbs are provided for you. You provide the corresponding affirmative and negative commands. Remember, the affirmative and negative commands can have different stems!

Verb	Affirmative Command	Negative Command
cantar	____________	____________
olvidar	____________	____________
sonreír	____________	____________
compartir	____________	____________
divertirse	____________	____________
volver	____________	____________

A. New and Review Vocabulary:

Spanish	English
____________	to go for a walk: I go for a walk, I went for a walk, I will go for a walk.
____________	to pass: I pass, I passed, I will pass
____________	to stick/hit: I stick/hit, I stuck/hit, I will stick/hit
____________	ask forgiveness: I ask forgiveness
____________	last
____________	past
____________	next, near
____________	since
____________	during
____________	last night
____________	to remember: I remember, I remembered, I will remember
____________	to ask: I ask, I asked, I will ask
____________	to seem: I seem, I seemed, I will seem
____________	to prepare: I prepare, I prepared, I will prepare
____________	until

B. Canto:

Fill in the boxes of this week's **canto**.

Tú Command Endings

	-ar Endings	-er and -ir Endings
tú command form: positive command	______	______
tú command form: negative command	______	______

Commands: **Pensar and Comer**

	-ar Endings	-er and -ir Endings
tú command form: positive command	______	______
tú command form: negative command	______	______

C. Grammar:

Let's make some more commands! The infinitives are provided for you, so just fill in the affirmative and negative command forms for each one.

Verb	Affirmative Command	Negative Command
preguntar	______	______
correr	______	______
acostarse	______	______

(Here's a hint: **acostar** is a stem-change verb and has the same change in all the "boot" forms.)

Frases:

¡Ven aquí!
¡Ponte el abrigo!
¡Sal de la sala! . . .
Y ¡no te vayas sin decir adiós!
sala = *a living room*

Canto:

Verb	Affirmative Tú Command Form	Negative Tú Command Form
ser	**sé**	**no seas**
ir	**ve**	**no vayas**
decir	**di**	**no digas**
hacer	**haz**	**no hagas**
tener	**ten**	**no tengas**
venir	**ven**	**no vengas**
poner	**pon**	**no pongas**
salir	**sal**	**no salgas**

Vocabulario:

Vocabulario nuevo

Spanish	English
reparar: reparo, reparé, repararé	to repair: I repair, I repaired, I will repair
responder: respondo, respondí, responderé	to respond/answer: I respond/answer, I responded/answered, I will respond/answer
funcionar: funciono, funcioné, funcionaré	to work/function: I work/function, I worked/functioned, I will work/function
organizar: organizo, organicé, organizaré	to organize: I organize, I organized, I will organize
llenar: lleno, llené, llenaré	to fill: I fill, I filled, I will fill
pero	but
juntos/juntas	together
casi	almost
jamás	never

Vocabulario de repaso

Spanish	English
explicar: explico, expliqué, explicaré	to explain: I explain, I explained, I will explain
contestar: contesto, contesté, contestaré	to answer: I answer, I answered, I will answer
servir: sirvo, serví, serviré	to serve: I serve, I served, I will serve
reír: río, reí, reiré	to laugh: I laugh, I laughed, I will laugh
siempre	always
nunca	never

Irregular Commands

Now that you've got the idea of command forms, let's talk about the irregulars. Do you remember what "irregulars" are? They're verbs that don't follow the normal rules of conjugation. You're memorizing the **tú**-form irregulars as your **canto** this week, but we'll talk about irregulars in other forms, too. Let's start with the *regulars* for the **usted** form. Remember, **usted** is a second-person pronoun (it's just a fancy way to say "you" to someone you respect), but a verb conjugated for **usted** has third-person endings.[1] **Ustedes** works the same way: it means "you all," but it takes the same verb endings as "them."

The first two irregular verbs we'll learn about are really easy. **Dar** and **estar** look similar to the rest of the regular verbs in the command form at first glance—but see if you can spot two big differences. Here are the **usted** and **ustedes** command forms for **dar** and **estar**:

Infinitive	Usted Command Form	Ustedes Command Form
dar	**dé**	**den**
estar	**esté**	**estén**

Can you tell what makes these guys irregular? The first thing that makes these irregular is that there's an accent on the last ***e*** of **dé**, **esté**, and **estén**. The second thing is that **dar** and **estar** don't look like they were put into the **yo** form before chopping and adding the command ending. (This is a good thing, since the **yo** form of **dar** is **doy**, and if you chop off the ***o*** of **doy**, what do you do with the ***y***?)

Let's see if you can use these irregular forms. Translate these commands using the **ustedes** forms.

Give me the ball (**la pelota**)! ______________________________

Be here at four o'clock! ______________________________

Here are some other verbs with irregular conjugations in the **usted** and **ustedes** command forms:

Infinitive	Usted Command Form	Ustedes Command Form
ir	**vaya**	**vayan**
ser	**sea**	**sean**
saber	**sepa**	**sepan**

See if you can come up with your own fun way to memorize these. Remember, in the **usted** form, the verb endings are the same whether you're giving an affirmative or a negative command.

Let's do some more translations. Use the **ustedes** form again, as though you're talking to a group of buddies.

Don't go! ______________________________

Don't be stupid (**estúpidos**)! ______________________________

1. Why do we learn the third-person command-form endings with **usted** and not with **él**, **ella**, and **ellos/as**? Because when you give someone a command, you're talking directly to that person (that makes it "second person"), which makes it impossible to give a command to a third person! We use the third person to talk about people indirectly. That's no good for giving commands.

Tú-Form Irregulars

Here's something important to remember: Even when **tú**-form commands are irregular, **the affirmative and negative forms are still different from each other**.

Verb	Affirmative Tú Command Form	Example	Negative Tú Command Form	Example
ser	**sé**	**Sé mi amigo.** (Be my friend.)	**seas**	**¡No seas tonto!** (Don't be dumb!)
ir	**ve**	**¡Vete!** (Leave!)	**vayas**	**No te vayas sin mí.** (Don't leave without me.)
decir	**di**	**Dime lo que tú quieres.** (Tell me what you want.)	**digas**	**No digas esas tonterías.** (Don't say those stupid things.)
hacer	**haz**	**Haz lo que quieres.** (Do what you want.)	**hagas**	**No hagas eso!** (Don't do that!)
tener	**ten**	**Ten paciencia.** (Have patience.)	**tengas**	**No tengas miedo.** (Don't be scared.)
venir	**ven**	**Ven aquí.** (Come here.)	**vengas**	**No vengas tarde.** (Don't come late.)
poner	**pon**	**Ponte un abrigo.** (Put on a coat.)	**pongas**	**No pongas la mesa sin** servilletas. (Don't set the table without napkins.)
salir	**sal**	**Sal con tus hermanos.** (Go out with your brothers.)	**salgas**	**No salgas sin abrigo.** (Don't go out without a coat.)

Some Other Verb Surprises

Do you remember learning about present-tense verbs that had what we call "spelling changers"?[2] These are verbs that have letters in them, such as ***g*** and ***c***, that can change their sounds depending on what letter comes after them. Here's a little chart to remind you how it works:

A Letter and the Sound It Makes:	When the Letter Makes That Sound:	Spanish Examples:
g – the English "g" sound, as in "gum"	before an ***a***, ***o***, or ***u***	**garaje, juego, guerra** (war)
g – the English "h" sound, as in "hat"	before an ***e*** or ***i***	**gente, girar** (to spin)
c – the English "k" sound, as in "king"	before an ***a***, ***o***, or ***u***	**casa, cola** (tail), **Cuzco** (a city in Peru)
c – the English "s" sound, as in "sell"	before an ***e*** or ***i***	**cepillo** (brush), **cilantro** (an herb)

When we conjugate verbs, sometimes we put on a new ending that would make a letter change its sound. Instead of switching the sound of its letters, often

2 . We talked about spelling changers in chapter 15 of *SFCA*. If you need some extra help after this section, you might want to go back and check it out.

a spelling-change verb will have . . . a *spelling change*! Did you see that one coming?

Since these letters only change their sounds when they're with an *e* instead of an *a*, or an *a* instead of an *e*, spelling changers don't do any changing with affirmative *tú* commands. That's because there's no switcheroo from an **-ar** to an **-er** or **-ir** ending with an affirmative **tú** command.

Here are three kinds of verbs that will need to have a spelling change:

1. Verbs that end in **-car**

Examples: **tocar**, **practicar**

What happens when you put these verbs into command form? The ***c*** changes to ***qu*** to keep the "k" sound. That's because ***c*** in front of an ***e*** would make an "s" sound.

No toquen! (Don't touch!)

2. Verbs that end in **-gar**

Examples: **jugar**, **cargar**

What happens when you put these verbs into command form? The ***g*** changes to ***gu*** so it keeps its sound and doesn't change to a "j" sound.

No cargues las pilas. (Don't charge the batteries.)

No juegues en la calle. (Don't play in the street.)

3. Verbs that end in **-zar**

Examples: **empezar**, **comenzar** (Both words are stem changers and mean "to begin.")

What happens when you do command-form conjugations? The ***z*** turns into a ***c***.

No empiecen tarde. (Don't start late.)

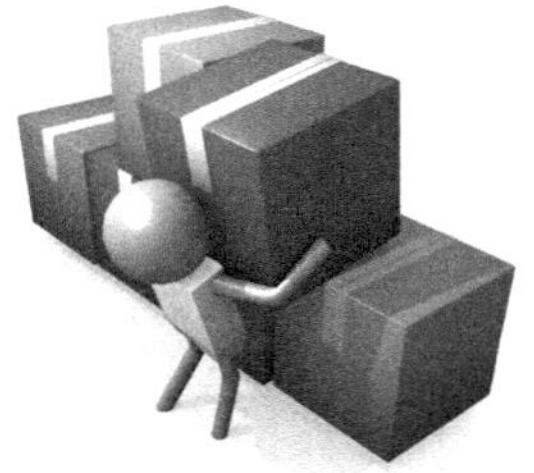

A. Translation:

1. **I repair**	______	9. **to fill**	______
2. **I explain**	______	10. **but**	______
3. **I respond**	______	11. **together**	______
4. **I answer (two translations)**	______ ______	12. **almost**	______
5. **I serve**	______	13. **always**	______
6. **I laugh**	______	14. **never**	______
7. **to function**	______	15. **never**	______
8. **to organize**	______		

B. Canto:

Fill in the boxes of this week's **canto**.

Verb	Affirmative Tú Command Form	Negative Tú Command Form
ser	______	______
ir	______	______
decir	______	______
hacer	______	______
tener	______	______
venir	______	______
poner	______	______
salir	______	______

C. Grammar:

1. Why do you sometimes see surprise letter changes when you're conjugating Spanish verbs?

____

____

2. **Usted**-form commands have one ending if they're affirmative and a different ending if they're negative. Circle one: True False

3. What type of command forms have one ending if they're affirmative and a different ending if they're negative?
   a. Only **usted**-form commands
   b. **Usted** and **ustedes** command forms
   c. All command forms
   d. Only **tú**-form commands
   e. **Usted** and **tú** command forms

D. ¡Hagamos mandatos!

Let's make some commands. You'll be given the verb and the pronoun for the person or persons you're bossing around, and then you will need to provide the affirmative and negative command forms. You know the drill! Make sure pronouns go in the right places in the commands. The first one is done as an example.

irse (**tú**)	vete	no te vayas
dar (**usted**)	______________	______________
practicar (**ustedes**)	______________	______________
comenzar (**tú**)	______________	______________
decir (**tú**)	______________	______________
hacer (**ustedes**)	______________	______________

A. New and Review Vocabulary:

Spanish	English
______________________	to repair: I repair, I repaired, I will repair
______________________	to respond/answer: I respond/answer, I responded/answered, I will respond/answer
______________________	to work/function: I work/function, I worked/functioned, I will work/function
______________________	to organize: I organize, I organized, I will organize
______________________	to fill: I fill, I filled, I will fill
______________________	but
______________________	together
______________________	almost
______________________	never
______________________	to explain: I explain, I explained, I will explain
______________________	to answer: I answer, I answered, I will answer
______________________	to serve: I serve, I served, I will serve
______________________	to laugh: I laugh, I laughed, I will laugh
______________________	always
______________________	never

B. Canto:

Fill in the boxes of this week's **canto**.

Verb	Affirmative Tú Command Form	Negative Tú Command Form
ser	______________	______________
ir	______________	______________
decir	______________	______________
hacer	______________	______________
tener	______________	______________
venir	______________	______________
poner	______________	______________
salir	______________	______________

C. Grammar:

Which of the following is the best thing to do when you see an irregular verb?

a. Memorize it.

b. Look it up in a dictionary or conjugation guide.

c. Try to guess which forms of the verb might be irregular and which ones might be regular.

d. Try to use the verb in a sentence.

e. Run the other way.

f. There is no "best way." Try all of these things to see what helps you the most!

Frases:

Venid fieles todos;

¡a Belén marchemos!

fieles todos = *all ye faithful*

Belén = *Bethlehem*

It may or may not be the right season for Christmas carols, but this traditional song is a great example of two grammar rules you'll be learning in this chapter.

Canto:

Nosotros and Vosotros Command Endings

	-ar Endings	-er and -ir Endings
vosotros affirmative command form	**-ad**	**-ed, id**
vosotros negative command form	**-éis**	**-áis**
nosotros command form	**-emos**	**-amos**

Dormir (to sleep) Command Forms

	Singular	Plural
1st person	N/A	(**nosotros**) **durmamos** (let's sleep) (**nosotros**) **no durmamos** (let's not sleep)
2nd-person familiar: affirmative	**(tú) duerme** (you sleep)	(**vosotros**) **dormid** (you all sleep)
2nd-person familiar: negative	**(tú) no duermas** (you don't sleep)	(**vosotros**) **no durmáis** (you all don't sleep)
2nd-person formal	**(usted) duerma** (you sleep) (**usted**) **no duerma** (you don't sleep)	**(ustedes) duerman** (you all sleep) **(ustedes) no duerman** (you all don't sleep)

Vocabulario:

Vocabulario nuevo

Spanish	English
marchar: marcho, marché, marcharé	to march/walk: I march/walk, I marched/walked, I will march/walk
marcharse: me marcho	to leave: I leave
corregir: corrijo, corregí, corregiré	to correct: I correct, I corrected, I will correct
cruzar: cruzo, crucé, cruzaré	to cross: I cross, I crossed, I will cross
decidir: decido, decidí, decidiré	to decide: I decide, I decided, I will decide
oler: huelo, olí, oleré	to smell: I smell, I smelled, I will smell
despacio	slowly
atrás	back, behind
el ejercicio	exercise
el examen	exam, test

Vocabulario de repaso

Spanish	English
probar: pruebo, probé, probaré	to try/taste: I try/taste, I tried/tasted, I will try/taste
venir: vengo, vine, vendré	to come: I come, I came, I will come
conseguir: consigo, conseguí, conseguiré	to get: I get, I got, I will get
vestirse: me visto, me vestí, me vestiré	to get dressed: I get dressed, I got dressed, I will get dressed
enviar: envío, envié, enviaré	to send: I send, I sent, I will send

Venid, ¡vámonos! (Come on, Guys, Let's Go!)

In this chapter, we're going to learn about the last two command forms: **nosotros** and **vosotros**. This chapter has two goals: By the end of the chapter, you should be able to recognize **vosotros** and **nosotros** commands, and you should be able to create them yourself. There are many different ways to make these commands, so you'll be given a lot of information. Hang in there until the end, though, and then you'll learn a cool shortcut you can use to make some commands easily when it's your turn to be the bossy one.

Vosotros Commands

As you should know by now, you only use **vosotros** forms if you go to Spain. So, let's go over these forms quickly so you can recognize them if you see them later somewhere. There are just three rules for **vosotros** commands, and they are fairly easy to learn. Here they are:

1. For an **affirmative command**, change the ***r*** at the end of the infinitive to a ***d***.
   Examples:
   ¡Venid! (Come!)
   ¡Id! (Go!)
   ¡Hablad! (Talk!)
   ¡Comed! (Eat!)
2. For a **negative command**, do the **yo**-chop-switch. An **-ar** verb gets an **-er/-ir vosotros** ending. An **-er** or **-ir** verb gets an **-ar vosotros** ending. If verbs are irregular in the other command forms, they're irregular in the **vosotros** form.
   ¡No vengáis! (Don't come!)
   ¡No vayáis! (Don't go!)
   ¡No habléis! (Don't talk!)
   ¡No comáis! (Don't eat!)
3. Watch out for stem-change verbs—they do some funny things in **nosotros** and **vosotros** command forms. You'll learn their patterns in just a minute.

Nosotros Commands

The hardest part about **nosotros** commands is keeping track of stem-change verbs that like to be tricky. You'll get to that part in a second; but first, let's talk about what a **nosotros** command *is*.

A **nosotros** command is how you get the fun started. It's similar to saying, "Let's ______." *Let's* wear our clothes inside out! *Let's* jump on mom and dad's bed while they're still asleep! *Let's* feed the goldfish to the dog! These might not be good ideas, but they're all **nosotros** commands. You're telling someone to do something, and by using a *first-person* plural form, you're saying that you'll do it, too.

There are six different patterns and rules you need to learn to be a pro at **nosotros** commands. Learning these is worth the effort, because you'll use these a lot. If it gets tough, you can always take a break and complete some of the exercises in the worksheet section. You should be able to start the first few groups of practice exercises before you finish reading this entire grammar section.

1. Regular **Yo**-Chop-Switch **Nosotros** Command Forms

You should know how to do these already, so here are your **nosotros** command-form endings: **Verbs ending in *-ar* get the command-form ending of *-emos*, and verbs ending in *-er* or *-ir* get the command-form ending of *-amos*.**

Verbs such as *tener* and *venir* that have irregular *yo* forms in the present tense are in this category.

¡Hablemos en español! (Let's speak in Spanish!)
¡Hagamos la tarea! (Let's do the homework!)
¡Pongamos la mesa! (Let's set the table!)
¡Tengamos fe! (Let's have faith!)
¡No vengamos tarde! (Let's not come late!)

2. No **Yo**-Chop-Switch: **-ar** and **-er** Stem-Change Verbs

The only command forms that don't do a **yo**-chop-switch are **-ar** and **-er** stem-change verbs in the **nosotros** and **vosotros** forms (except for the *really* wacky ones you already memorized in chapter 29[1]). With these guys, you just start with your infinitive, chop off the last two letters, and add the **nosotros** command-form ending. Can you handle that? *No* **yo**-chop-switching, **just an infinitive chop-and-switch**. No **yo** form involved. Got it? Let's see a few:

pensar = pensemos **probar = probemos** **mover = movamos** **volver = volvamos**

3. Spelling-Change Verbs Still Have a Spelling Change

Those spelling changers, verbs ending in **-car**, **-gar**, and **-zar**, all have spelling changes in the **nosotros** form, too. Do you remember making the verb **jugar** into a command? It's an **-ar** verb, so we don't have to start by converting it to the **yo** form. Let's start with the infinitive form:

jugar

We take off the **-ar** and add the **nosotros** command-form ending:

jugemos

But wait—that sounds ridiculous! With this change, we would pronounce that ***g*** as an "h" sound. So, that would change the pronunciation to "hoo-hay-mos." That's wrong! It just sounds awful. To fix this, let's add a ***u*** to the ***g*** to restore it to its usual sound in this word:

juguemos

---

1. Also, there are the **vosotros** affirmative-command forms, but those are so crazy and rare that you'll hardly ever run into them.

Much better! That works. Here are a few more:

llegar = lleguemos **pagar = paguemos** **practicar = practiquemos**
sacar = saquemos **buscar = busquemos**

4. Stem-Change Verbs Ending in -ir

Stem-change verbs ending in **-ir** appear to be the craziest of all. Guess what: These guys *do* start in the **yo** form when you conjugate them. That's right! Even though **-ar** and **-er** verbs don't do a **yo**-chop-switch in the **nosotros** form, **-ir** verbs do. It's rare that you would ever conjugate one "verb family" differently than you would the others, but that's exactly what you're going to do here.

So, here are the steps to conjugating **-ir** stem-change verbs:

A. Start with your **yo** form.
B. *Change the stem change.*

What? Change a stem change? You read that correctly. These **-ir** verbs only have *one letter* of their stem changes here. So, let's look at our options. Here are the different kinds of stem-change verbs and how you have to change them to make **nosotros** command forms. You'll only use the *first* letter of each stem-change vowel group.

Stem Change Category	Example Verb	Normal Yo Form	Special Yo Stem for Nosotros Commands	Nosotros Command Form
o » ue	**dormir**	**duermo**	**durm-**	**durmamos**
e » ie	**sentir**	**siento**	**sint-**	**sintamos**
e » i[2]	**pedir**	**pido**	**pid-**	**pidamos**

Here are a few more, just so you can get the hang of it:

seguir = sigamos **conseguir = consigamos** **vestir = vistamos** **repetir = repitamos**

5. The Really Irregular Guys

Remember the *really* irregular verbs for which you learned command forms in chapter 29? Here are their **nosotros** command forms. Only two of them are different from what you would get with a good old **yo**-chop-switch. See if you can figure out which ones they are, and circle them.

ser **ir** **decir** **hacer** **tener** **venir**

poner **salir** **seamos** **vayamos**

digamos **hagamos** **tengamos** **vengamos** **pongamos** **salgamos**

6. Advanced Material: Fun with Pronouns

Here you are—you finally made it to the last rule for making **nosotros** commands. You already know this rule: For a command in the **nosotros** form, **pronouns go *before* the verb in a negative command and *after* the verb in an affirmative command.**

2. In the case of the **e » i** stem changers, the *first* letter of the stem-change vowel group just so happens to be the *only* letter of the stem-change vowel group! That means you don't need to worry about figuring out which letter to drop.

No <u>nos</u> vistamos de princesas; ¡vistámo<u>nos</u> de vampiros!
(Let's not dress like princesses; let's dress like vampires!)

Enviamos los regalos a mis hermanos. Enviémo<u>selos</u>.
(Let's send the presents to my brothers. Let's send them them.)

One thing you might have noticed is that **when we stick a pronoun onto the end of a *nosotros* command, we drop the last letter *s*.** We only have to do that when the pronouns start with ***n*** (**nos**) or ***s*** (**se**). Dropping the ***s*** just makes the command easier to say.

Quick Quiz: Let's add some pronouns to some commands. Circle the commands that lost an ***s***:

tirémos + **se** + **lo** = **tirémoselo** (let's throw them it)

comámos + **lo** = **comámoslo** (let's eat it)

lavémos + **nos las manos** = **lavémonos las manos** (let's wash our hands)

vámos + **nos** = **vámonos** (let's go)

The Secret Shortcut

You made it to the end of the section about **nosotros** and **vosotros** commands. Great job! Now it's time for the super-cool shortcut. Unfortunately, **you can only use this shortcut when you're giving an affirmative command**. But it's still nice to know the shortcut. Here it is:

Just use the near-future tense.
(**ir** + **a** + infinitive verb)

Here's what it looks like:
¡Vamos a nadar! ("We're going to swim!" or "Let's swim!")
¡Vamos a bailar! ("We're going to dance!" or "Let's dance!")
¡Vamos a divertirnos! ("We're going to have fun!" or "Let's have fun!")

That's it? Yes—it is! The people listening to you will just guess from the way you're talking whether you're saying, "Let's do something," or "We are going to do something."

This shortcut is pretty cool, huh? The only bummer is that you can never use this for negative commands, just positive ones. The only verb that would sound really funny in this form is **ir**, since you'd already be using the verb as a helping verb in the near-future tense. So, to say, "Let's go," you can just say:

¡Vamos! (Let's go!) (affirmative command)

Or, you can put a reflexive pronoun on the end to say, "Let's leave!":

¡Vámonos! (Let's go! Let's leave!)

Remember, this only works for *affirmative* commands. You still have to use all the rules to figure out the negative command form.

A. Translation:

1. **marchar**	______	9. **conseguir**	______
2. **marcharse**	______	10. **enviar**	______
3. **corregir**	______	11. **vestirse**	______
4. **cruzar**	______	12. **despacio**	______
5. **decidir**	______	13. **atrás**	______
6. **oler**	______	14. **el ejercicio**	______
7. **probar**	______	15. **el examen**	______
8. **venir**	______		

B. Canto:

Fill in the boxes of this week's **canto**.

Nosotros and Vosotros Command Endings

	-ar Endings	-er and -ir Endings
vosotros affirmative command form	-ad	-ed, -id
vosotros negative command form	-éis	-áis
nosotros command form	______	______

Dormir (to sleep) Command Forms

	Singular	Plural
1st person	N/A	______ ______
2nd-person familiar: affirmative	______	(vosotros) dormid
2nd-person familiar: negative	______	(vosotros) no durmáis
2nd-person formal	______ ______	______ ______

C. Grammar:

1. Where will you use **vosotros** forms? ______
2. What's the affirmative **vosotros** ending? Circle one:
   a. **-áis** or **-éis** c. **-id**
   b. **-ís** d. **-er**

3. What do you use for *negative* **vosotros** commands? Circle one:
   a. You use nothing because they don't exist. c. Use the **ustedes** command form.
   b. Use the **yo**-chop-switch. d. Just use the regular **usted** form.
4. What is the English equivalent of a **nosotros** command? Circle one:
   a. Do something! c. Let's ___________!
   b. Don't do something! d. There is no English equivalent.
5. What kinds of commands are different depending on whether the command is affirmative or negative? Circle one:
   a. **tú**-form commands and **vosotros** commands
   b. **vosotros** and **nosotros** commands
   c. Every kind of command
   d. **tú**-form commands, **vosotros** commands, and **nosotros** commands (if you're using the shortcut)
6. What do you do that's unusual when you add pronouns to the end of a **nosotros** command?

   ____

7. What's the secret shortcut to making easy **nosotros** commands? When can you use it?

   ____

   ____

D. Using the Rules

For each rule listed, conjugate the provided verbs to write affirmative and negative **nosotros** commands, and write your answers on the lines provided.

1. Regular **yo**-chop-switch

   hacer ______________ ______________
2. *No* **yo**-chop-switch

   probar ______________ ______________
3. Spelling-change verbs

   buscar ______________ ______________
4. Stem-change verbs ending in **-ir** (Hint: "Change the stem change . . .")

   dormir ______________ ______________
5. The *really* irregular guys (Let's do two since they're so weird.)

   ser ______________ ______________

   ir ______________ ______________
6. Pronouns

   te lo enviar ______________ ______________
7. Shortcuts

   pensar ______________ ______________

A. New and Review Vocabulary

Spanish	English
__________________	to march/walk: I march/walk, I marched/ walked, I will march/walk
__________________	to leave: I leave
__________________	to correct: I correct, I corrected, I will correct
__________________	to cross: I cross, I crossed, I will cross
__________________	to decide: I decide, I decided, I will decide
__________________	to smell: I smell, I smelled, I will smell
__________________	slowly
__________________	back, behind
__________________	exercise
__________________	exam, test
__________________	to try/taste: I try/taste, I tried/tasted, I will try/taste
__________________	to come: I come, I came, I will come
__________________	to get: I get, I got, I will get
__________________	to get dressed: I get dressed, I got dressed, I will get dressed
__________________	to send: I send, I sent, I will send

B. Canto:

Fill in the boxes of this week's **canto**.

Nosotros and Vosotros Command Endings

	-ar Endings	-er and -ir Endings
vosotros affirmative command form	**-ad**	**-ed, -id**
vosotros negative command form	**-éis**	**-áis**
nosotros command form	______________	______________

Dormir (to sleep) Command Forms

	Singular	Plural
1st person	N/A	______________ ______________
2nd-person familiar: affirmative	______________	**(vosotros) dormid**
2nd-person familiar: negative	______________	**(vosotros) no durmáis**
2nd-person formal	______________ ______________	______________ ______________

C. Grammar:

For the following sentences, circle the commands, cross out the sentences that aren't commands, and draw a box around any that could be either.

No vayamos.	**No nos pongamos los abrigos.**
Jugamos.	**No nos ponemos los abrigos.**
No vamos.	**Vamos a jugar.**
Durmamos.	**Vamos a hacer la tarea.**
Vamos.	**No hacemos la tarea.**
No dormimos.	**No hagamos la tarea.**

Repaso de vocabulario

We've reached the end of another unit, and you know what that means—another set of review vocabulary words. Let's see how well you did at memorizing them. If there are any that you forgot, try writing them backwards on your forehead so you see them every time you look in a mirror. Or, a simpler (and less messy) idea would be to use the forgotten words in several creative sentences; just write the sentences several times on a separate piece of paper to memorize the use of the words.

Chapter 26

1. **danger**	5. **it's hot**	9. **I am careful**	13. **I agree**
2. **dangerous**	6. **it's cold**	10. **I am scared**	14. **I command**
3. **hot**	7. **I'm cold**	11. **I am right**	15. **I sting**
4. **cold**	8. **I'm hot**	12. **I'm eleven years old**	

Chapter 27

16. **happy (three words)**	20. **beautiful (two words)**	24. **poor**	27. **ugly**
17. **talk to me**	21. **calm**	25. **good-looking**	28. **I'm sorry**
18. **rich**	22. **relaxed**	26. **nice (two words)**	29. **excuse me**
19. **equal**	23. **pardon me**		

Chapter 28

30. **I go for a walk**	34. **I ask**	38. **I ask forgiveness**	42. **next**
31. **I pass**	35. **I seem**	39. **last**	43. **since**
32. **I stick/hit**	36. **I prepare**	40. **last night**	44. **during**
33. **I remember**	37. **until**	41. **past**	

Chapter 29

45. **I repair**	49. **I serve**	53. **to fill**	57. **always**
46. **I explain**	50. **I laugh**	54. **but**	58. **never**
47. **I respond**	51. **to work/function**	55. **together**	59. **never**
48. **I answer (two translations)**	52. **to organize**	56. **almost**	

Chapter 30

	60. I march		**63. I cross**		**67. I taste**		**71. slowly**
	61. I leave (You know four ways to say "I leave" in English, if you include "I go out." List them all!)		**64. I decide**		**68. I get**		**72. back**
			65. I smell		**69. I send**		**73. exercise**
	62. I correct		**66. I come**		**70. I get dressed**		**74. exam**

Cantos

Complete the following chart, which contains all the command-form endings from the individual **cantos** in chapters 26–30.

Command Endings (Chapters 26, 27, 28, 29, and 30)

	-ar Endings	-er and -ir Endings
tú command form: affirmative command	____________	____________
tú command form: negative command	____________	____________
usted command form	____________	____________
nosotros command form	____________	____________
vosotros affirmative command form	**-ad**	**-ed, -ied**
vosotros negative command form	**-éis**	**-áis**
ustedes command form	____________	____________

Tú-Form Irregulars (Chapter 29)

Verb	Affirmative Tú Command Form	Negative Tú Command Form
ser	____________	____________
ir	____________	____________
decir	____________	____________
hacer	____________	____________
tener	____________	____________
venir	____________	____________
poner	____________	____________
salir	____________	____________

Dormir (to sleep) Command Forms (Chapter 30)

	Singular	Plural
		______
1st person	N/A	______
2nd-person familiar: affirmative	______	(vosotros) **dormid**
2nd-person familiar: negative	______	(vosotros) **no durmáis**
	______	______
2nd-person formal	______	______

Commands: **Pensar** and **Tener** (Chapter 26)

	-ar Endings	-er and -ir Endings
usted command form	______	______
ustedes command form	______	______

Commands: **Pensar** and **Comer** (Chapter 28)

	-ar Endings	-er and -ir Endings
tú command form: affirmative command	______	______
tú command form: negative command	______	______

Chapter 27

Write out the **canto** from chapter 27. Write the Spanish on the left and the English translation on the right.

Spanish	English
Dígame, ______	Tell me, ______
______	______
______	______
______	______

Más casillas (More Boxes)

You've learned lots of rules for making command forms, but there can be so many different forms for each verb that you may be confused. Insert what you do know into the following boxes so that you can keep it all straight. Remember, you usually don't need to use subject pronouns when you're giving a command, but they're there in the boxes of the following charts to make it clear which verb forms you need to use.

Hacer (to make/do) Command Forms

	Singular	Plural
1st person: affirmative	N/A	**nosotros** ________________
1st person: negative	N/A	**nosotros** ________________
2nd-person familiar: affirmative	**tú** ____________________	vosotros haced
2nd-person familiar: negative	**tú** ____________________	vosotros no hagáis
2nd-person formal	**usted** __________________	**ustedes** ________________

Ir (to go) Command Forms

	Singular	Plural
1st person: affirmative	N/A	**nosotros** ________________
1st person: negative	N/A	**nosotros** ________________
2nd-person familiar: affirmative	**tú** ____________________	vosotros id
2nd-person familiar: negative	**tú** ____________________	vosotros no vayáis
2nd-person formal	**usted** __________________	**ustedes** ________________

Jugar (to play) Command Forms

	Singular	Plural
1st person: affirmative	N/A	**nosotros** ____________________
1st person: negative	N/A	**nosotros** ____________________
2nd-person familiar: affirmative	**tú** __________________	vosotros jugad
2nd-person familiar: negative	**tú** __________________	vosotros no juguéis
2nd-person formal	**usted** ________________	**ustedes** ______________________

Comer (to eat) Command Forms

	Singular	Plural
1st person: affirmative	N/A	**nosotros** ______
1st person: negative	N/A	**nosotros** ______
2nd-person familiar: affirmative	**tú** ______	vosotros comed
2nd-person familiar: negative	**tú** ______	vosotros no comáis
2nd-person formal	**usted** ______	**ustedes** ______

For the last one, you pick a verb.

______ Command Forms

	Singular	Plural
1st person: affirmative	N/A	**nosotros** ______
1st person: negative	N/A	**nosotros** ______
2nd-person familiar: affirmative	**tú** ______	vosotros ______
2nd-person familiar: negative	**tú** ______	vosotros ______
2nd-person formal	**usted** ______	**ustedes** ______

Thinking on Your Feet

Here is a list of situations. Imagine you're actually in each described scenario, and think of a command you might give in each case. You can write any command that would make sense according to the described situation, as long as your grammar is correct.

1. Your little brother is looking hungrily at your lunch.

______

2. A policeman is giving you directions, but he's talking too quickly.

______

3. You want all your friends to help you drink the rest of the lemonade (**limonada**).

______

4. You want all your friends to leave your house (maybe you have a lot of homework). You're not going to leave with them.

______

5. Your mom is leaving for a meeting, and she forgot some important papers.

____

6. Your little brother and sister are supposed to wash the dishes, but they're watching TV.

____

7. Your dog is hogging the bed and keeping you awake.

____

8. Your teacher is about to trip over a backpack.

____

Vamos a jugar "Simón dice" (Simon Says)

Here are some verbs that are great for **Simón dice**. Write the **ustedes** command forms of the verbs on the provided lines, and then play the game with your friends, using the list of **las partes del cuerpo** to tell them what to raise, touch, etc.

Verb	**Ustedes** Command Form
saltar (jump)	______________
dar una vuelta (turn around)	______________
ponerse de pie (stand up)	______________
sentarse (sit down)	______________
levantar . . . (raise . . .)	______________
tocar . . . (touch. . .)	______________

Las partes del cuerpo:
la nariz (nose)
la cabeza (head)
los hombros (shoulders)
los pies (feet)
los brazos (arms)
las manos (hands)

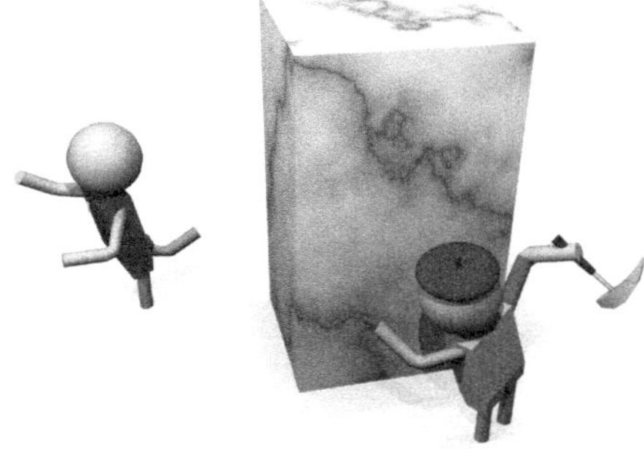

Repaso de vocabulario

Let's see how you've done memorizing all of your vocabulary words! If there are any words that you still don't know, spend some time using those words to write sentences.

Unit 1 Review

Chapter 1

- [ ] 1. **desayunar**
- [ ] 2. **cortar**
- [ ] 3. **el lápiz**
- [ ] 4. **el bolígrafo**
- [ ] 5. **el papel**
- [ ] 6. **el cuaderno**
- [ ] 7. **las tijeras**
- [ ] 8. **la mochila**
- [ ] 9. **la palabra**
- [ ] 10. **la página**
- [ ] 11. **hablar**
- [ ] 12. **cantar**
- [ ] 13. **bailar**
- [ ] 14. **correr**
- [ ] 15. **abrir**
- [ ] 16. **vivir**

Chapter 2

- [ ] 17. **mostrar**
- [ ] 18. **bajar**
- [ ] 19. **venir**
- [ ] 20. **el almuerzo**
- [ ] 21. **el desayuno**
- [ ] 22. **la fiesta**
- [ ] 23. **la bebida**
- [ ] 24. **la fruta**
- [ ] 25. **las verduras**
- [ ] 26. **el postre**
- [ ] 27. **querer**
- [ ] 28. **tener**
- [ ] 29. **poder**
- [ ] 30. **poner**
- [ ] 31. **hacer**
- [ ] 32. **ver**

Chapter 3

- [ ] 33. **empezar**
- [ ] 34. **almorzar**
- [ ] 35. **conducir**
- [ ] 36. **reducir**
- [ ] 37. **creer**
- [ ] 38. **el aeropuerto**
- [ ] 39. **el avión**
- [ ] 40. **el autobús**
- [ ] 41. **el barco**
- [ ] 42. **la maleta**
- [ ] 43. **decir**
- [ ] 44. **saber**
- [ ] 45. **estar**
- [ ] 46. **dormir**
- [ ] 47. **pedir**

Chapter 4

- [ ] 48. **limpio/a/os/as**
- [ ] 49. **sucio/a/os/as**
- [ ] 50. **feliz/felices**
- [ ] 51. **triste/es**
- [ ] 52. **divertido/a/os/as**
- [ ] 53. **aburrido/a/os/as**
- [ ] 54. **difícil/difíciles**
- [ ] 55. **fácil/fáciles**
- [ ] 56. **diferente/es**
- [ ] 57. **mismo/a/os/as**
- [ ] 58. **yo mismo/ yo misma**
- [ ] 59. **grande/es**
- [ ] 60. **pequeño/a/os/as**
- [ ] 61. **bueno/a/os/as**
- [ ] 62. **malo/a/os/as**

Chapter 5

- 63. **siempre**
- 64. **nunca**
- 65. **todavía**
- 66. **también**
- 67. **tarde**
- 68. **temprano**
- 69. **tampoco**
- 70. **sólo**
- 71. **solo/a/os/as**
- 72. **demasiado**
- 73. **demasiado/a/os/as**
- 74. **por**
- 75. **para**
- 76. **a**
- 77. **de**
- 78. **con**
- 79. **sin**

Chapter 6

- 80. **temer**
- 81. **escoger**
- 82. **enviar**
- 83. **las noticias**
- 84. **la flor, las flores**
- 85. **el parque**
- 86. **la carta**
- 87. **el problema**
- 88. **el idioma**
- 89. **el programa**
- 90. **el poema**
- 91. **gustar**
- 92. **tirar**
- 93. **usar**
- 94. **beber**
- 95. **recibir**

Unit 2 Review

Chapter 8

- 96. **arreglar**
- 97. **recoger**
- 98. **pasar**
- 99. **pasar la aspiradora**
- 100. **la aspiradora**
- 101. **el dormitorio**
- 102. **la alfombra**
- 103. **la almohada**
- 104. **la manta**
- 105. **el juguete**
- 106. **el muñeco de peluche**
- 107. **el huevo**
- 108. **limpiar**
- 109. **el jardín**
- 110. **el árbol**
- 111. **el libro**
- 112. **la cama**
- 113. **hacer la cama**

Chapter 9

- 114. **soñar con**
- 115. **odiar**
- 116. **mirar la tele**
- 117. **tocar música**
- 118. **tocar el piano**
- 119. **jugar videojuegos**
- 120. **pasar tiempo con los amigos**
- 121. **practicar deportes**
- 122. **jugar al fútbol**
- 123. **el sueño**
- 124. **amar**
- 125. **salir**
- 126. **la tarea**
- 127. **hacer la tarea**
- 128. **el tiempo**

Chapter 10

- 129. **la hora**
- 130. **¿Qué hora es?**
- 131. **Es hora de . . .**
- 132. **medio/a**
- 133. **el cuarto**
- 134. **la medianoche**
- 135. **el mediodía**
- 136. **la tarde**
- 137. **menos**
- 138. **el/la menos**
- 139. **el sol**
- 140. **comenzar**
- 141. **hoy**
- 142. **la luna**
- 143. **la noche**
- 144. **el día**
- 145. **la mañana/mañana**
- 146. **el reloj**

Unit 3 Review

Chapter 12

- 147. **proteger**
- 148. **continuar**
- 149. **contar**
- 150. **contar con**
- 151. **de repente**
- 152. **había**
- 153. **había una vez . . .**
- 154. **el pájaro**
- 155. **nadie**
- 156. **alguien**
- 157. **trabajar**
- 158. **nacer**
- 159. **conseguir**
- 160. **deber**
- 161. **dejar**

Chapter 13

- 162. **el juego**
- 163. **el lugar**
- 164. **el mar**
- 165. **el hogar**
- 166. **el ejemplo**
- 167. **la luz**
- 168. **la llave**
- 169. **la vez**
- 170. **la fecha**
- 171. **la parte**
- 172. **descansar**
- 173. **dibujar**
- 174. **descubrir**
- 175. **encontrar**

Chapter 14

- 176. **cerrar**
- 177. **cansar**
- 178. **abrir**
- 179. **ocupar**
- 180. **cubrir**
- 181. **escribir**
- 182. **freír**
- 183. **decir**
- 184. **hacer**
- 185. **ver**
- 186. **poner**
- 187. **morir**
- 188. **romper**
- 189. **volver**
- 190. **nadar**
- 191. **necesitar**
- 192. **olvidar**
- 193. **pagar**
- 194. **parar**

Unit 4 Review

Chapter 16

- 195. **montar**
- 196. **el patinete**
- 197. **la bicicleta**
- 198. **la ropa**
- 199. **el casco**
- 200. **los pantalones**
- 201. **la chaqueta**
- 202. **la falda**
- 203. **el vestido**
- 204. **las gafas**
- 205. **llevar**
- 206. **prestar**
- 207. **la camisa**
- 208. **los zapatos**
- 209. **el abrigo**

Chapter 17

- 210. **este/esta**
- 211. **ese/esa**
- 212. **estos/estas**
- 213. **esos/esas**
- 214. **aquel/aquella**
- 215. **aquellos/aquellas**
- 216. **libre/libres**
- 217. **listo/a/os/as**
- 218. **cada**
- 219. **ayudar**
- 220. **comprar**
- 221. **compartir**
- 222. **buscar**
- 223. **contestar**
- 224. **todo/a/os/as**

Chapter 18

225. **derecha**	229. **detrás de**	233. **fuera de**	237. **comprender**
226. **izquierda**	230. **cerca de**	234. **dentro de**	238. **cocinar**
227. **encima de**	231. **lejos de**	235. **debajo de**	239. **la gente**
228. **delante de**	232. **entre**	236. **cambiar**	240. **la cosa**

Chapter 19

241. **mejorar**	245. **peor**	249. **menos que**	253. **morir**
242. **añadir**	246. **el/la peor**	250. **menor/es**	254. **morder**
243. **mejor**	247. **más**	251. **mayor/es**	255. **molestar**
244. **el/la mejor**	248. **más que**	252. **mover**	256. **menos**

Chapter 20

257. **probar**	261. **caro/a/os/as**	265. **fuerte/es**	269. **inteligente/es**
258. **tratar de**	262. **barato/a/os/as**	266. **cómico/a/os/as**	270. **alto/a/os/as**
259. **tratar**	263. **rápido/a/os/as**	267. **el mundo**	271. **bajo/a/os/as**
260. **empujar**	264. **lento/a/os/as**	268. **el joven, la joven**	272. **joven/jóvenes**

Unit 5 Review

Chapter 22

273. **cubrir**	277. **el dibujo**	281. **el chiste**	284. **seguir**
274. **el país**	278. **el cambio**	282. **vender**	285. **saltar**
275. **la vida**	279. **la razón**	283. **sonreír**	286. **volver**
276. **la salud**	280. **tener razón**		

Chapter 23

287. **bañarse**	291. **peinarse**	295. **el cuerpo**	299. **la mano**
288. **vestirse**	292. **el peine**	296. **la cara**	300. **el baño**
289. **levantarse**	293. **el cepillo**	297. **el vestido**	301. **el pelo**
290. **acostarse**	294. **los dientes**	298. **lavar**	

Chapter 24

302. **sentirse**	306. **sentarse**	310. **apresurarse**	314. **incluir**
303. **divertirse**	307. **quejarse (de)**	311. **enamorarse (de)**	315. **guardar**
304. **despertarse**	308. **casarse (con)**	312. **irse**	316. **gritar**
305. **preocuparse (por)**	309. **quitarse**	313. **imaginar**	317. **ganar**

Unit 6 Review

Chapter 26

- 318. **mandar**
- 319. **picar**
- 320. **tener cuidado**
- 321. **tener miedo**
- 322. **tener razón**
- 323. **estar de acuerdo**
- 324. **el peligro**
- 325. **peligroso/a/os/as**
- 326. **caliente/es**
- 327. **frío/a/os/as**
- 328. **hace calor**
- 329. **hace frío**
- 330. **tengo once años**
- 331. **tengo frío**
- 332. **tengo calor**

Chapter 27

- 333. **discúlpeme**
- 334. **perdóneme**
- 335. **dígame**
- 336. **bello/a/os/as, hermoso/a/os/as**
- 337. **simpático/a/os/as**
- 338. **contento/a/os/as, alegre/es**
- 339. **tranquilo/a/os/as**
- 340. **pobre/es**
- 341. **rico/a/os/as**
- 342. **igual/es**
- 343. **feliz/felices**
- 344. **guapo/a/os/as**
- 345. **amable/amables**
- 346. **feo/a/os/as**
- 347. **lo siento**

Chapter 28

- 348. **pasear**
- 349. **pasar**
- 350. **pegar**
- 351. **pedir perdón**
- 352. **último/a/os/as**
- 353. **pasado/a/os/as**
- 354. **próximo/a/os/as**
- 355. **desde**
- 356. **durante**
- 357. **anoche**
- 358. **recordar**
- 359. **preguntar**
- 360. **parecer**
- 361. **preparar**
- 362. **hasta**

Chapter 29

- 363. **reparar**
- 364. **responder**
- 365. **funcionar**
- 366. **organizar**
- 367. **llenar**
- 368. **pero**
- 369. **juntos/juntas**
- 370. **casi**
- 371. **jamás**
- 372. **explicar**
- 373. **contestar**
- 374. **servir**
- 375. **reír**
- 376. **siempre**
- 377. **nunca**

Chapter 30

- 378. **marchar**
- 379. **marcharse**
- 380. **corregir**
- 381. **cruzar**
- 382. **decidir**
- 383. **oler**
- 384. **despacio**
- 385. **atrás**
- 386. **el ejercicio**
- 387. **el examen**
- 388. **probar**
- 389. **venir**
- 390. **conseguir**
- 391. **vestirse**
- 392. **enviar**

Grammar

Unit 2 (Chapters 8–11)

1. Circle the phrases you could finish with an infinitive verb. Then, finish all the sentences by filling in the blanks. Make sure you use the right part of speech or verb form to finish each one.

Yo quiero ____________.

____________ es muy divertido.

Hay ____________.

Yo ____________ a las siete y media.

Ahora yo estoy ____________.

Vamos a ____________.

Hay que ____________.

¿Tienes que ____________?

Tú tienes ____________.

2. What are the person and number of the verb **hay**? What is its tense?

____

3. What gender do you use when you are telling time? (Circle one.)
   a. Masculine
   b. Feminine
   c. It depends.
4. What verb do you use to tell what time it is? (Circle one.)
   a. **Estar**
   b. **Ser**
   c. **Haber**
   d. **Tener**
5. What is the only hour that isn't plural?

____

6. You use articles when you're telling time in Spanish. Circle one: True False

Unit 3 (Chapters 12–15)

1. Here are the rules for using the preterit and imperfect tenses. However, there's a problem: In the following sentences, the words "preterit" and "imperfect" have been erased. Carefully read the incomplete sentences, and fill in either "preterit" or "imperfect" to complete the rules.

For an action in the past that happens again and again, use the ________________ tense.

We use the ________________ tense for actions that have a clear beginning and end.

We use the ________________ tense for actions that don't have a clear beginning and end.

We use the ________________ tense for actions that were ongoing.

We use the ________________ tense for actions that happened once.

Past-tense descriptions are in the ________________ tense.

________________-tense actions interrupt ________________-tense actions.

________________ actions don't happen "suddenly."

We use the ________________ tense for emotions and "brain-action" verbs.

2. Here are pairs of phrases. In each pair, one phrase should be in the preterit tense, and one should be in the imperfect tense. It's up to you to figure out which is which! On the line next to each sentence, write the tense you would use to translate it into Spanish.

Sentence	Tense
My balloon popped.	________________
My balloon was yellow.	________________
I used to practice piano every afternoon.	________________
I played the piano for one hour this morning.	________________
One time, I packed a bread sandwich for lunch.	________________
I thought bread sandwiches were really cool.	________________
I used to wish I had yellow eyes like an owl.	________________
Once I saw an owl in the woods behind our house.	________________
My grandfather was Hungarian.	________________
He immigrated to the United States in 1927.	________________

3. You know how to use the near-future tense, but what happens if you conjugate **ir** in the imperfect tense? Let's find out!

First, write a sentence using the near-future tense:

____

Next, rewrite your sentence, putting the verb **ir** in the imperfect tense instead:

____

Finally, translate your sentence into English:

____

4. How do you make a past participle?

____

____

5. Choose a verb, and make a past participle of that verb:

   Verb: ______________________________

   Past participle: ______________________________

6. What are the two rules for using a past participle as an adjective? (Hint: One rule tells you where to put it in the sentence, and the other rule you hear all the time.)

   Rule 1: ______________________________

   ____

   Rule 2: ______________________________

   ____

7. Take the past participle you just made in question 5, and use it in a sentence:

   ____

   ____

Unit 4 (Chapters 16–21)

1. What is a possessive pronoun?

   ____

2. What are three rules for using a possessive pronoun?

   ____

   ____

   ____

3. When is the only time you don't need an article with a possessive pronoun?

   ____

   ____

4. What is a demonstrative?

   ____

   ____

5. Why are there so many more demonstrative forms in Spanish than in English?

   ____

   ____

   ____

6. What's the big spelling difference between demonstrative pronouns and demonstrative adjectives?

   ____

   ____

7. What does it mean if we say a word is *neuter*?

   ____

8. When can you use neuter demonstrative pronouns?

____

____

____

____

9. When you use a comparative, what are you doing?

____

10. What words can you add to adjectives in Spanish to make them into comparatives?

____

____

11. What are the three Spanish phrases you can use to compare two things? (Hint: In English, they're "more . . . than," "less. . . than," and "as . . . as.")

____

____

12. What is a superlative?

____

13. What do you add to a comparative to make it a superlative?

____

14. What are four adjectives that don't follow the usual pattern to become comparatives or superlatives?

____

____

Unit 5 (Chapters 22–25)

1. What is the indefinite pronoun in Spanish?

____

2. What kinds of sentences have an indefinite pronoun as a subject?

____

____

3. Give an example of a sentence using the indefinite pronoun as the subject.

____

____

4. How will you know when a verb is a reflexive verb? (Circle one.)
   a. It will have a reflexive pronoun around it somewhere.
   b. It will be conjugated differently from other verbs.
   c. It won't have an **-ar**, **-er**, or **-ir** ending.

5. Why are some verbs, such as **bañarse** and **afeitarse**, reflexive?

6. Where does a reflexive pronoun go if the verb is conjugated?

7. Circle the actions that would most likely be expressed using reflexive verbs in Spanish:

scratching your head — painting a picture

running in the park — stubbing your toe

Unit 6 (Chapters 26–31)

1. What is an affirmative command?

2. What is a negative command?

3. Write out the steps to turning an infinitive into a command.

4. When you're giving an affirmative command, and you want to use a direct- or indirect-object pronoun, where do you put the pronoun?

5. Give an affirmative command with an object pronoun. Use the **usted** form.

6. Where do you put an object pronoun when you're giving a negative command?

7. Make the command you provided as the answer for question 5 a negative command.

8. What do you use to give an affirmative **tú**-form command? How about a negative **tú**-form command?

R

9. Give an affirmative **tú**-form command. Then, give the same command again, but make it negative.

____

____

10. Why do we sometimes have spelling changes when making command-form verbs?

____

____

11. What is the English equivalent of a **nosotros** command? ____________

12. How do you make a **nosotros** command?

____

____

13. What's the secret shortcut to making easy **nosotros** commands? When can you use it?

____

____

Hay and Había

You know that **hay** means "there is" or "there are," and **había** means "there was" or "there were." These words are great for describing places. Start this exercise by describing a place in the present tense. Write three or four sentences using **hay** to describe the place where you are working right now.

____

____

____

____

____

Now, describe a place using the imperfect tense. Think of a place where you were a long time ago. You can even make up an imaginary place. Then, write three or four sentences using **había** to describing this long-ago place.

____

____

____

____

____

Telling Time

¿Qué hora es? Draw hands on these clocks. On the first line under each clock, write out in Spanish what time it is. Use complete sentences! Then, for each clock write a sentence starting with the phrase "**Es la hora de . . .**"

Using the Imperfect

Choose seven verbs that are actions you have done before.

1. ______________________________
2. ______________________________
3. ______________________________
4. ______________________________
5. ______________________________
6. ______________________________
7. ______________________________

Think about how you did each action (each verb). If you did the action over and over, or over a long period of time, mark an *I* next to the verb for "imperfect tense." If the action had a clear beginning and end, or if you did the action once (or only a few times), mark a *P* next to the verb for "preterit tense."

Now, go back and conjugate all of your verbs in the **yo** form. If you have labeled the verb with *P*, conjugate it in the preterit tense. If the verb is labeled with an *I*, conjugate it in the imperfect tense.

1. ______________________________
2. ______________________________
3. ______________________________
4. ______________________________

5. ______________________________

6. ______________________________

7. ______________________________

Finally, use these verbs to write a story about your life! Start the story with this phrase: **Cuando yo era niño/a . . .** (When I was a kid. . .).

____

____

____

____

____

Robot Reflexives

What were you doing in the bathroom for so long? We know the truth: You were perfecting your secret weapon, a robot that looks just like a human, which will help you take over the world! But your babysitter doesn't know that. She thinks you were just getting ready for bed. Here is a list of actions that you did to put the finishing touches on your amazing robot. You'll notice that they're reflexive verbs. To prevent your babysitter from knowing what you were up to, you need to tell her that you did all of these actions to yourself (instead of to your robot) to explain all of the sounds she heard emanating from the bathroom. Rewrite each sentence using the provided verb to say that you did the action to yourself. For example, if the sentence says you buttoned your robot's shirt, you would need to change the sentence to say *you* buttoned *your* shirt.

You brushed your robot's teeth (**cepillarse los dientes**).

____

You combed your robot's hair (**peinarse**).

____

You washed your robot's hands (**lavarse las manos**).

____

You gave your robot a bath (**bañarse**).

____

You dressed your robot (**vestirse**).

____

Despite your explanations to the babysitter, she is smarter than you thought and discovers your robot. When you see her reaction to your plan for global domination, you realize that maybe creating a robot to take over the world wasn't such a good idea after all. You feel sorry about it (**arrepentirse**) and apologize (**disculparse**) by filling in the reflexive pronouns in the following sentences.

Yo ____________ arrepiento.

Yo ____________ disculpo.

Review of Cantos

Chapters 1–7 **Cantos**

Review of Verb Endings

	Present-Tense -**ar** Verb Endings	Present-Tense -**er** Verb Endings	Present-Tense -**ir** Verb Endings	Preterit-Tense -**ar** Verb Endings	Preterit-Tense -**er**/-**ir** Verb Endings	Future-Tense Verb Endings
1st-person singular (**yo**)	________	________	________	________	________	________
2nd-person singular (**tú**)	________	________	________	________	________	________
3rd-person singular (**él/ella/usted**)	________	________	________	________	________	________
1st-person plural (**nosotros**)	________	________	________	________	________	________
2nd-person plural (**vosotros**)	**-áis**	**-éis**	**-ís**	**-asteis**	**-isteis**	**-éis**
3rd-person plural (**ellos/ustedes**)	________	________	________	________	________	________

Review of **Ser** (to be), **Estar** (to be), and **Ir** (to go) Present-Tense Forms

Ser (to be: characteristics and "permanent" qualities)

	Singular	Plural
1st person	________________	________________
2nd person	________________	**sois** (you all are)
3rd person	________________	________________

Estar (to be: location, condition, and "temporary" qualities)

	Singular	Plural
1st person	________________	________________
2nd person	________________	**estáis** (you all are)
3rd person	________________	________________

Ir (to go)

	Singular	Plural
1st person	______	______
2nd person	______	**vais** (you all go)
3rd person	______	______

Review of **Ser** and **Ir** Preterit-Tense Forms

Ser Preterit-Tense Forms

	Singular	Plural
1st person	______	______
2nd person	______	**fuisteis** (you all were)
3rd person	______	______

Ir Preterit-Tense Forms

	Singular	Plural
1st person	______	______
2nd person	______	**fuisteis** (you all went)
3rd person	______	______

Review of Articles and Adjective Endings

Definite Articles

	Singular	Plural
Masculine	______	______
Feminine	______	______

Indefinite Articles

	Singular	Plural
Masculine	______	______
Feminine	______	______

Adjective Endings

	Singular	Plural
Masculine	______	______
Feminine	______	______

Review of Prepositions

Fill in the prepositions. On the lines to the right, write the English translation of each preposition.

Spanish	**English**
Preposiciones _______________ la ardilla	______________________
La ardilla va:	
_______________ **mi casa**	______________________
_______________ **descanso**	______________________
_______________ **el parque**	______________________
_______________ **su hogar**	______________________
_______________ **el árbol**	______________________
_______ _______ _______ **lago.**	______________________
Llega _______________ **su nido**	______________________
_______________ **una nuez**	______________________
__________ _______ **correr**	______________________
__________ _______ **comer.**	______________________

Review of Pronouns

	Subject Pronouns	Direct-Object Pronouns	Indirect-Object Pronouns
1st-person singular	______________	______________	______________
2nd-person singular	______________	______________	______________
2nd-person formal	______________	______________	______________
3rd-person singular	______________	______________	______________
1st-person plural	______________	______________	______________
2nd-person plural	**vosotros/vosotras** (you all)	**os** (you all)	**os** (you all)
2nd-person plural formal (Latin American "you all")	______________	______________	______________
3rd-person plural	______________	______________	______________

Chapters 8–11 **Cantos**

Remember, all of these **cantos** were poems you memorized. The first line of each **canto** has been provided for you. Complete the **cantos**.

Hay

____
____
____
____
____
____

Infinitives

____
____
____
____
____
____

Telling Time

____
____
____
____
____
____
____
____
____
____
____
____
____
____
____
____

Chapters 12–15 **Cantos**

Imperfect Tense

Hablar Imperfect-Tense Forms

	Singular	Plural
1st person	**yo** ____________	**nosotros** ____________
2nd person	**tú** ____________	**vosotros hablabais**
3rd person	**él, ella** ____________	**ellos** ____________

Comer Imperfect-Tense Forms

	Singular	Plural
1st person	**yo** ____________	**nosotros** ____________
2nd person	**tú** ____________	**vosotros comíais**
3rd person	**él, ella** ____________	**ellos** ____________

Ser Imperfect-Tense Forms

	Singular	Plural
1st person	**yo** ____________	**nosotros** ____________
2nd person	**tú** ____________	**erais**
3rd person	**él, ella** ____________	**ellos** ____________

Ir Imperfect-Tense Forms

	Singular	Plural
1st person	**yo** ____________	**nosotros** ____________
2nd person	**tú** ____________	**ibais**
3rd person	**él, ella** ____________	**ellos** ____________

Ver Imperfect-Tense Forms

	Singular	Plural
1st person	**yo** ____________	**nosotros** ____________
2nd person	**tú** ____________	**veíais**
3rd person	**él, ella** ____________	**ellos** ____________

Past Participles

Write out the past participles of each of these verbs. Then, translate the **canto** into English.

Verb	Past Participle	Translation
cerrar	____________	____________
cansar	____________	____________
abrir	____________	____________

Verb	Past Participle	Translation
ocupar		
cubrir		
escribir		
freír		
decir		
hacer		
ver		
poner		
morir		
romper		
volver		

Chapters 16–21 **Cantos**

Possessive Pronouns

	Singular	Plural
1st person		
2nd-person familiar		**vuestro/a/os/as**
2nd-person formal		
3rd person		

Demonstrative Adjectives

Something "Near You" (this, these)

	Singular	Plural
Masculine		
Feminine		

Something "Farther from You" (that, those)

	Singular	Plural
Masculine	________	________
Feminine	________	________

Something "Over There" (that "over there," those "over there")

	Singular	Plural
Masculine	________	________
Feminine	________	________

Demonstrative Pronouns

Something "Near You" (this, these)

	Singular	Plural
Masculine	________	________
Feminine	________	________
Neuter	________	N/A

Something "Farther from You" (that, those)

	Singular	Plural
Masculine	________	________
Feminine	________	________
Neuter	________	N/A

Something "Over There" (that "over there," those "over there")

	Singular	Plural
Masculine	________	________
Feminine	________	________
Neuter	________	N/A

Comparisons

Yo soy _________ __________ _________ mi madre,

y ___________ ___________ ________ mi padre.

Ya que yo nací ________ temprano,

yo _________ ____________ _________ mi hermano.

Pero aunque a su lado salto,

mi hermanito es _________ ___________.

Yo soy ___________ ________ mi prima,

y aquí concluyo la rima.

Superlatives

¡Nuestro equipo es _____ ______________ !

Sí, ¡sí, señor!

Tenemos los jugadores ________ rápidos.

(¡Los jugadores son _______ _______ _______________ !)

Las jugadores son _______ ____________ ___________.

(¡Son _______ ____________ ____________ !)

¡Nuestro equipo ______ ______ ______________ !

Sí, ¡sí, señor!

Chapters 22–25 **Cantos**

Remember, this is a **canto** you memorized. See if you can write it out.

The Pronoun **Se**

Aquí ______________________ español,

aquí ______________________ voleibol.

Allí ______________________ chino,

______________________ muy fino.

Reflexive Pronouns

	Singular	Plural
1st person	________	________
2nd-person familiar	________	os
2nd-person formal	________	________
3rd person	________	________

Bañarse (to take a bath) Present-Tense Forms

	Singular	Plural
1st person	________	________
2nd-person familiar	________	**vosotros os bañáis**
2nd-person formal	________	________
3rd person	________	________

Irse (to leave) Present-Tense Forms

	Singular	Plural
1st person	________	________
2nd-person familiar	________	**vosotros os vais** (you all leave)
2nd-person formal	________	________
3rd person	________	________

R

Chapters 26–31 **Cantos**

Command Endings

	-ar Endings	-er and -ir Endings
tú command form: affirmative command	________	________
tú command form: negative command	________	________
usted command form	________	________
nosotros command form	________	________
vosotros affirmative command form	**-ad**	**-ed, -id**
vosotros negative command form	**-éis**	**-áis**
ustedes command form	________	________

Tú-Form Irregulars

Verb	Affirmative Tú Command Form	Negative Tú Command Form
ser	________	________
ir	________	________
decir	________	________
hacer	________	________
tener	________	________
venir	________	________
poner	________	________
salir	________	________

Dormir (to sleep) Command Forms

	Singular	Plural
		________
1st person	________	________
2nd-person familiar: affirmative	________	**(vosotros) dormid**
2nd-person familiar: negative	________	**(vosotros) no durmáis**
	________	________
2nd-person formal	________	________

Commands: **Pensar** and **Tener**

	-ar Endings	-er and -ir Endings
usted command form	________	________
ustedes command form	________	________

Commands: **Pensar** and **Comer**

	-ar Endings	-er and -ir Endings
tú command form: affirmative command	________	________
tú command form: negative command	________	________

Commands with Pronouns

Remember, this is a **canto** you memorized. Write the Spanish on the left and the English translation on the right.

Spanish	English
Dígame, ________	________
________	________
________	________
________	________

GLOSSARY BY CHAPTER

Chapter 1

Vocabulario nuevo

Spanish	English
desayunar: desayuno, desayuné, desayunaré	to eat breakfast: I eat breakfast, I ate breakfast, I will eat breakfast
cortar: corto, corté, cortaré	to cut: I cut, I cut, I will cut
el lápiz	pencil
el bolígrafo	pen
el papel	paper
el cuaderno	notebook
las tijeras	scissors
la mochila	backpack
la palabra	word
la página	page

Vocabulario de repaso

Spanish	English
hablar: hablo, hablé, hablaré	to speak: I speak, I spoke, I will speak
cantar: canto, canté, cantaré	to sing: I sing, I sang, I will sing
bailar: bailo, bailé, bailaré	to dance: I dance, I danced, I will dance
correr: corro, corrí, correré	to run: I run, I ran, I will run
abrir: abro, abrí, abriré	to open: I open, I opened, I will open
vivir: vivo, viví, viviré	to live: I live, I lived, I will live

Chapter 2

Vocabulario nuevo

Spanish	English
mostrar: muestro, mostré, mostraré	to show: I show, I showed, I will show
bajar: bajo, bajé, bajaré	to go down: I go down, I went down, I will go down
venir: vengo, vine, vendré	to come: I come, I came, I will come
el almuerzo	lunch
el desayuno	breakfast
la fiesta	party
la bebida	drink
la fruta	fruit
las verduras	vegetables
el postre	dessert

Vocabulario de repaso

Spanish	English
querer: quiero, quise, querré	to want/love: I want/love, I wanted/loved, I will want/love
tener: tengo, tuve, tendré	to have: I have, I had, I will have
poder: puedo, pude, podré	to be able to: I can, I could, I will be able to
poner: pongo, puse, pondré	to put/place: I put/place, I put/placed, I will put/place
hacer: hago, hice, haré	to make/do: I make/do, I made/did, I will make/do
ver: veo, vi, veré	to see: I see, I saw, I will see

Chapter 3

Vocabulario nuevo

Spanish	English
empezar: empiezo, empecé, empezaré	to begin: I begin, I began, I will begin
almorzar: almuerzo, almorcé, almorzaré	to eat lunch: I eat lunch, I ate lunch, I will eat lunch
conducir: conduzco, conduje, conduciré	to drive: I drive, I drove, I will drive
reducir: reduzco, reduje, reduciré	to reduce: I reduce, I reduced, I will reduce
creer: creo, creí, creeré	to believe: I believe, I believed, I will believe
el aeropuerto	airport
el avión	airplane
el autobús	bus
el barco	boat
la maleta	suitcase

Vocabulario de repaso

Spanish	English
decir: digo, dije, diré	to say/tell: I say/tell, I said/told, I will say/tell
saber: sé, supe, sabré	to know: I know, I knew, I will know
estar: estoy, estuve, estaré	to be: I am, I was, I will be
dormir: duermo, dormí, dormiré	to sleep: I sleep, I slept, I will sleep
pedir: pido, pedí, pediré	to ask for: I ask for, I asked for, I will ask for

Chapter 4

Vocabulario nuevo

Spanish	English
limpio/a/os/as	clean
sucio/a/os/as	dirty
feliz/felices	happy
triste/es	sad
divertido/a/os/as	fun
aburrido/a/os/as	boring
difícil/difíciles	difficult
fácil/fáciles	easy

Spanish	English
diferente/es	different
mismo/a/os/as	same
yo mismo/yo misma	myself

Vocabulario de repaso

Spanish	English
grande/es	big
pequeño/a/os/as	little
bueno/a/os/as	good
malo/a/os/as	bad

Chapter 5

Vocabulario nuevo

Spanish	English
siempre	always
nunca	never
todavía	still
también	also
tarde	late
temprano	early
tampoco	neither
sólo	only
solo/a/os/as	alone
demasiado	too (plus an adjective)
demasiado/a/os/as	too much, too many

Vocabulario de repaso

Spanish	English
por	for, by, through
para	for, toward
a	at, to
de	from, of
con	with
sin	without

Chapter 6

Vocabulario nuevo

Spanish	English
temer: temo, temí, temeré	to fear: I fear, I feared, I will fear
escoger: escojo, escogí, escogeré	to choose: I choose, I chose, I will choose
enviar: envío, envié, enviaré	to send: I send, I sent, I will send

Spanish	English
las noticias	news
la flor, las flores	flower, flowers
el parque	the park
la carta	letter
el problema	problem
el idioma	language
el programa	program
el poema	poem

Vocabulario de repaso

Spanish	English
gustar: me gusta, me gustó, me gustará	to be pleasing: it is pleasing to me, it was pleasing to me, it will be pleasing to me
tirar: tiro, tiré, tiraré	to throw: I throw, I threw, I will throw
usar: uso, usé, usaré	to use: I use, I used, I will use
beber: bebo, bebí, beberé	to drink: I drink, I drank, I will drink
recibir: recibo, recibí, recibiré	to receive: I receive, I received, I will receive

Chapter 8

Vocabulario nuevo

Spanish	English
arreglar: arreglo, arreglé, arreglaré	to tidy: I tidy, I tidied, I will tidy
recoger: recojo, recogí, recogeré	to pick up: I pick up, I picked up, I will pick up
pasar: paso, pasé, pasaré	to pass: I pass, I passed, I will pass
pasar la aspiradora	to vacuum
la aspiradora	vacuum cleaner
el dormitorio	bedroom
la alfombra	rug
la almohada	pillow
la manta	blanket
el juguete	toy
el muñeco de peluche	stuffed animal
el huevo	egg

Vocabulario de repaso

Spanish	English
limpiar: limpio, limpié, limpiaré	to clean: I clean, I cleaned, I will clean
el jardín	garden, yard
el árbol	tree
el libro	book
la cama	bed
hacer la cama	to make the bed

Chapter 9

Vocabulario nuevo

Spanish	English
soñar con: sueño con, soñé con, soñaré con	to dream about: I dream about, I dreamed about, I will dream about
odiar: odio, odié, odiaré	to hate: I hate, I hated, I will hate
mirar la tele	to watch TV
tocar música	to play music (on a musical instrument)
tocar el piano	to play the piano
jugar videojuegos	to play video games
pasar tiempo con los amigos	to spend time with friends
practicar deportes	to play sports
jugar al fútbol	to play soccer
el sueño	dream

Vocabulario de repaso

Spanish	English
amar: amo, amé, amaré	to love: I love, I loved, I will love
salir: salgo, salí, saldré	to go out: I go out, I went out, I will go out
la tarea	homework
hacer la tarea	to do homework
el tiempo	time, weather

Chapter 10

Vocabulario nuevo

Spanish	English
la hora	hour
¿Qué hora es?	What time is it?
Es hora de . . . (finish this sentence with an infinitive)	It's time to…
medio/a	half, middle
el cuarto	quarter, fourth, room
la medianoche	midnight
el mediodía	noon
la tarde	afternoon
menos	minus, less
el/la menos	the least
el sol	sun

Vocabulario de repaso

Spanish	English
comenzar: comienzo, comencé, comenzaré	to begin: I begin, I began, I will begin
hoy	today
la luna	the moon
la noche	night
el día	day
la mañana/mañana	morning/tomorrow
el reloj	clock, watch

Chapter 12

Vocabulario nuevo

Spanish	English
proteger: protejo, protegí, protegeré	to protect: I protect, I protected, I will protect
continuar: continúo, continué, continuaré	to continue: I continue, I continued, I will continue
contar: cuento, conté, contaré	to count/tell: I count/tell, I counted/told, I will count/tell
contar con	to count on
de repente	suddenly
había	there was, there were
había una vez . . .	once upon a time there was . . .
el pájaro	bird
nadie	no one, nobody
alguien	someone, somebody

Vocabulario de repaso

Spanish	English
trabajar: trabajo, trabajé, trabajaré	to work: I work, I worked, I will work
nacer: nazco, nací, naceré	to be born: I am born, I was born, I will be born
conseguir: consigo, conseguí, conseguiré	to get: I get, I got, I will get
deber: debo, debí, deberé	to owe/ought to: I owe/should, I owed/should have, I will owe/should
dejar: dejo, dejé, dejaré	to leave (something): I leave (something), I left (something), I will leave (something)

Chapter 13

Vocabulario nuevo

Spanish	English
el juego	game
el lugar	place

Spanish	English
el mar	sea
el hogar	home
el ejemplo	example
la luz	light
la llave	key
la vez	time (instance, occasion)
la fecha	date (on a calendar)
la parte	part

Vocabulario de repaso

Spanish	English
descansar: descanso, descansé, descansaré	to rest: I rest, I rested, I will rest
dibujar: dibujo, dibujé, dibujaré	to draw: I draw, I drew, I will draw
descubrir: descubro, descubrí, descubriré	to discover: I discover, I discovered, I will discover
encontrar: encuentro, encontré, encontraré	to find/meet: I find/meet, I found/met, I will find/meet

Chapter 14

Vocabulario nuevo

Spanish	English
cerrar: cerrado	to close: closed
cansar: cansado	to tire: tired
abrir: abierto	to open: open (opened)
ocupar: ocupado	to occupy: busy, occupied
cubrir: cubierto	to cover: covered
escribir: escrito	to write: written
freír: frito	to fry: fried
decir: dicho	to say: said
hacer: hecho	to make/do: made, done
ver: visto	to see: seen
poner: puesto	to put/place: put, placed
morir: muerto	to die: died, dead
romper: roto	to break: broken
volver: vuelto	to return: returned

Vocabulario de repaso

Spanish	English
nadar: nado, nadé, nadaré	to swim: I swim, I swam, I will swim
necesitar: necesito, necesité, necesitaré	to need: I need, I needed, I will need
olvidar: olvido, olvidé, olvidaré	to forget: I forget, I forgot, I will forget
pagar: pago, pagué, pagaré	to pay: I pay, I paid, I will pay
parar: paro, paré, pararé	to stop: I stop, I stopped, I will stop

Chapter 16

Vocabulario nuevo

Spanish	English
montar: monto, monté, montaré	to ride: I ride, I rode, I will ride
el patinete	scooter
la bicicleta	bicycle
la ropa	clothes
el casco	helmet
los pantalones	pants
la chaqueta	jacket
la falda	skirt
el vestido	dress
las gafas	glasses

Vocabulario de repaso

Spanish	English
llevar: llevo, llevé, llevaré	to carry/wear: I carry/wear, I carried/wore, I will carry/wear
prestar: presto, presté, prestaré	to loan: I loan, I loaned, I will loan
la camisa	shirt
los zapatos	shoes
el abrigo	coat

Chapter 17

Vocabulario nuevo

Spanish	English
este/esta	this
ese/esa	that
estos/estas	these
esos/esas	those
aquel/aquella	that over there
aquellos/aquellas	those over there
libre/libres	free
listo/a/os/as	ready, smart
cada	each, every

Vocabulario de repaso

Spanish	English
ayudar: ayudo, ayudé, ayudaré	to help: I help, I helped, I will help
comprar: compro, compré, compraré	to buy: I buy, I bought, I will buy
compartir: comparto, compartí, compartiré	to share: I share, I shared, I will share
buscar: busco, busqué, buscaré	to look for: I look for, I looked for, I will look for
contestar: contesto, contesté, contestaré	to answer: I answer, I answered, I will answer
todo/a/os/as	all

Chapter 18

Vocabulario nuevo

Spanish	English
derecha	right
izquierda	left
encima de	on top of
delante de	in front of
detrás de	behind
cerca de	near
lejos de	far from
entre	between
fuera de	out of
dentro de	inside of
debajo de	underneath

Vocabulario de repaso

Spanish	English
cambiar: cambio, cambié, cambiaré	to change: I change, I changed, I will change
comprender: comprendo, comprendí, comprenderé	to understand: I understand, I understood, I will understand
cocinar: cocino, cociné, cocinaré	to cook: I cook, I cooked, I will cook
la gente	people
la cosa	thing

Chapter 19

Vocabulario nuevo

Spanish	English
mejorar: mejoro, mejoré, mejoraré	to improve (something): I improve (something), I improved (something), I will improve (something)
añadir: añado, añadí, añadiré	to add: I add, I added, I will add
mejor	better
el/la mejor	the best
peor	worse
el/la peor	the worst
más	more
más que	more than
menos que	less than
menor/es	younger
mayor/es	older

Vocabulario de repaso

Spanish	English
mover: muevo, moví, moveré	to move: I move, I moved, I will move
morir: muero, morí, moriré	to die: I die, I died, I will die
morder: muerdo, mordí, morderé	to bite: I bite, I bit, I will bite
molestar: molesto, molesté, molestaré	to bother: I bother, I bothered, I will bother
menos	minus, less

Chapter 20

Vocabulario nuevo

Spanish	English
probar: pruebo, probé, probaré	to try/taste: I try/taste, I tried/tasted, I will try/taste
tratar de: trato de, traté de, trataré de	to try to: I try to, I tried to, I will try to
tratar: trato, traté, trataré	to treat: I treat, I treated, I will treat
empujar: empujo, empujé, empujaré	to push: I push, I pushed, I will push
caro/a/os/as	expensive
barato/a/os/as	inexpensive
rápido/a/os/as	fast
lento/a/os/as	slow
fuerte/es	strong
cómico/a/os/as	funny
el mundo	world
el joven, la joven	young man, young woman

Vocabulario de repaso

Spanish	English
inteligente/es	intelligent, smart
alto/a/os/as	tall, high
bajo/a/os/as	short, low
joven/jóvenes	young

Chapter 22

Vocabulario nuevo

Spanish	English
cubrir: cubro, cubrí, cubriré	to cover: I cover, I covered, I will cover
el país	country
la vida	life
la salud	health
el dibujo	drawing
el cambio	change

Spanish	English
la razón	reason
tener razón	to be right
el chiste	joke

Vocabulario de repaso

Spanish	English
vender: vendo, vendí, venderé	to sell: I sell, I sold, I will sell
sonreír: sonrío, sonreí, sonreiré	to smile: I smile, I smiled, I will smile
seguir: sigo, seguí, seguiré	to follow: I follow, I followed, I will follow
saltar: salto, salté, saltaré	to jump: I jump, I jumped, I will jump
volver: vuelvo, volví, volveré	to return: I return, I returned, I will return

Chapter 23

Vocabulario nuevo

Spanish	English
bañarse: me baño, me bañé, me bañaré	to take a bath: I take a bath, I took a bath, I will take a bath
vestirse: me visto, me vestí, me vestiré	to get dressed: I get dressed, I got dressed, I will get dressed
levantarse: me levanto, me levanté, me levantaré	to get up: I get up, I got up, I will get up
acostarse: me acuesto, me acosté, me acostaré	to go to bed: I go to bed, I went to bed, I will go to bed
peinarse: me peino, me peiné, me peinaré	to comb one's hair: I comb my hair, I combed my hair, I will comb my hair
el peine	comb
el cepillo	brush
los dientes	teeth
el cuerpo	body
la cara	face
el vestido	dress

Vocabulario de repaso

Spanish	English
lavar: lavo, lavé, lavaré	to wash: I wash, I washed, I will wash
la mano	hand
el baño	bathroom
el pelo	hair

Chapter 24

Vocabulario nuevo

Spanish	English
sentirse: me siento	to feel: I feel
divertirse: me divierto	to have fun: I have fun
despertarse: me despierto	to wake up: I wake up
preocuparse (por): me preocupo	to worry (about): I worry
sentarse: me siento	to sit: I sit
quejarse (de): me quejo	to complain (about): I complain
casarse (con): me caso	to get married (to): I get married
quitarse: me quito	to take off: I take off
apresurarse: me apresuro	to hurry: I hurry
enamorarse (de): me enamoro	to fall in love (with): I fall in love
irse: me voy	to leave: I leave

Vocabulario de repaso

Spanish	English
imaginar: imagino, imaginé, imaginaré	to imagine: I imagine, I imagined, I will imagine
incluir: incluyo, incluí, incluiré	to include: I include, I included, I will include
guardar: guardo, guardé, guardaré	to keep: I keep, I kept, I will keep
gritar: grito, grité, gritaré	to yell: I yell, I yelled, I will yell
ganar: gano, gané, ganaré	to win/earn: I win/earn, I won/earned, I will win/earn

Chapter 26

Vocabulario nuevo

Spanish	English
mandar: mando, mandé, mandaré	to command/send: I command/send, I commanded/sent, I will command/send
picar: pico, piqué, picaré	to sting/bite: I sting/bite, I stung/bit, I will sting/bite
tener cuidado: tengo cuidado	to be careful: I am careful
tener miedo: tengo miedo	to be scared: I am scared
tener razón: tengo razón	to be right: I am right
estar de acuerdo: estoy de acuerdo	to agree: I agree
el peligro	danger
peligroso/a/os/as	dangerous
caliente/es	hot
frío/a/os/as	cold

Vocabulario de repaso

Spanish	English
hace calor	it's hot
hace frío	it's cold
tengo once años	I'm eleven years old
tengo frío	I'm cold
tengo calor	I'm hot

Chapter 27

Vocabulario nuevo

Spanish	English
discúlpeme	excuse me
perdóneme	pardon me
dígame	talk to me (a way to answer the phone)
bello/a/os/as, hermoso/a/os/as	beautiful
simpático/a/os/as	nice
contento/a/os/as, alegre/es	happy
tranquilo/a/os/as	calm, relaxed
pobre/es	poor
rico/a/os/as	rich
igual/es	equal

Vocabulario de repaso

Spanish	English
feliz/felices	happy
guapo/a/os/as	good-looking
amable/amables	nice
feo/a/os/as	ugly
lo siento	I'm sorry

Chapter 28

Vocabulario nuevo

Spanish	English
pasear: paseo, paseé, pasearé	to go for a walk: I go for a walk, I went for a walk, I will go for a walk.
pegar: pego, pegué, pegaré	to stick/hit: I stick/hit, I stuck/hit, I will stick/hit
pedir perdón: pido perdón	to ask forgiveness: I ask forgiveness
último/a/os/as	last
pasado/a/os/as	past
próximo/a/os/as	next, near
desde	since
durante	during
anoche	last night

Vocabulario de repaso

Spanish	English
recordar: recuerdo, recordé, recordaré	to remember: I remember, I remembered, I will remember
preguntar: pregunto, pregunté, preguntaré	to ask: I ask, I asked, I will ask
parecer: parezco, parecí, pareceré	to seem: I seem, I seemed, I will seem
preparar: preparo, preparé, prepararé	to prepare: I prepare, I prepared, I will prepare
pasar: paso, pasé, pasaré	to pass: I pass, I passed, I will pass
hasta	until

Chapter 29

Vocabulario nuevo

Spanish	English
reparar: reparo, reparé, repararé	to repair: I repair, I repaired, I will repair
responder: respondo, respondí, responderé	to respond/answer: I respond/answer, I responded/answered, I will respond/answer
funcionar: funciono, funcioné, funcionaré	to work/function: I work/function, I worked/functioned, I will work/function
organizar: organizo, organicé, organizaré	to organize: I organize, I organized, I will organize
llenar: lleno, llené, llenaré	to fill: I fill, I filled, I will fill
pero	but
juntos/juntas	together
casi	almost
jamás	never

Vocabulario de repaso

Spanish	English
explicar: explico, expliqué, explicaré	to explain: I explain, I explained, I will explain
contestar: contesto, contesté, contestaré	to answer: I answer, I answered, I will answer
servir: sirvo, serví, serviré	to serve: I serve, I served, I will serve
reír: río, reí, reiré	to laugh: I laugh, I laughed, I will laugh
siempre	always
nunca	never

Chapter 30

Vocabulario nuevo

Spanish	English
marchar: marcho, marché, marcharé	to march/walk: I march/walk, I marched/walked, I will march/walk
marcharse: me marcho	to leave: I leave
corregir: corrijo, corregí, corregiré	to correct: I correct, I corrected, I will correct
cruzar: cruzo, crucé, cruzaré	to cross: I cross, I crossed, I will cross
decidir: decido, decidí, decidiré	to decide: I decide, I decided, I will decide
oler: huelo, olí, oleré	to smell: I smell, I smelled, I will smell
despacio	slowly
atrás	back, behind
el ejercicio	exercise
el examen	exam, test

Vocabulario de repaso

Spanish	English
probar: pruebo, probé, probaré	to try/taste: I try/taste, I tried/tasted, I will try/taste
venir: vengo, vine, vendré	to come: I come, I came, I will come
conseguir: consigo, conseguí, conseguiré	to get: I get, I got, I will get
vestirse: me visto, me vestí, me vestiré	to get dressed: I get dressed, I got dressed, I will get dressed
enviar: envío, envié, enviaré	to send: I send, I sent, I will send

GLOSSARY BY Alphabet

Spanish	English	Chapter
a	at, to	5
abrigo, el	coat	16
abrir: abierto	to open: open (opened)	14
abrir: abro, abrí, abriré	to open: I open, I opened, I will open	1
aburrido/a/os/as	boring	4
acostarse: me acuesto, me acosté, me acostaré	to go to bed: I go to bed, I went to bed, I will go to bed	23
aeropuerto, el	airport	3
alegre/es	happy	27
alfombra, la	rug	8
alguien	someone, somebody	12
almohada, la	pillow	8
almorzar: almuerzo, almorcé, almorzaré	to eat lunch: I eat lunch, I ate lunch, I will eat lunch	3
almuerzo, el	lunch	2
alto/a/os/as	tall, high	20
amable/amables	nice	27
amar: amo, amé, amaré	to love: I love, I loved, I will love	9
añadir: añado, añadí, añadiré	to add: I add, I added, I will add	19
anoche	last night	28
apresurarse: me apresuro	to hurry: I hurry	24
aquel/aquella	that over there	17
aquellos/aquellas	those over there	17
árbol, el	tree	8
arreglar: arreglo, arreglé, arreglaré	to tidy: I tidy, I tidied, I will tidy	8
aspiradora, la	vacuum cleaner	8
atrás	back, behind	30
autobús, el	bus	3
avión, el	airplane	3
ayudar: ayudo, ayudé, ayudaré	to help: I help, I helped, I will help	17
bailar: bailo, bailé, bailaré	to dance: I dance, I danced, I will dance	1
bajar: bajo, bajé, bajaré	to go down: I go down, I went down, I will go down	2
bajo/a/os/as	short, low	20

Spanish	English	Chapter
bañarse: me baño, me bañé, me bañaré	to take a bath: I take a bath, I took a bath, I will take a bath	23
baño, el	bathroom	23
barato/a/os/as	inexpensive	20
barco, el	boat	3
beber: bebo, bebí, beberé	to drink: I drink, I drank, I will drink	6
bebida, la	drink	2
bello/a/os/as	beautiful	27
bicicleta, la	bicycle	16
bolígrafo, el	pen	1
bueno/a/os/as	good	4
buscar: busco, busqué, buscaré	to look for: I look for, I looked for, I will look for	17
cada	each, every	17
caliente/es	hot	26
cama, la	bed	8
cambiar: cambio, cambié, cambiaré	to change: I change, I changed, I will change	18
cambio, el	change	22
camisa, la	shirt	16
cansar: cansado	to tire: tired	14
cantar: canto, canté, cantaré	to sing: I sing, I sang, I will sing	1
cara, la	face	23
caro/a/os/as	expensive	20
carta, la	letter	6
casarse (con): me caso	to get married (to): I get married	24
casco, el	helmet	16
casi	almost	29
cepillo, el	brush	23
cerca de	near	18
cerrar: cerrado	to close: closed	14
chaqueta, la	jacket	16
chiste, el	joke	22
cocinar: cocino, cociné, cocinaré	to cook: I cook, I cooked, I will cook	18
comenzar: comienzo, comencé, comenzaré	to begin: I begin, I began, I will begin	10
cómico/a/os/as	funny	20
compartir: comparto, compartí, compartiré	to share: I share, I shared, I will share	17
comprar: compro, compré, compraré	to buy: I buy, I bought, I will buy	17

Spanish	English	Chapter
comprender: comprendo, comprendí, comprenderé	to understand: I understand, I understood, I will understand	18
con	with	5
conducir: conduzco, conduje, conduciré	to drive: I drive, I drove, I will drive	3
conseguir: consigo, conseguí, conseguiré	to get: I get, I got, I will get	12, 30
contar: cuento, conté, contaré	to count/tell: I count/tell, I counted/told, I will count/tell	12
contar con	to count on	12
contento/a/os/as	happy	27
contestar: contesto, contesté, contestaré	to answer: I answer, I answered, I will answer	17, 29
continuar: continuo, continué, continuaré	to continue: I continue, I continued, I will continue	12
corregir: corrijo, corregí, corregiré	to correct: I correct, I corrected, I will correct	30
correr: corro, corrí, correré	to run: I run, I ran, I will run	1
cortar: corto, corté, cortaré	to cut: I cut, I cut, I will cut	1
cosa, la	thing	18
creer: creo, creí, creeré	to believe: I believe, I believed, I will believe	3
cruzar: cruzo, crucé, cruzaré	to cross: I cross, I crossed, I will cross	30
cuaderno, el	notebook	1
cuarto, el	quarter, fourth, room	10
cubrir: cubierto	to cover: covered	14
cubrir: cubro, cubrí, cubriré	to cover: I cover, I covered, I will cover	22
cuerpo, el	body	23
de	from, of	5
de repente	suddenly	12
debajo de	underneath	18
deber: debo, debí, deberé	to owe/ought to: I owe/should, I owed/should have, I will owe/should	12
decidir: decido, decidí, decidiré	to decide: I decide, I decided, I will decide	30
decir: dicho	to say: said	14
decir: digo, dije, diré	to say/tell: I say/tell, I said/told, I will say/tell	3
dejar: dejo, dejé, dejaré	to leave (something): I leave (something), I left (something), I will leave (something)	12
delante de	in front of	18
demasiado	too (plus an adjective)	5
demasiado/a/os/as	too much, too many	5
dentro de	inside of	18

Spanish	English	Chapter
derecha	right	18
desayunar: desayuno, desayuné, desayunaré	to eat breakfast: I eat breakfast, I ate breakfast, I will eat breakfast	1
desayuno, el	breakfast	2
descansar: descanso, descansé, descansaré	to rest: I rest, I rested, I will rest	13
descubrir: descubro, descubrí, descubriré	to discover: I discover, I discovered, I will discover	13
desde	since	28
despacio	slowly	30
despertarse: me despierto	to wake up: I wake up	24
detrás de	behind	18
día, el	day	10
dibujar: dibujo, dibujé, dibujaré	to draw: I draw, I drew, I will draw	13
dibujo, el	drawing	22
dientes, los	teeth	23
diferente/es	different	4
difícil/difíciles	difficult	4
dígame	talk to me (a way to answer the phone)	27
discúlpeme	excuse me	27
divertido/a/os/as	fun	4
divertirse: me divierto	to have fun: I have fun	24
dormir: duermo, dormí, dormiré	to sleep: I sleep, I slept, I will sleep	3
dormitorio, el	bedroom	8
durante	during	28
ejemplo, el	example	13
ejercicio, el	exercise	30
empezar: empiezo, empecé, empezaré	to begin: I begin, I began, I will begin	3
empujar: empujo, empujé, empujaré	to push: I push, I pushed, I will push	20
enamorarse (de): me enamoro	to fall in love (with): I fall in love	24
encima de	on top of	18
encontrar: encuentro, encontré, encontraré	to find/meet: I find/meet, I found/met, I will find/meet	13
entre	between	18
enviar: envío, envié, enviaré	to send: I send, I sent, I will send	6, 30
Es hora de . . . (finish this sentence with an infinitive)	It's time to…	10
escoger: escojo, escogí, escogeré	to choose: I choose, I chose, I will choose	6
escribir: escrito	to write: written	14
ese/esa	that	17
esos/esas	those	17

Spanish	English	Chapter
estar: estoy, estuve, estaré	to be: I am, I was, I will be	3
estar de acuerdo: estoy de acuerdo	to agree: I agree	26
este/esta	this	17
estos/estas	these	17
examen, el	exam, test	30
explicar: explico, expliqué, explicaré	to explain: I explain, I explained, I will explain	29
fácil/fáciles	easy	4
falda, la	skirt	16
fecha, la	date (on a calendar)	13
feliz/felices	happy	4, 27
feo/a/os/as	ugly	27
fiesta, la	party	2
flor, la; flores, las	flower, flowers	6
freír: frito	to fry: fried	14
frío/a/os/as	cold	26
fruta, la	fruit	2
fuera de	out of	18
fuerte/es	strong	20
funcionar: funciono, funcioné, funcionaré	to work/function: I work/function, I worked/functioned, I will work/function	29
gafas, las	glasses	16
ganar: gano, gané, ganaré	to win/earn: I win/earn, I won/earned, I will win/earn	24
gente, la	people	18
grande/es	big	4
gritar: grito, grité, gritaré	to yell: I yell, I yelled, I will yell	24
guapo/a/os/as	good-looking	27
guardar: guardo, guardé, guardaré	to keep: I keep, I kept, I will keep	24
gustar: me gusta, me gustó, me gustará	to be pleasing: it is pleasing to me, it was pleasing to me, it will be pleasing to me	6
había	there was, there were	12
había una vez . . .	once upon a time there was . . .	12
hablar: hablo, hablé, hablaré	to speak: I speak, I spoke, I will speak	1
hace calor	it's hot	26
hace frío	it's cold	26
hacer: hago, hice, haré	to make/do: I make/do, I made/did, I will make/do	2
hacer: hecho	to make/do: made, done	14
hacer la cama	to make the bed	8
hacer la tarea	to do homework	9

Spanish	English	Chapter
hasta	until	28
hermoso/a/os/as	beautiful	27
hogar, el	home	13
hora, la	hour	10
hoy	today	10
huevo, el	egg	8
idioma, el	language	6
igual/es	equal	27
imaginar: imagino, imaginé, imaginaré	to imagine: I imagine, I imagined, I will imagine	24
incluir: incluyo, incluí, incluiré	to include: I include, I included, I will include	24
inteligente/es	intelligent, smart	20
irse: me voy	to leave: I leave	24
izquierda	left	18
jamás	never	29
jardín, el	garden, yard	8
joven, el; joven, la	young man, young woman	20
joven/jóvenes	young	20
juego, el	game	13
jugar al fútbol	to play soccer	9
jugar videojuegos	to play video games	9
juguete, el	toy	8
juntos/juntas	together	29
lápiz, el	pencil	1
lavar: lavo, lavé, lavaré	to wash: I wash, I washed, I will wash	23
lejos de	far from	18
lento/a/os/as	slow	20
levantarse: me levanto, me levanté, me levantaré	to get up: I get up, I got up, I will get up	23
libre/libres	free	17
libro, el	book	8
limpiar: limpio, limpié, limpiaré	to clean: I clean, I cleaned, I will clean	8
limpio/a/os/as	clean	4
listo/a/os/as	ready, smart	17
llave, la	key	13
llenar: lleno, llené, llenaré	to fill: I fill, I filled, I will fill	29
llevar: llevo, llevé, llevaré	to carry/wear: I carry/wear, I carried/wore, I will carry/wear	16
lo siento	I'm sorry	27
lugar, el	place	13

Spanish	English	Chapter
luna, la	the moon	10
luz, la	light	13
maleta, la	suitcase	3
malo/a/os/as	bad	4
mañana, la/mañana	morning/tomorrow	10
mandar: mando, mandé, mandaré	to command/send: I command/send, I commanded/sent, I will command/send	26
mano, la	hand	23
manta, la	blanket	8
mar, el	sea	13
marchar: marcho, marché, marcharé	to march/walk: I march/walk, I marched/walked, I will march/walk	30
marcharse: me marcho	to leave: I leave	30
más	more	19
más que	more than	19
mayor/es	older	19
media, la	half, middle, sock	10
medianoche, la	midnight	10
medio/a	half, middle	10
mediodía, el	noon	10
mejor	better	19
mejor, el/la	the best	19
mejorar: mejoro, mejoré, mejoraré	to improve (something): I improve (something), I improved (something), I will improve (something)	19
menor/es	younger	19
menos	minus, less	10, 19
menos, el/la	the least	10
menos que	less than	19
mirar la tele	to watch TV	9
mismo/a/os/as	same	4
mochila, la	backpack	1
molestar: molesto, molesté, molestaré	to bother: I bother, I bothered, I will bother	19
montar: monto, monté, montaré	to ride: I ride, I rode, I will ride	16
morder: muerdo, mordí, morderé	to bite: I bite, I bit, I will bite	19
morir: muero, morí, moriré	to die: I die, I died, I will die	19
morir: muerto	to die: died, dead	14
mostrar: muestro, mostré, mostraré	to show: I show, I showed, I will show	2
mover: muevo, moví, moveré	to move: I move, I moved, I will move	19
mundo, el	world	20

Spanish	English	Chapter
muñeco de peluche, el	stuffed animal	8
nacer: nazco, nací, naceré	to be born: I am born, I was born, I will be born	12
nadar: nado, nadé, nadaré	to swim: I swim, I swam, I will swim	14
nadie	no one, nobody	12
necesitar: necesito, necesité, necesitaré	to need: I need, I needed, I will need	14
noche, la	night	10
noticias, las	news	6
nunca	never	5, 29
ocupar: ocupado	to occupy: busy, occupied	14
odiar: odio, odié, odiaré	to hate: I hate, I hated, I will hate	9
oler: huelo, olí, oleré	to smell: I smell, I smelled, I will smell	30
olvidar: olvido, olvidé, olvidaré	to forget: I forget, I forgot, I will forget	14
organizar: organizo, organicé, organizaré	to organize: I organize, I organized, I will organize	29
pagar: pago, pagué, pagaré	to pay: I pay, I paid, I will pay	14
página, la	page	1
país, el	country	22
pájaro, el	bird	12
palabra, la	word	1
pantalones, los	pants	16
papel, el	paper	1
para	for, toward	5
parar: paro, paré, pararé	to stop: I stop, I stopped, I will stop	14
parecer: parezco, parecí, pareceré	to seem: I seem, I seemed, I will seem	28
parque, el	the park	6
parte, la	part	13
pasado/a/os/as	past	28
pasar: paso, pasé, pasaré	to pass: I pass, I passed, I will pass	8, 28
pasar la aspiradora	to vacuum	8
pasar tiempo con los amigos	to spend time with friends	9
pasear: paseo, paseé, pasearé	to go for a walk: I go for a walk, I went for a walk, I will go for a walk.	28
patinete, el	scooter	16
pedir: pido, pedí, pediré	to ask for: I ask for, I asked for, I will ask for	3
pedir perdón: pido perdón	to ask forgiveness: I ask forgiveness	28
pegar: pego, pegué, pegaré	to stick/hit: I stick/hit, I stuck/hit, I will stick/hit	28
peinarse: me peino, me peiné, me peinaré	to comb one's hair: I comb my hair, I combed my hair, I will comb my hair	23

Spanish	English	Chapter
peine, el	comb	23
peligro, el	danger	26
peligroso/a/os/as	dangerous	26
pelo, el	hair	23
peor	worse	19
peor, el/la	the worst	19
pequeño/a/os/as	little	4
perdóneme	pardon me	27
pero	but	29
picar: pico, piqué, picaré	to sting/bite: I sting/bite, I stung/bit, I will sting/bite	26
pobre/es	poor	27
poder: puedo, pude, podré	to be able to: I can, I could, I will be able to	2
poema, el	poem	6
poner: pongo, puse, pondré	to put/place: I put/place, I put/placed, I will put/place	2
poner: puesto	to put/place: put, placed	14
por	for, by, through	5
postre, el	dessert	2
practicar deportes	to play sports	9
preguntar: pregunto, pregunté, preguntaré	to ask: I ask, I asked, I will ask	28
preocuparse (por): me preocupo	to worry (about): I worry	24
preparar: preparo, preparé, prepararé	to prepare: I prepare, I prepared, I will prepare	28
prestar: presto, presté, prestaré	to loan: I loan, I loaned, I will loan	16
probar: pruebo, probé, probaré	to try/taste: I try/I taste, I tried/I tasted, I will try/I will taste	20, 30
problema, el	problem	6
programa, el	program	6
proteger: protejo, protegí, protegeré	to protect: I protect, I protected, I will protect	12
próximo/a/os/as	next, near	28
¿Qué hora es?	What time is it?	10
quejarse (de): me quejo	to complain (about): I complain	24
querer: quiero, quise, querré	to want/love: I want/love, I wanted/loved, I will want/love	2
quitarse: me quito	to take off: I take off	24
rápido/a/os/as	fast	20
razón, la	reason	22

Spanish	English	Chapter
recibir: recibo, recibí, recibiré	to receive: I receive, I received, I will receive	6
recoger: recojo, recogí, recogeré	to pick up: I pick up, I picked up, I will pick up	8
recordar: recuerdo, recordé, recordaré	to remember: I remember, I remembered, I will remember	28
reducir: reduzco, reduje, reduciré	to reduce: I reduce, I reduced, I will reduce	3
reír, río, reí, reiré	to laugh: I laugh, I laughed, I will laugh	29
reloj, el	clock, watch	10
reparar: reparo, reparé, repararé	to repair: I repair, I repaired, I will repair	29
responder: respondo, respondí, responderé	to respond/answer: I respond/answer, I responded/answered, I will respond/answer	29
rico/a/os/as	rich	27
romper: roto	to break: broken	14
ropa, la	clothes	16
saber: sé, supe, sabré	to know: I know, I knew, I will know	3
salir: salgo, salí, saldré	to go out: I go out, I went out, I will go out	9
saltar: salto, salté, saltaré	to jump: I jump, I jumped, I will jump	22
salud, la	health	22
seguir: sigo, seguí, seguiré	to follow: I follow, I followed, I will follow	22
sentarse: me siento	to sit: I sit	24
sentirse: me siento	to feel: I feel	24
servir: sirvo, serví, serviré	to serve: I serve, I served, I will serve	29
siempre	always	5, 29
simpático/a/os/as	nice	27
sin	without	5
sol, el	sun	10
solo/a/os/as	alone	5
sólo	only	5
soñar con: sueño con, soñé con, soñaré con	to dream about: I dream about, I dreamed about, I will dream about	9
sonreír: sonrío, sonreí, sonreiré	to smile: I smile, I smiled, I will smile	22
sucio/a/os/as	dirty	4
sueño, el	dream	9
también	also	5
tampoco	neither	5
tarde, la	afternoon	10
tarde	late	5
tarea, la	homework	9
temer: temo, temí, temeré	to fear: I fear, I feared, I will fear	6

Spanish	English	Chapter
temprano	early	5
tener: tengo, tuve, tendré	to have: I have, I had, I will have	2
tener cuidado: tengo cuidado	to be careful: I am careful	26
tener miedo: tengo miedo	to be scared: I am scared	26
tener razón: tengo razón	to be right: I am right	26
tener razón	to be right	22
tengo calor	I'm hot	26
tengo frío	I'm cold	26
tengo once años	I'm eleven years old	26
tiempo, el	time, weather	9
tijeras, las	scissors	1
tirar: tiro, tiré, tiraré	to throw: I throw, I threw, I will throw	6
tocar el piano	to play the piano	9
tocar música	to play music (on a musical instrument)	9
todavía	still	5
todo/a/os/as	all	17
trabajar: trabajo, trabajé, trabajaré	to work: I work, I worked, I will work	12
tranquilo/a/os/as	calm, relaxed	27
tratar: trato, traté, trataré	to treat: I treat, I treated, I will treat	20
tratar de: trato de, traté de, trataré de	to try to: I try to, I tried to, I will try to	20
triste/es	sad	4
último/a/os/as	last	28
usar: uso, usé, usaré	to use: I use, I used, I will use	6
vender: vendo, vendí, venderé	to sell: I sell, I sold, I will sell	22
venir: vengo, vine, vendré	to come: I come, I came, I will come	2, 30
ver: veo, vi, veré	to see: I see, I saw, I will see	2
ver: visto	to see: seen	14
verduras, las	vegetables	2
vestido, el	dress	16, 23
vestirse: me visto, me vestí, me vestiré	to get dressed: I get dressed, I got dressed, I will get dressed	23, 30
vez, la	time (instance, occasion)	13
vida, la	life	22
vivir: vivo, viví, viviré	to live: I live, I lived, I will live	1
volver: vuelto	to return: returned	14
volver: vuelvo, volví, volveré	to return: I return, I returned, I will return	22
yo mismo/yo misma	myself	4
zapatos, los	shoes	16

Preterit
Puzzle
Did you solve all the **piedra** puzzles and uncover the images of the **piedras**? (You should have eight images!) If you did, flip the page, and start your way through the maze using the images (in order) to guide you. Can you find the statue?

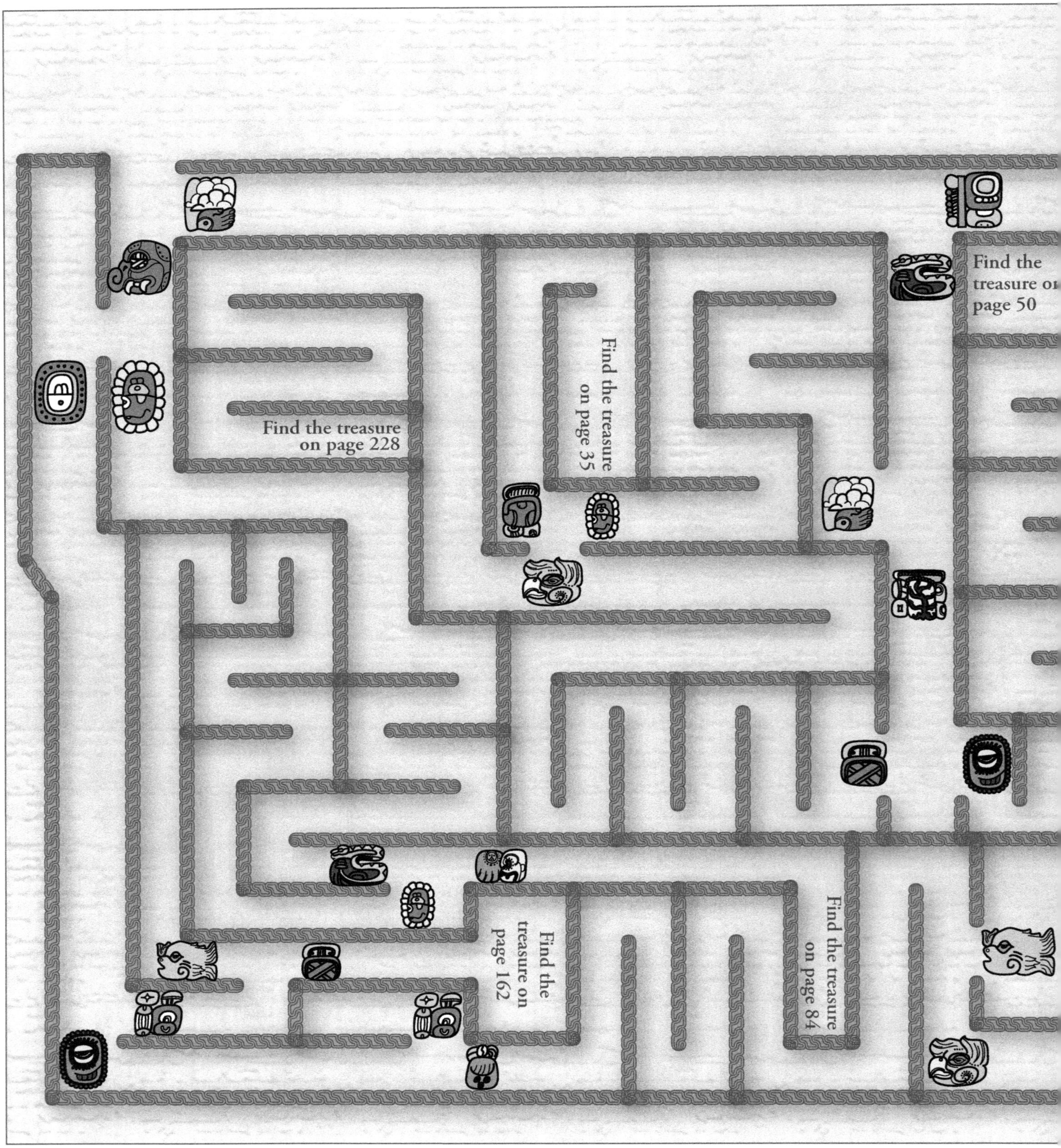

Find the treasure on page 228

Find the treasure on page 35

Find the treasure on page 50

Find the treasure on page 162

Find the treasure on page 84

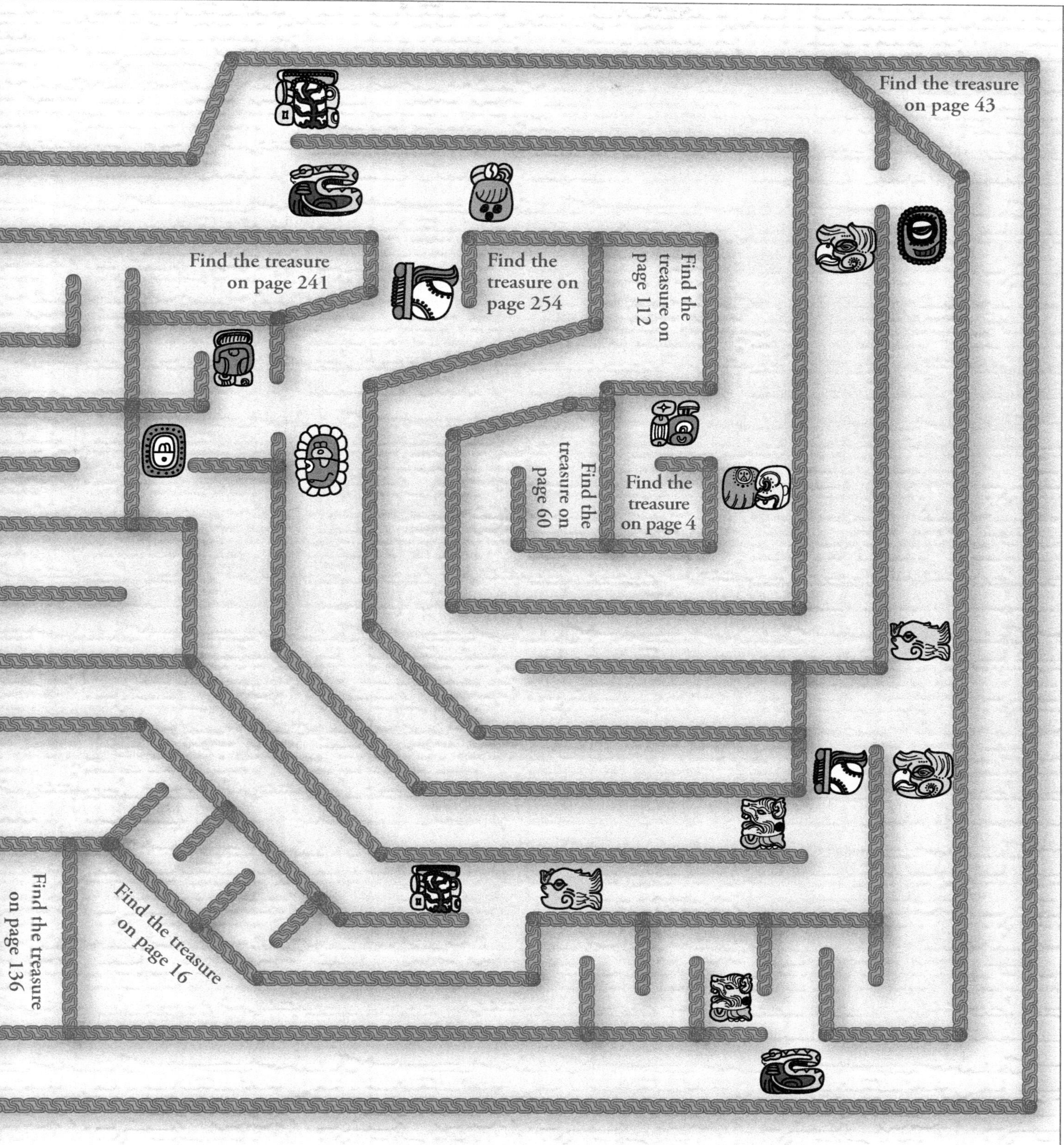
Find the treasure on page 43
Find the treasure on page 241
Find the treasure on page 254
Find the treasure on page 112
Find the treasure on page 60
Find the treasure on page 4
Find the treasure on page 16
Find the treasure on page 136

Logic

We use logic every day, especially to distinguish *logical* arguments from those that are unreasonable. As a fundamental part of the trivium, logic is a paradigm subject by which we evaluate, assess, and learn other subjects, growing ever closer to their mastery.

Informal Logic
(Grades 7–12)

Formal Logic
(Grades 8–12)

Logic/Pre-Rhetoric
(Grades 8–12)

Speech & Debate
(Grades 8–12)

> "French for Children has a very immersion-style feel to the program! It uses lots of dialogue, translation, vocabulary, dictation, grammar, and there are quizzes too. This is all presented in such a way that it really is quite enjoyable!"
>
> —Schoolhouse Review Crew

French for Children

by Joshua Kraut

A classical, beautiful, and widely spoken language, French will be a treasure for children to learn. There is a distinction, however, between just learning common words and phrases, which is the approach of many French programs, and knowing the language well enough to communicate fluently and accurately. The French for Children series teaches elementary students in grade 4 and up this dynamic language, both classically and creatively, at a time when students soak up language like sponges. This book employs the pedagogy and structure of our popular Latin for Children series combined with immersion-style dialogues and vocabulary so that the French language will be taught well and enjoyed thoroughly.

Free samples and videos at ClassicalAcademicPress.com